Disaster and Development

Disaster and Development
The Politics of Humanitarian Aid

Neil Middleton and Phil O'Keefe

Pluto  Press
LONDON • CHICAGO, ILLINOIS
In Association with ETC (UK)

First published 1998 by Pluto Press
345 Archway Road, London N6 5AA
and 1436 West Randolph,
Chicago, Illinois 60607, USA

British Library Cataloguing-in-Publication Data
A catalogue record for this book is available from the British Library

ISBN 0 7453 1229 2 hbk

Designed and produced for Pluto Press by
Chase Production Services, Chadlington, OX7 3LN
Typeset from disk by Stanford DTP Services, Northampton
Printed in Great Britain

Contents

Maps and Figures

Tables

ETC

This book is an ETC project. Founded in The Netherlands in 1974 and now established in India, Sri Lanka, Kenya, Britain and Ireland, ETC exists to encourage and support local initiatives towards sustainable development. It is organised under the umbrella of ETC International which is located in The Netherlands. It recognises that local knowledge and experience are the building blocks for any developmental activity and that those communities for whom aid projects of any kind are constructed must have substantial influence on their design. Employing people from many and varied backgrounds, ETC can offer expertise in sustainable agriculture, agroforestry, energy, water supplies, humanitarian assistance, institutional development and training and extension courses. For further information write to ETC UK, 117 Norfolk Street, North Shields, Tyne & Wear NE30 1NQ.

Acknowledgements

We, the authors, are grateful to John Kirkby of ETC and the University of Northumbria and Ian Convery of ETC for their generosity in allowing us to use their research, particularly in the chapter on Kenya. We have drawn extensively on John Kirkby's experience in leading or taking part in eight evaluations of complex emergencies and on Ian Convery's work on similar evaluations in Ethiopia and the Caucasus. Our special thanks go to Geraldine Mitchell for her support during the writing, for her tireless help in reading and commenting on each chapter as it was written and for rescuing us from our most egregious mistakes. Donna Porter was endlessly patient and helpful in organisational matters; we thank her too. It remains, of course, that despite these invaluable contributions, all the opinions and errors in the text are our very own.

Our thanks go also to the University of Northumbria for the grant which contributed towards producing the final draft of this book.

The authors and Pluto Press gratefully acknowledge permission to reproduce 'The Great Famine', verse VI, by Sorley MacLean, from *Somhairle: Dàin is Deilbh: A celebration on the 80th birthday of Sorley MacLean*, published by Acair Ltd, 7 James Street, Stornoway, Isle of Lewis, 1991.

Cò às a thug sibh a' choiseachd
'Nur triùir chompanach an-
    iochdmhor,
A' ghort 's an laige 's an calar?
Cò às a thàinig sibh le 'r sgreamh,
Cò às a thàinig sibh idir?
'N ann às an aineolos rag,
No às an leisg gun shuim,
As a' pheacahd bheag,
No às a' pheacadh mhòr,
No às an fhèinealachd choma,
No às an aingidheachd fhèin
No às a' ghamhlas as miosa,
Is mac an duine cho còir
Cho iochdmhor coibhneil laghach,
Cho cùramach mu chor a'
    chloinne?

From where have you walked,
you three merciless companions,
famine weakness and cholera?
From where have you come with
    your loathsomeness,
From where have you come at all?
Is it from stubborn ignorance,
or from the uncaring laziness,
from the small sin,
or from the great sin,
or from the indifferent selfishness
or from wickedness itself
or from the worst malice,
though mankind is so generous,
so merciful, kind and pleasant,
so careful of the state of his
    children.

A' Ghort Mhòr,
    Somhairle MacGill-eain

The Great Famine,
    Sorley MacLean

Acronyms and Abbreviations

ACAS	Association of Concerned African Scholars
AMRU	*Associação Moçambicana para o Desenvolvimento da Mulher Rural* (Mozambican Association for the Development of Rural Women)
ANC	African National Congress
APEC	Asia-Pacific Economic Cooperation
APR	*Armée Patriotique Rwandaise* (Rwandese Patriotic Army – RPA)
ASEAN	Association of South East Asian Nations
CARE	Christian American Relief Everywhere
CDR	*Coalition pour la Défence de la République* (Coalition for the Defence of the Republic)
CEAR	*Comisión Española de Ayuda a Refugiados* (*Comissão Espanhola de Ajuda aos Refugiados* – Spanish Commission of Aid to Refugees)
CEMIRDE	*Comissão Episcopal para Migrantes, Refugiados e Deslocados* (Episcopal Commission for Migrants, Refugees and Displaced Persons)
CENTO	Central Treaty Organisation
CEPGL	Economic Community of the Great Lakes
CIA	Central Intelligence Agency
CIS	Commonwealth of Independent States
CIIR	Catholic Institute of International Relations
CRS	Catholic Relief Services
CVM	*Cruz Vermelha de Moçambique* (Mozambique Red Cross)
ECMEP	*Empresa de Construção e Manutenção Estrades e Pontes* (Roads and Bridges Construction and Maintenance Company – a Mozambican parastatal)
ECOSOC	Economic and Social Council of the United Nations
ECOWAS	Economic Community of West African States
EFF	Extended Fund Facility (attached to ESAF)
ESAF	Enhanced Structural Adjustment Facility
EU	European Union
FAO	Food and Agriculture Organisation
FAR	*Forces Armées Rwandaises* (Rwandese Armed Forces)

FRELIMO	*Frente de Libertação de Moçambique* (Front for the Liberation of Mozambique)
FPR	*Front Patriotique Rwandaise* (Rwandan Patriotic Front – RPF)
GATT	General Agreement on Tariffs and Trade
GDP	Gross domestic product
GEMA	Gikuyu, Embu and Meru Association
GNP	Gross National Product
HRW	Human Rights Watch
HRW/A	Human Rights Watch/Africa
HRWAP	Human Rights Watch Arms Project
IBRD	International Bank for Reconstruction and Development (World Bank)
ICRC	International Committee of the Red Cross
IDP	Internally displaced person
IGADD	Intergovernmental Agency for Drought and Development
ILO	International Labour Office
IMF	International Monetary Fund
INGO	International non-governmental organisation
IRC	International Rescue Committee
ITeM	*Instituto del Tercer Mundo*
ITO	International Trade Organisation
JEEAR	Joint Evaluation of Emergency Assistance to Rwanda
KANU	Kenya African National Union
KULIMA	*Organismo para o Desenvolvimento Sócio-Económico Integrado* (Organisation for the Development of Socio-Economic Integration)
MAR	*Marins san Frontières*
MFC	Mechanised Farming Corporation
MRND	*Mouvement Révolutionnaire National pour le Développment* (National Revolutionary Movement for Development)
MSF	*Médecin sans Frontières* (followed by country: Es – Spain; Fr – France; Sw – Switzerland)
NAFTA	North American Free Trade Association
NAR	*Nucleo do Apoio aos Refugiados* (Refugee Support Bureau)
NCPB	National Cereals and Produce Board
NGO	Non-governmental organisation
NIF	National Islamic Front
NRC	Norwegian Refugee Council
OAU	Organisation for African Unity
OECD	Organisation for Economic Cooperation and Development
OLS	Operation Lifeline Sudan

PDPA	People's Democratic Party of Afghanistan
PFA	People's Front of Azerbaijan
PTA	Preferential Trade Area for East and Southern Africa
QIP(s)	Quick Impact Project(s)
RENAMO	*Resistencia Nacional Moçambicana* (National Resistance of Mozambique)
RPA	See APR
RPF	See FPR
RRR	National Ecumenical Committee Programme for Repatriation, Resettlement and Rehabilitation
RS	UNHCR Reintegration Strategy
SA	Structural adjustment
SADC	Southern African Development Community (formerly SADCC, the Southern African Development Coordination Conference)
SALT	Strategic Arms Limitation Treaty
SAP	Structural adjustment programme
SCF	Save the Children Fund (Commonly followed by country)
SEAS	*Secretaria de Estado para Acção Social* (State Secretariat for Social Action)
SEATO	South-East Asia Treaty Organisation
SPLA	Sudan People's Liberation Army
SRCS	Somali Red Crescent Society
STS	Supplies and Transport Section (of UNHCR)
TNC	Transnational corporation
UDEAC	Customs and Economic Union of Central Africa
UNAMIR	United Nations Aid Mission to Rwanda
UNAMO	National Union of Mozambique
UNDHA	United Nations Department for Humanitarian Affairs
UNDMT	United Nations Disaster Management Team
UNDP	United Nations Development Programme
UNESCO	United Nations Educational, Scientific and Cultural Organisation
UNHCR	United Nations High Commission for Refugees
UNICEF	United Nations Children's Fund
UNITAF	Unified Task Force
UNOSOM	United Nations Operation in Somalia
USAID	United States Agency for International Development
USC	United Somali Congress
UXO	Unexploded ordnance
WFP	World Food Programme
WHO	World Health Organisation
WCRWC	Women's Commission for Refugee Women and Children
WRI	World Relief International
WTO	World Trade Organisation

Part 1

Politics and Assistance

CHAPTER 1

Introduction: The Politics of Analysis

On the morning that this paragraph was written, newspaper reports were published of a massive bomb attack in central Colombo in which up to a hundred people were killed and a far larger number injured.[1] In the scale of things, horrible though it was, it constituted a small disaster, but a disaster nonetheless. Journalists immediately commented on the policies of the Tamil Tigers and the probable responses of both the Sri Lankan government and of the Sinhalese 'hawks'. There could be no doubt about its political origin, nor that its consequences would be equally political. Fuller analyses will, no doubt, point to the difficulties which spring from divisions aggravated by poverty, weak economic bases, the lack of resources available to the poor and the use of terror as a political weapon. In this book we argue that the elements of all other disasters, even those which some commentators are apt to describe as 'triggered by natural events',[2] are necessarily just as susceptible to political analysis as the horror in Colombo. We shall also contend that unless we are prepared to consider the role of humanitarian 'disasters' or 'emergencies' (the words are frequently used interchangeably) in international politics, then our analyses of developmental policies and of the relationships of the industrialised world to the developing world will be seriously flawed.

Floods, earthquakes, volcanoes and droughts all present dangers to human life; sometimes large numbers of people die following such events, often as direct casualties and, quite commonly, for a range of reasons of which the event itself may only be one. In some instances their scale compels the attention of the industrialised nations and 'emergencies' are declared – 'disaster' is recognised. We will return in later chapters to the ways in which this happens, but it is worth pointing out that in societies where extreme poverty is rife *everyday life* is dangerous. In 1993 an estimated 1.3 billion people lived below the level described by the World Bank as 'absolute poverty' (Commission on Global Governance, 1995, p. 21), and this number could rise to 1.5 billion by 2025 (Watkins, 1995). Phrases like 'life expectancy', 'maternal mortality', 'infant mortality', even 'malnutrition', somehow sanitise the reality that women, children and men are dying in huge numbers from being too poor – this is the chronic humanitarian disaster within which intermittent emergencies are declared, but it is rarely seen as such.

Poverty is one of the principal reasons why people become vulnerable to natural hazards (Sen, 1981; Blaikie et al., 1994), but, as we may see from Table 1.1, natural disasters themselves do not usually end in the losses of life, the gigantic refugeeism and the long-term destruction of livelihoods on the scale of the major catastrophes with which we are concerned in this book. This remains largely true even if we include events like the eruption of Mont Pelée in Martinique in 1902, which killed 28,000 people in moments. It follows that alleviating poverty and helping people towards economic self-reliance, sometimes called 'development', must be high among the strategies for dealing with both chronic and intermittent disasters which are political and economic in origin. This must be particularly true if we follow Sen in suggesting that individuals, families, even whole regions or societies can reduce their vulnerability by increasing the range of commodities they have to sell. Their 'entitlement' to food, shelter and other necessities depends on having more than, for example, simply their labour with which to bargain (Sen, 1981).

Even though Sen's view of entitlements is open to question, few would question this assertion as a generalised proposition, but the means of achieving economic self-reliance are not so commonly agreed. Blaikie et al. offer the example of Bangladesh, one of the most densely populated countries in the world. UN estimates for 1992 (quoted in UNDP, 1995) give the population as 112.7 million which means that there are 799 people for each square kilometre – we may compare this with China's 123, The Netherlands' 450 and Britain's 250 (excluding Northern Ireland) per square kilometre. Not least because of fierce Northern protectionism (Watkins, 1992), the industrial base in Bangladesh is extremely fragile: the most recent figures suggest that only 2 per cent of the workforce is employed in the formal industrial sector, another 13.5 per cent scrapes a living in non-waged and largely home-based industry (World Bank, 1995). Eighty-five per cent of the population depend on agriculture, yet 'between 40 and 60 per cent own no land' (Blaikie et. al., 1994, p. 35). Durable solutions depend on land reform as well as on the development of non-agricultural employment, but at present, political and economic priorities, both national and international, render both improbable. One major consequence of this failure of political will is that a large vulnerable population of Bangladeshis, with few entitlements, continues to live perpetually threatened by 'natural' hazards.

Famine is the most uncomfortable of human disasters, certainly to the people it visits, but also to those who observe from a distance, social or geographical. Unlike floods, earthquakes or even epidemics, its onset seems slow and its effects, if not examined too closely, all-engulfing; its duration can be long and recognising its end can be problematic. Decent, liberal folk, informed by their media of such an event, will think in terms of lending a hand to those smitten by this calamity and give generously to charity; they will add their voices in support of those multilateral agencies supposedly designed to meet extremes of human need. Their discomfort lies in a largely unfocused sense that they may be implicated in famine's causes or, at least, that its existence calls into question their own relatively easy circumstances.

Table 1.1 Natural and Environmental Disasters 1995*

Disaster	Date	Places	Dead
Earthquakes	January	Japan/Colombia	5503
Avalanche	January	India	63
Earthquakes	February	Colombia/Cyprus	36
Earthquakes	March	Colombia	8
Floods	March	Botswana	20
Landslide	March	Afghanistan	350
Storms	April	Argentina/Bangladesh	125
Earthquakes	May	Indonesia/Russian Federation	1827
Floods	May	Indonesia/Sri Lanka/ Ethiopia/ Tanzania	82
Earthquake	June	Greece	26
Floods	June	Bangladesh	66
Landslide	June	Nepal	85
Earthquakes	July	Chile/Myanmar/China	5
Floods	July	China/Azerbaijan/ Georgia/Ghana	1218
Rainstorms	July	Pakistan	451
Floods	August	Morocco/Korea N. & S.	336
Floods	September	Philippines/Myanmar	99
Hurricane (Luis)	September	Caribbean	5
Earthquakes	October	Turkey/Ecuador/ Indonesia/Mexico	227
Floods	October	Benin/El Salvador/ Azerbaijan	20
Storms	October	Philippines	845
Floods	November	Turkey/Somalia	82
Typhoon (Zack)	November	Vietnam	253
Floods	December	South Africa	161

*Only those disasters which led to fatalities, or for which the numbers killed are available, have been included.
Source: Compiled from Retrospective DHA 1995, UNDHA.

For many people in the industrialised world the first images of famine, usually acquired in schools, come from the Bible. In Old Testament times, famines, common in Palestine and Egypt, are often interpreted as weapons in God's armoury (see, for example, Isaiah 14: 30 and 51: 19), or as punishments (Ezekiel 5: 16 and Jeremiah 11: 22), or threats (Jeremiah 27: 13). An early example of developing food security against future drought is pithily, if dramatically, described in Genesis 41. Of all the biblical images of famine, probably the most compelling is that of the mounted, apocalyptic angel in Revelation 8: 6–13, and we may legitimately wonder which satirist was responsible for naming a well known delicacy 'Angels on Horseback'. Causes, in biblical famines, are presented simply: crops are destroyed either by drought, pests or, occasionally, flood and everyone, apparently without exception, suffers. There are hints that it is possible for famine to be selective, that not everyone is necessarily affected – an example may be seen in Solomon's prayer for the people in 1 Kings 8: 22–40. But, in general, biblical descriptions would lead one to suppose that famine, when it occurred, was an indiscriminate calamity visited on a people lax in doctrine.

These impressions have survived in popular imagination and they are supported by dictionaries: Oxford gives, as its first definition, 'Extreme and general scarcity of food, in a town, country, etc.; an instance of this, a period of extreme and general dearth' (*OED*, 1971), while Collins has 'a severe shortage of food, as through a crop failure or overpopulation [sic]' (*Collins*, 1989). For generations food shortages have been thought of as general in the areas where they occurred and were thought to affect more or less everyone, and even if the better-off had some cushion against their worst ravages, eventually they, too, would suffer. Above all, famine is widely understood as a 'natural disaster', although, paradoxically, it is not altogether unusual to find the accompanying opinion that the afflicted are also, somehow, to blame for their own predicament. A whiff of this may be caught in the ascription, in the Collins definition, of overpopulation as a cause of famine.

Contemporary analyses of famines and of all other disasters are, of course, substantially more sophisticated than this and are constantly developing. Writers who fail to observe that people afflicted by famine are those who are denied access to resources or are too poor to buy them are now fortunately rare. Our purpose, in this introduction, is to suggest other consequences of the more simplistic account and to see to what extent, if at all, it has conditioned the framework within which debate now moves. This is an apposite moment for questions of this sort because one major European famine, that in Ireland in the 1840s, is being extensively debated and reassessed in that country and, as a result, historians, in support of their differing interpretations, have made substantial bodies of evidence generally available.

There has been a curious and unfortunate divorce, in the Irish debate, between development theorists and geographers on the one hand and historians on the other. The former have long recognised, particularly since the ground-breaking work of Amartya Sen (Sen, 1981), that thorough socio-economic analyses of famines are called for. Sen defined terms like 'poverty', 'vulnerability', 'entitlement' and the economic bases on which they rested, in order to show who suffers and who does not in a famine. In doing so, he immeasurably increased the scope of the debate about *all* famines, not the least by making space for subsequent political analyses even though these, in turn, have led to substantial modification and development of some of his work and important criticism of his concepts (see, for example, Swift 1996). Sen and subsequent authors have, with few exceptions, been ignored by Irish historians and where they are referred to (for example, Ó Gráda, 1993, 1995) they are often either used selectively or are misunderstood. Wider political and social battles may well lie behind the Irish desire to see the mid-nineteenth-century disaster as unique in both nature and scale, but the failure to hear what geographers and others are saying has resulted in a hugely detailed but conceptually restricted account of relations between Ireland and Westminster at the time. Terry Eagleton, in a brilliant and important essay (Eagleton, 1995), contrives, through a Gramscian analysis, to annexe wider political territory; but he, too, seems to accept Ó Gráda's view that Sen's analysis does not quite work in the case of Ireland.

We shall return, indirectly, to the broad issues at stake in these discussions throughout this book, but we will first look at the framework of some popular assumptions: famines are natural disasters, or a common consequence of them, and there are ways in which its victims, possibly because of some fecklessness, are, at least in part, responsible for their own dilemmas. An opposing account is summed up in a popular Irish saying: 'God sent the potato blight, but the English caused the Famine' (quoted in Kiberd, 1995). The intellectual and moral climate in which these differing positions were held in the case of the Irish Famine is set out neatly in an essay entitled 'Ideology and the Famine' by Peter Gray (Póirtéir, 1995). It is a wider essay dealing with the political shifts in the British government of the time, but in it he describes the politico-ethical categories in which the authorities thought. It is remarkable how alike they are to those common in the Britain of Margaret Thatcher and her successors.

Classical economics, formulated in the work of, among others, Malthus and Ricardo had, by the 1840s, been elaborated by a new generation which assumed that Ireland could be developed

sufficiently to overcome its problems, but not without aid. By this
they meant the provision by the government of infrastructure and
education, but not, incidentally, relief for the poor, which they saw
as draining 'scarce resources away from employment into "useless"
relief to the able-bodied' (Póirtéir, 1995, p. 89). They were opposed,
principally, by two other groups of economists, one known as the
'Manchester School' and another, unnamed, which included in its
number John Stuart Mill. Both saw the Irish form of the
landlord–tenant relationship as destructive and, in slightly different
ways, saw the end of that system and the creation of a free market
in land as means of encouraging more broadly based investment
which would allow the emergence of a land-owning peasantry.
Gray remarks, rather acidly, that 'Detailed suggestions as to how
such a revolution in agrarian power relationships could be brought
about were more troublesome ...' (Póirtéir, 1995, pp. 90–1), but
many commentators of the period saw the Famine as an opportunity
for modernising reform, for, in practice, the consolidation of an
agricultural capitalism. These economic quarrels took place at a
time when, among Christians, particularly Protestants, there was
a growing belief that 'human affairs are regulated by a divine
agency for human good'. Potato blight in Ireland, so far as Protestant
ultras were concerned, was sent by God as vengeance for government
backsliding in the question of Roman Catholicism. It was this
'providentialism', combined with the Manchester School version
of free-market economics, that persuaded large sections of the
British middle classes that the blame for Irish problems was due
to 'the moral failings of Irishmen of all classes' (Póirtéir, 1995, p.
92). Little of this is central to Gray's powerful and sophisticated
argument; it is closer to a comment in passing, but its importance
for our purposes lies in the description of the ancestry of a continuing
prejudice which now, as then, has distressing political consequences.

　　Detailed historical discussion of the Irish Famine continues to
be published at an astonishing rate and it comes from all shades
within the political spectrum. While there is little serious doubt about
the train of events, fierce argument continues about the scale, the
causes and, above all, the responsibility for the catastrophe. Is
blame to be laid at the door of, at best, ill-informed and criminally
slow, at worst, politically self-serving and racialist British officials?
Were landlords, the system of sub-letting land and the powerful
Catholic 'middlemen' (Whelan, 1996) the main villains? Was the
misery turned to disaster with the help of, among others, small,
grasping, Irish tradesmen-cum-money-lenders (the 'gombeen'
men) and land-agents with an eye to the main chance? These
questions oversimplify the debate, but, nonetheless, the extent to
which the arguments have largely ignored the complexity of the
colonial relationship is surprising. Eagleton (1995), although he

approaches the question from a different perspective, does fill the gap by describing the economic and intellectual influences on Irish responses to British rule, and the ways in which that particular relationship worked. Colonialism is an institution which presupposes specific power-relationships between the coloniser and the colonised, but as Liam O'Dowd, summarising Albert Memmi, pointed out '... colonizer and colonized are linked together in a reciprocal but mutually destructive relationship within which the identity of each is forged' (O'Dowd, 1990, p. 40).

Obviously, in Ireland, as elsewhere, colonialism was the politically conditioning superstructure within which the economic and political decisions, which killed up to a million people and forced somewhere in the region of a million and a half into becoming refugees, could be made. Thus while much of the present argument in Ireland about degrees of responsibility for the Great Famine may be invaluable in throwing up new evidence and new political and historical insights, it will fail in serious purpose if it does not lead to analyses of that 'mutually destructive relationship'. The popular saying quoted by Kiberd was right in distinguishing the failure of the potato crop from the totality of the famine, but wrong in attributing the blame to the 'English'. Potato blight may or may not have come from God, but British colonialism, from which huge numbers of English people also suffered (see, among others, Thompson, 1980; Hutton, 1996), lay at the root of that disaster.

Our point is that while, lunatic fringes apart, the crude teleology of mid-nineteenth-century ultras may no longer have the slightest intellectual respectability, its influence is not over. That powerful alliance of providentialism with some of the main currents in economic thinking during the heyday of capitalism, with its accompanying colonisation of resource-rich regions, has left present-day industrialised or post-industrial society with an abiding suspicion of the 'undeserving poor'. It is difficult for the settled, urbanised world of the North to accept that the rush of people to the cities in the Third World, with its consequent and gross expansion of unspeakable slums in patently unsafe areas, is, in existing political and economic circumstances, inevitable. Nor does it understand, for example, why people settle on marginal land, particularly in plainly dangerous places like silt islands in the Ganges Delta. Prejudice, sometimes barely if at all conscious, suggests 'fecklessness' as part of the problem – the poor must in some way be complicit in their own misfortunes. It is a pernicious mythology, memorably illustrated by Norman Tebbitt's suggestion that the unemployed in Britain should stop whining, get on their bikes and look for work.

Margaret Thatcher's notorious announcement that there is no society was simply a rhetorical reaffirmation of the Conservative idol of individual entrepreneurship. It may be a matter of some astonishment that such an idol should still attract worshippers in a world where 80 per cent of all trade is controlled not by individuals, but by giant transnational corporations (TNCs); just ten of them, for example, 'control virtually every aspect of the worldwide food chain' (Vidal, 1997). However, that commitment to the pre-eminent responsibility of the individual for her or his own well-being, so central to Toryism, is also part and parcel of the legacy left by the alliance described by Gray. It is easy enough to deride the absurdities of a Tebbitt, a Thatcher or a Ross Perrot, but it is also easy to miss the strength of the morally narrow ideology for which they have been both the propagandists and the manipulators in the interests of a *laissez-faire* economy. This is not the place in which to discuss the nature of that ideology – other writers have done so extensively (for example, Eagleton, 1991; Marx and Engels, 1965; Marx 1867/1975; Hutton, 1996) – we are, instead, offering it as one explanation for the directions taken by many Northern reactions to human disaster in the 'developing' world.

The days when 'models of best practice' in development theory were based on a general view, formulated in the industrialised world, of what was good for the poor, what was most efficient for achieving their economic well-being, may almost be over, at least among some NGOs and a few enlightened donor states. But until we have irrefutable evidence that the major institutions of development, the multilateral agencies and, above all, the TNCs have changed their actual practice, we should hesitate to congratulate ourselves on the demise of paternalistic theorising – Kwame Nkrumah (1963), Kenneth Kaunda (1966) and Samir Amin (1973) all characterised it as 'neo-colonialism'. Its origins lie in crude self-interest on the part of those powers strong enough to exercise it, but it fits happily with the providentialist inheritance. More to the point, it has fixed the terms of debate in a very particular way.

In their illuminating book, *At Risk*, Blaikie and his fellow authors offer a brisk rejection of 'environmental determinism' as an adequate account of human disasters (Blaikie et al., 1994, p, 12). They also describe the straightforward linking of poverty with vulnerability to disaster as lacking '... an explanation of how one gets from very *widespread conditions* such as "poverty" to very *particular vulnerabilities* that link the political economy to the actual hazards that people face' (ibid., emphasis in original). This is, of course, unexceptionable and the authors follow it with excellent, if generalised, examinations of the sorts of social and, to a limited extent, economic conditions which render particular poor people, families or groups exceptionally vulnerable to hazard. In passing they make the point that it is not necessary to be of the exploited poor to be vulnerable to disastrous natural events; exploitation does not usually cause earthquakes. This is said largely to avoid what they see as the opposite trap of economic determinism.

However, in general, poor people are more likely to be settled or working in areas prone to disaster and are more likely to find themselves in the path of resource or territorial conflicts, simply because they lack the means to be anywhere else. What Blaikie et al. do is to consider the web of social conditions affecting those who suffer most in a complex emergency in which one of the contributing factors is some kind of natural hazard. Included in their analysis are all those factors that others have discussed: size of population, class, ethnicity, caste, gender, age, disability, religion, occupation and so on. They then add to this a discussion of the social and economic factors to do with access to the means for livelihoods and go on to consider what conditions that access. Within this context they also consider the social and economic strategies evolved by people who have to live in a wide variety of hazardous conditions and remark on their value as bases for creating less fragile circumstances.

Work of this sort is invaluable not only because it points to new ways of thinking about development planning, but because it also subverts the inclination in the industrialised world to discount the abilities of the poor, the inclination to tend towards convenient prejudice. But *At Risk* stops short of tackling the larger complex in which the world's poor are so vulnerable. In suggesting that socio-economic issues be included in development planning and in directly confining their examination to unquestionably important detail, the authors add the fateful words that they do so in order not to oversimplify and not to produce 'a theory that is of little use to managers, planners and policy-makers' (p. 13). Any book which, with some success, provides such people with valuable new approaches is to be applauded, but we are bound to ask whether the authors have not imposed too great a limit on themselves. Differing orders of socio-economic process impinge upon one another. What the Commission on Global Governance (1995) described as the institutions of governance, national, international and global, governmental and corporate, have both direct and indirect effects on those smaller institutions summed up in the social factors that the authors do consider. Theories which fail to take these effects into account must, as it were, be reactive and can, in the longer run, be little more than palliative. It cannot be right to regard the macro-economic and political causes as issues too large to be usefully addressed because a general refusal to criticise the role of the larger institutions of governance is simply another example of that nineteenth-century hangover. If, as we argue, many, possibly most, of the problems spring from the unregulated exercise of global power, then solely to search for all the answers among the institutions of the poor is precisely to collude in the prejudice that they are responsible, at least in part, for their own predicament.

Blaikie et al. acknowledge that the causes of disaster lie beyond any 'natural trigger'. We are inclined to think, however, that at the heart of their analyses of these causes there is a conceptual error which undermines the proper use of their insight. They offer two models for analysing vulnerability 'in specific hazard situations'; they call the first of these the 'pressure and release model' (p. 21) and the second the 'access model' (p. 46). The first is designed to show 'how disasters occur when natural hazards affect vulnerable people' (pp. 21–2), the second is constructed to overcome the simplifications of the first and 'focuses on the way unsafe conditions arise in relation to the economic and political processes that allocate assets, income and other resources in a society' (p. 46). With some cogency these authors argue that both models, although discrete and fulfilling different functions, must be applied together in any successful analysis.

We have already observed that despite their robust intentions, these authors still seem trapped in a circular argument: people are vulnerable because they are poor and lack resources, and because they are poor and lack resources they are vulnerable. This triumph of reason arises, we think, not so much because Blaikie et al. are unaware of the wider forces producing poverty and vulnerability, but quite possibly because of a fault in the logic of their models. They have adopted a very simplistic Aristotelian, if not Thomistic, form in their 'pressure and release' model, in which 'cause and effect' may be understood in such a way as to produce a 'chain of explanation' (pp. 22–3). We reproduce a modified version of it in Figure 1.1. They do not offer the same sort of universal schema for their 'access model'; the closest that they come to it is a more sophisticated chart illustrating 'Access to resources to maintain livelihoods' (p. 50).

Set out in this form, the 'power and release' model consists, of course, of a number of generalised headings and each of its columns is replaced with more specific 'causes', 'pressures' and 'conditions' when it is applied in a specific case. We may see this in the authors' application of the model to the Irish Famine of 1845–8 (the authors put it in 1847, but the potato crop failed in 1845 and the famine lasted for the succeeding three years), where the 'root causes' are listed as the penal laws,[3] corn laws, discrimination against Catholics and economic dependency on England. 'Dynamic pressures' are given as rapid population growth, population density in the west of Ireland, the export of food to England, the small farms plots worked by most people, few alternative forms of employment. The 'unsafe conditions' are a diet heavily dependent on potatoes, low

THE PROGRESSION OF VULNERABILITY

1	2	3		
Root Causes	Dynamic Pressures	Unsafe Conditions	Disaster	Hazards
		Fragile environment: dangerous locations, unprotected buildings and infrastructure		Earthquake
	Lack of: institutions, training, skills, investments, markets, free press, ethical standards in public life			Storm
Limited access to: power, structures, resources		**Fragile local economy:** livelihoods at risk, low incomes		Flood
			Risk = Hazard + Vulnerability	Volcanic eruption
Ideologies: political and economic systems	**Macro-forces:** rapid population growth, rapid urbanisation, arms expenditure, external debt servicing, deforestation, degraded soils	**Vulnerable society:** special groups at risk, lack of local institutions		Landslide
		Public actions: lack of disaster preparedness, uncontrolled endemic disease		Drought
				Viruses & pests

Figure 1.1 The Blaikie et al. model for 'the progression of vulnerability'

Source: Based on *At Risk*, Table 2.1, p. 23.

incomes, high food prices, chronic poor health and poor sanitation and the limited genetic diversity of the potato in Ireland. These three elements in 'the progression of vulnerability' form the causal chain leading to that disaster; the direct hazards were the blight and the slightly unusual weather at the time which encouraged its spread (p. 109).

Blaikie et al. recognise that this model is a trifle mechanistic and, indeed, that is why they modified it with their 'access' model. Unfortunately, the recognition has not rescued them from the simple mechanism of causal chains and an almost syllogistic analysis. Even if we treat their three links in the progression not as links, but as accumulating waves, we are, as their accompanying text makes plain, still talking about a *progression*. In applying the model to the Irish Famine they make the mistake obvious: there are elements in their description which may be categorised under all three of their heads, others which work in both directions simultaneously, yet more (such as an attempted, if not, according to Eagleton, wholly successful, colonial hegemony), which are not susceptible to such an analysis. It may also be significant that they failed to include some central factors such as the use of the Famine as an occasion to dispossess the peasantry (a factor which will appear in our examinations of several contemporary humanitarian disasters), the role of the small trader, the collapse of the linen industry as a consequence of a wider colonial policy, primogeniture in landholding, to name but a few. No matter how carefully the two forms of analysis proposed by these authors are brought together, the combination of the essential circularity of their argument and, above all, their distaste for the larger political issues leave them trapped in an intellectual corner. Their analysis fails because they have rejected politics as an analytical tool – we shall have occasion to return to this point in our subsequent case studies.

It is often pointed out that some natural cataclysm may be among the events leading to disaster, often acting as a trigger, but there are plenty of cases in which this is not so. We have, for example, only to think of Cambodia, Iraq, Rwanda and Sudan; in each of these cases disaster has been caused by economic and political conflict. Disasters and hazards, natural and constructed, abound, but not all of them are regarded by international agencies as humanitarian emergencies, the Indonesian destruction of East Timor being an example. It has become commonplace to refer to humanitarian emergencies as 'complex' precisely so as to avoid the pitfall of supposing that there is one simple cause and, in consequence, addressing the wrong questions and providing the wrong answers. Emergencies are usually multifarious, each part reinforcing and modifying the other, but central to them all is the fact that they are *recognised* as emergencies.

As we consider the wider context of some specific examples, we must also point to ambiguities in the ways in which a human disaster is identified as a humanitarian emergency. We expect to make clear that humanitarian emergencies are always political events and play a role in national and international politics. Similarly, humanitarian assistance is 'complex' in its effects but also in its origins, which are frequently an uneasy mix of politics and philanthropy and, as in the policy of USAID, unashamedly to do with a national political agenda (USAID, 1995). Its complexity may, above all, lie in the use which can be made of it quite beyond its function in addressing the particular problems for which it is supposedly designed.

With the exception of the Caucasus, a disaster importantly different in its political origins, and Afghanistan, we have confined ourselves to crises in the continent of Africa even though it is entirely possible to extend our argument to, for example, Iraq, East Timor and Salvador. If we had chosen any of these, or any one among many others, the argument would have been much the same. Africa is special because it is the continent in which the rapacity of the world's banking systems, commodity markets, TNCs and some bilateral donors (particularly Britain and the US[4]) has been most obviously destructive and in which its effects can most widely be seen (Tandon, 1996). It is also the continent in which, despite its array of despotic and venal governments, alternative economic and political structures may yet emerge (Barratt Brown, 1995).

Before we turn to the seven particular disasters from which we draw the evidence for our argument, we must first look, in a general sort of way, at the context in which they happen. Each of them has occurred since the cataclysmic end of the Cold War and each has either involved, or been affected by, some form of civil conflict. 'Civil' is a problematic word, since in none of these cases has the conflict within national boundaries been unaffected by the actions and political choices, in some cases the armed forces, of the industrialised nations and their agencies. Wars have aims and it is our contention that these have consistently centred, no matter what ideological, racialist or even clan agenda may be involved, around resources and trade. Issues raised in this chapter, and in the next, will be illustrated by our seven examples and discussed in our conclusions.

CHAPTER 2

Hot and Cold Running Trade Wars

It is unusual to come across commentary on contemporary humanitarian emergencies which does not, somewhere, point to the end of the Cold War, and the consequent change in geopolitics, as part of the complexity of their causes. Africa is the continent in which this is most demonstrably true. Nation states, created by colonialism and rendered fragile both by that history and by a frequently brutal fight by the metropolitan powers against decolonisation, were subsequently widely tied to the structures of their former rulers by the process described as 'neo-colonialism'. Often governed by dubious regimes, many of which were installed with the connivance of the former colonising states, they were repeatedly propped up by one or other of the competing powers. With the abrupt withdrawal of the USSR, the slower, but no less definite decline in US interest (except in some resource rich states like Angola and Nigeria) and the realignment of European commitments, several of those states have tumbled into a kind of anarchy or into yet more repressive regimes which seem, like Abacha's government in Nigeria or Mobutu's tyranny in Zaire (renamed, since his defeat, The Democratic Republic of the Congo), solely concerned with simple extortion. Perhaps the most obvious change came when South Africa's policy of apartheid, profoundly weakened by a well-organised and highly principled indigenous and international opposition, could not survive without the monolithic polarities of Cold War politics – the wall in Berlin was not the only one to collapse.

But without some wider thought about the nature of the Cold War and its historical place, it is difficult to do much more than acknowledge that both its course and its ending continue to influence the politics of Third World development. A disjunction becomes apparent: we accept that the end of the Cold War produced a new situation in many developing countries, particularly in the poorest, but we continue our analyses almost as if it had not happened. Somehow the context has vanished with the result that much writing about the problems of developing countries treats each crisis as separate and backs away from making the connections which might allow of alternative strategies. Matters like the Bretton Woods organisations' ruthless insistence on peddling patently unsuccessful nostrums, the collapse of Somalia or the problems associated with contract agriculture in, for example, Kenya are often seen as bearing on one another, but rarely as intimately linked by world politics. Even changes in the nature of the interest evinced by the industrialised world in the developing world or, more crudely, by the rich in the poor, tend to be treated as if they were a temporary hitch and not, themselves, a product of a wider agenda. This is a pity since a clearer understanding might spare us the spectacle of well-meaning members of international development NGOs trying hard to persuade their national treasuries to be decent fellows and spare an extra dime or two for alleviating poverty.

Battle lines for the Cold War were essentially drawn up at Yalta and the West's most public opening gambit was the infamous Gehlen roll-back in which so much of the Nazi bureaucracy was retained to facilitate Western hegemony (Stone, 1960). From that moment until Yeltsin's precarious presidency, aid to developing countries was rarely far from the issues raised by world confrontation. It was frequently used by both sides as a lever to disrupt the shaky agreements between the 'non-aligned' states, to persuade some into one camp or the other. Development aid was also extensively employed as a tool for securing resources which were simultaneously regarded as essential for the economic survival of the Powers and as strategically important. Despite the simple ideology expressed in those quaint words 'evil empire', used by President Ronald Reagan to describe the USSR, the Cold War was not a crusade, but a calculated war waged by the US to defend its international interests and, simultaneously, to bury Rooseveltian politics at home (Hobsbawm, 1994, p. 249). It grew out of changes in the world economy that, whenever they began, were shaped by, as they themselves helped to shape, the events from 1914 to 1945. Hobsbawm makes the case for seeing the two mass hot wars, commonly called World War I and World War II, as the opening and closing episodes in a continuous, 31-year war. In both phases of mass conflict and, in particular, the second, the international commitment of people and *matériel* for such extended periods was only possible in a world of enormous industrial capital. Yet in order to wage those vastly expensive wars, it became necessary for governments largely to take control of economic management, rather than leaving matters to be regulated by the mechanisms of the market (Hobsbawm, 1994, p. 46). It is not inconceivable that the popularity of nationalisation in Britain in the years following the war was due to the success and, indeed, the comparative equity of wartime state economic control, particularly as it followed the appalling hardships inflicted on working people by the Great Depression.

In looking at the problems of the developing world, most writers (the present authors included) inculpate, in some way, the TNCs' domination of world trade, yet, as in the case of the Cold War, the point frequently remains unexamined. Empire and industry, or as Hutton (1996) convincingly argues, the stock exchange, may well have been the foundation of contemporary economic globalisation, the scale of Britain's overseas investment as long ago as 1914 illustrates this (Hobsbawm, 1987), but the instruments of its present pre-eminence were forged in those moments of the centralisation of economic effort in the two hottest phases of Hobsbawm's 31-year war. Walden Bello suggests that the same sort of process, involving intense state intervention, was at work in the apparent success of the South-East Asian 'tiger' economies (Bello, 1990). What took place in both instances was the creation by the state of a 'launch-pad' from which the TNCs and indigenous industrial production could grow. Capital movement, foreign exchange, social conditions and much investment were tightly regulated by the states concerned; leaving that development to the vagaries of corporate capital, the market, was not thought to be a sensible vehicle for such growth. State intervention was, and still is, directed at creating an environment in which TNCs can exist. Huge assumptions lie behind this kind of state activity, not least among them the identification of national interest, even identity, with capital growth. Another is the common equation between capital movement, chiefly through the medium of international stock exchanges, and national wealth creation. Yet others are to do with the necessity of creating the conditions in which a 'free' market can regulate international and national trade and production. Regions in which these assumptions may be correct are also strategic; they exist only where overall conditions permit, and it is unclear how far they can be reproduced.

The General Agreement on Tariffs and Trade (GATT) came into existence in 1948, and its purpose was to regulate international trade on a less cut-throat basis than had been the case before World War II, when the industrialised world, faced with a massive slump, turned its back on free trade and opted for a fierce protectionism (Hobsbawm, 1994, p. 94). The Agreement was governed by a series of conferences called 'Rounds', the first of which took place in 1964. National protectionist trade policies had increasingly become a nuisance for the TNCs and for their associated financial institutions, and so, too, had the tendency of certain trading blocs to use protectionism as a means of advancing common trading advantage. In 1986 the eighth Round was begun in Uruguay to address these problems, but because of the scope of the agreement it was trying to forge and the difficulties advanced by many of the more powerful states, the Round was not concluded until 1993. However, the results of the Uruguay Round were formally accepted in principle (absolute acceptance depended on ratification of the agreement by the parliaments of the participating nations) at a conference of ministers held in Marrakesh in April 1994. A statement known as the 'Marrakesh Declaration' was issued which said that the ministers of '124 governments and the European Communities ...'

Confirm their resolution to strive for greater global coherence of policies in the fields of trade, money and finance, including cooperation between the WTO, the IMF and the World Bank for that purpose. (GATT, 1994)

In this declaration lies the most significant achievement of the Uruguay Round – the establishment, with a legal identity, of the World Trade Organisation (WTO) which replaces the existing GATT. Its origins lie in the 31-year war, in particular its second hot phase, which proved to be an economic blessing for the US. The United States was the first industrialised nation to begin to emerge from the Great Depression, which finally and completely disappeared for it in the massive productivity of World War II, the war which made it the world's most powerful economy; it was determined to consolidate that position. Comparisons of the relative positions of the US and the USSR and the history of the differences between them, although bearing heavily on our subject, do not belong here (see, *inter alia*, Hobsbawm, 1994; Harris, 1983). Other Western states, strongly influenced by the work of John Maynard Keynes and with the memory of 1930s protectionism fresh in their minds, particularly of the Draconian US Tariff Act of 1930, were also anxious to find ways of stabilising international trade relations. Between them they invented the idea of an International Trade Organisation (ITO) which, in those more generous days, would have made substantial provision for growth in the still largely colonial world. It came to nothing when, in 1947, ratification was denied by the US Congress, still largely dominated by the struggles around isolationism (Watkins, 1992).

The ITO had been among the proposals made, in 1944, at the Bretton Woods Conference at which the governments of the US, Canada and Britain laid down the ground-rules for post-war international financial systems. Bretton Woods, of course, led to the foundation of the International Bank for Reconstruction and Development (IBRD – now known simply as the World Bank) and of the UN's International Monetary Fund (IMF). It was also responsible for inventing the General Agreement on Tariffs and Trade, the effectiveness of which could, in the eyes of the participants in the Conference, only be complete if it was implemented by an internationally accepted body with policing powers and which would ultimately, itself, replace GATT. It is for this reason that the creation of the WTO, decades after the defeat of the ITO, came to be such a central part of the negotiations in the Uruguay Round. It also explains why the brief Marrakesh Declaration (eight short paragraphs) concentrated on its establishment claiming that it 'ushers in a new era of global economic cooperation' (GATT, 1994).

Current financial uncertainties may yet lead to a chequered future for the WTO. For example, the US shows many signs of wanting to return to its former isolationist politics (even if its practice is a little more internationalist) and, on the European side of the Atlantic, newspapers utter awful warnings.[1] But the globalisation of the economy and the vastly increased power of supply capital mean that there is a limit to how far these tendencies can go. Much has been made in development debates of the ability of TNCs to move to areas of cheap labour and fewer environmental restraints, and plenty of examples of this kind of movement exist. Seriously polluting chemical industries setting up shop in Ireland with the connivance of a venal and largely anti-environmentalist bureaucracy is a case in point; another is the sight of a corrupt Tory government in Britain supine, until their defeat, before the interests of oil giants and followed by 'new' Labour unwilling to be too precise about carbon emission targets. Yet most of the world's biggest TNCs stay in their countries of origin and, no matter how widespread their activities may be, the profits of their investments remain within the industrialised world. While corporations and capital may, in theory, be very mobile, most TNCs have preferred to operate within the confines of the industrialised club-room. 'Globalisation', frequently misunderstood,[2] has meant three things: the first is the concentration of world trade into the hands of the TNCs, the second is the monopolisation of world markets and the third is the increased ability to move production to countries with low-wage economies.

In our introduction we have already remarked that TNCs control 80 per cent of world trade, half of which is intra-company (Watkins, 1995, p. 113). Commodity markets have, since the rise of capitalism, been in corporate control, but now, more than ever before, companies owned by TNCs are fighting for the control of the exchange of even the most basic elements of life. The drive to persuade health authorities in deprived regions to buy expensive oral rehydration kits rather than to promote simple and cheap home-made procedures and the attempts to dissuade mothers from breast-feeding and to choose, instead, less nourishing and protective diets of powdered milk are both notorious examples. Even more insidious have been the increasingly successful attempts at patenting genetic material, and an interesting example may be seen in the World Bank's determination to compel Zimbabwe to give TNCs virtually free access to its protected national seed bank.

A succinct account of this form of piracy was given by Professor Carol Thompson, of North Arizona University.[3]

Transnational corporations are not recent phenomena; we have only to think, for example, of the breakup of the Standard Oil Company in 1911 and its regrouping as a complex of companies under the control of the Rockefeller group (Baran and Sweezy, 1966). What is relatively new is the global extent of their reach, and it is to facilitate this that financial and trade 'liberalisation' and the construction of the WTO have taken place. It is significant that, following the aims of the Bretton Woods conferees, it is the third partner in that trade and finance ruling triumvirate, the WTO, which now has the world-wide legal power to enforce the rules of the global market. The importance of this for our argument lies in recognising the effects of their combined policies on the capacity of the poor, not just poor countries, but the poor everywhere, to protect their own resources. One of the strands within resurgent isolationism in the US is the recognition by many working people that these policies affect them too. It is unfortunate that their response has often taken the ultra-right and racialist path of 'Fortress America'.

Just as the Cold War was, in a sense, a war about resources, about protecting spheres of economic influence and about securing the pre-eminent position of the US and, to a lesser extent, Western Europe and Japan, so the WTO is the TNCs' protectionist organisation. Its purpose is to render national boundaries as porous as possible to 'free' trade. Within this arrangement the various trade blocs or customs unions (for example, the EU, NAFTA, APEC) are scrambling for improved trading positions. NAFTA, in particular, illustrates a growing problem for the poor. It was negotiated against the background of a considerable history of US industry, particularly the motor industry, subcontracting its assembly processes to factories in Mexico (*maquiladoras*) which depended on cheap labour and unregulated working conditions (Browne et al., 1994). This process really took off (see Table 2.1) after major devaluations of the peso. Given Mexico's most recent financial collapses, together with the United States' predatory 'rescue' policy, we may well see an even greater acceleration of the process.

Enthusiasts for world governance might descry in all this at least a step in the right direction and, indeed, it is in that optimistic light that the World Bank sees it. Waxing almost lyrical it remarks:

> These are revolutionary times in the global economy. The embrace of market-based development by many developing and former centrally planned economies, the opening of international markets, and great advances in the ease with which goods, capital, and ideas flow around the world are bringing new opportunities, as well as risks, to billions of people. (World Bank, 1995, p. 1)

This optimism (always saving the 'risks') is based on unexamined, and in some instances, patently false, assumptions. Among them is that large capital investment is always good for economies, that state regulation discourages investment or renders it less efficient, that any economy which puts its house in order can eventually compete in the big league, that cheap labour and unregulated environmental conditions are not particularly important in the pantheon of international investors and, most importantly, a free market will level all things out. There are several more.

Table 2.1 Maquila Industry 1980–92

Year	Plants, No.	Employees	Value added[†]	Hourly pay[‡]
1980	620	119,546	771	2.41
1981	605	130,973	974	2.57
1982	585	127,048	812	1.78
1983	600	150,867	825	1.28
1984	672	199,684	1161	1.43
1985	760	211,968	1266	1.39
1986	890	249,833	1295	1.02
1987	1125	305,423	1635	1.04
1988	1369	369,489	2339	1.17
1989	1655	429,725	3057	1.30
1990	1930	460,293	3362	1.34
1991	1954	489,000	4100	1.60
1992	2129	511,000	4300	1.64

[†] Millions of 1992 US$ (not adjusted). [‡] Average wage, includes direct wages and all benefits, bonuses, payroll taxes and vacations – given in 1992 US$.
Source: Browne et al.,1994.

There are differences in the approaches of the World Bank, the IMF and the WTO, but their practices are intimately linked. One result of this phenomenon may be observed in the wildly inappropriate structural adjustment programmes attached to loans, or loan rescheduling, by the World Bank and the IMF. These loans, broadly and theoretically speaking, are designed, in one form or another, to help the borrowing states improve their economies; even rescheduling may, with an effort, be considered in this way. Simultaneously the lending institutions demand reductions in social provision, in, therefore, the protection and restoration of the human capital on which any future recovery among the borrowers might be built. Peter was destitute to begin with, but he is to be squeezed yet further to pay Paul. This is important because structural adjustment most clearly illustrates the impossibility of applying unregulated free-market mechanisms to substantial numbers of marginalised countries. The cheerful observation that 'Their limitations have been sufficiently analyzed in recent years' (IOV, 1991) does not, unfortunately, mean that these programmes are no longer applied. Nor, strictly speaking, is it true, since such analysis as has appeared seems to have left the practice largely untouched. For evidence of this we have only to look at the recent joint loan to Argentina in which the World Bank and the IMF are major partners. 'The IMF team, which is negotiating a new £1.4 billion loan in exchange for a tougher economic programme ...'.[4]

In case we should be in any doubt that market principles are to dominate, we should turn to the provisions of GATT:

3) Members shall seek to avoid the imposition of new quantitative restrictions for balance-of-payments purposes unless ... price based measures cannot arrest a sharp deterioration in the external payments position ...

4) Members confirm that restrictive import measures taken for balance-of-payment purposes may only be applied to control the general level of imports ... the importing Member shall provide adequate justification as to the criteria used to determine which products are subject to restriction ... [except for] certain essential products ... which meet basic consumption needs ... [or] capital goods needed for production. (GATT, 1994 pp. 27–8)

This requirement will make life even more difficult for the weakest economies. In the section of the Agreement headed 'Ministerial Decisions and Declarations' (p. 440) there is a 'Decision on Measures in Favour of Least-Developed Countries' which allows the tempering of the wind to the shorn lamb. However, this decision lacks teeth or definition and is only offered as a possibility. For a more concrete example of what it can mean we may turn to paragraphs 6 and 8 of the balance-of-payments provision (pp. 28–9) which simply offers the least developed countries easier consultation periods with the 'Committee for the Balance of Payments' which will assist the developing country in managing the issues. Since there is no suggestion that the rules might be modified in these cases, we may be free to fear that stricter application of the favourite Bretton Woods solutions will form an integral part of that management.

Perhaps solutions to the problems of the 'least developed countries' may lie in arranging matters of international trade so that it is possible for them, collectively or severally, to enter the world trading system by means which will allow them to survive independently and equitably. However, the provisions of the GATT and the activities of customs unions and TNCs at present treat them, when they are considered at all, simply as exploitable markets. One example may stand for all. Article VI of the 1947–8 GATT has been incorporated into the 1994 Agreement and the conditions of its implementation are to be found in Annex 1A (GATT, 1994, p. 168). It is the measure designed to stop dumping, which Article 2 of the Agreement on Implementation defines as the introduction 'into the commerce of another country [of a product] at less than its normal value' (clause 2.1). 'Normal value' is defined in differing ways which include the price paid by customers for the product in the country which is exporting it. Effectively the exported goods should not be sold in the recipient country at a price below the cost of production 'plus a reasonable amount for administrative, selling and general costs and for profits' (clause 2.2). Goods would also be sold below normal value by an exporter where the selling price to the importing country is lower than the selling price for the same thing in the exporter's own home market. In a footnote to clause 2.2, normal value is said to be established in the domestic market of the exporter when sales are equivalent to 5 per cent or more of what is to be exported to any given country.

Bearing these rules in mind we must note that agriculture has been brought within the provisions of the GATT for the first time. Turning to Annex 2 to the Agreement on Agriculture we find that domestic support for agricultural products must have 'no, or at most minimal, trade distorting effects' and that support 'shall not have the effect of providing price support to producers' (GATT, 1994, p. 56). Cheap food produced by Northern agribusiness has repeatedly distorted domestic markets in poor countries; it is estimated that 'each American farmer receives a subsidy of about $29,000'.[5] Subsidised imports into developing countries have reduced, if not destroyed, domestic production to the point where no comparison can be made which might demonstrate that imported food had effectively been dumped. Similarly, the Agreement on Agriculture removes, or at least reduces, the ability of governments to support the lowering of domestic prices. Much of the cheap food imported from the developed world has been, effectively, a sop to urban demands and many governments in poor countries do not see combating cheap imports as in their short-term interests.

Obvious consequences for the poorer developing countries flow from all this: in many of them prices, depressed for so long by cheap imports, have become one of the issues governing industrialised exporters' prices. Farmers faced with competition from cheap imported food notoriously try to compete by working themselves and their land much harder and in unsustainable ways. Poor countries, already deep in debt, are compelled to find additional hard currency to pay for the imports, thus impoverishing themselves yet further. Cheap food imports, because of demographic pressures and poor infrastructure, are principally confined to urban areas, so migration to the towns is further encouraged. There are other, more insidious, consequences which have to do with changed diets, increased energy use and so on. What the Agreement, to be operated and policed by the WTO, has done is to allow the commonly subsidised industrialised food producers, who have the machinery, economic conditions, distribution and marketing ability to keep prices as low as circumstances demand, to enter into direct competition with Third World farmers. Competition between such unequally matched groups may well satisfy rules dreamt up in the Humpty-Dumpty world of Bretton Woods, where 'free' in relation to 'market' seems to be defined by whomever is 'master'. It does not satisfy a common sense of justice. Watkins quotes a woman called Rosa who farms in the Philippines: 'I don't understand how the Americans can sell us maize so cheaply ... we cannot compete, our prices are going down, our children are going hungry, and our community is dying.'[6]

Throughout the Cold War the danger of an irruption into a hot and nuclear war was always present, but, that apart, it engendered a kind of stability. Western capital was contained and the command economies of the Warsaw Pact managed, somehow, to be a credible alternative model for at least some states in the developing world. Widespread instability has followed the collapse of the Soviet Union and emerging nationalisms, often inspired by an eye to the main economic chance, have led to internecine wars, even in that quondam socialist economy rejected by Stalin and his successors, the former Yugoslavia. The industrialised world's response has been instructive. Large-scale aid and investment have been directed at integrating the industrial, largely European, sectors of the former Union into the world market economy, even to the point of acquiring substantial parts of it (Middleton et al., 1993). Other survivors of the Cold War, China and Vietnam, also until recently outside the world of the free market, are being drawn into the World Trade Organisation (Watkins, 1995). It is not stretching the evidence too far to see in this confirmation of our analysis of US and European motivation in waging the Cold War, but, more importantly, we may also see the merging of political and financial objectives in binding former 'enemies' into the WTO. Investment may be led by the multilateral banks, but is only possible on any effective scale if they are accompanied and, in the end, overshadowed by the TNCs.

At the centre of this new world order lies a neo-liberal economic ideology which has elevated 'competition' to the status of a law of nature, even, occasionally, invoking a spurious Darwinism in support of its arguments. In a nightmarish simplification of Marx's theory of exchange value (Marx, 1867, 1968), it begins with the breathtaking assumption that all social relations are the relations of the market. Thus workers, producers, financiers, states, institutions are all offering bundles of commodities (we take the phrase from Sen – services of all kinds become commodified in this perception of the world) in exchange for their survival. Failure to possess a bundle sufficient to meet need is a consequence not of the relations of production, but of personal inadequacy which can end in starvation, bankruptcy or takeover. Competition, in this surreal account, is not only between differing groups or nations, but between individual members of the same group. So it is that, among others, workers must compete with one another in enhancing their capacity to sell. Thus is the issue fudged and the pretence that all parties in competition are either equal or have the capacity to be so is maintained. In passing we should note that this neo-liberal ideology is only possible as a product of the urban world of capital; it can only respond to alternative, rural peasant economies by trying to destroy them.

It was in the gradual formation of this bizarre world that the older forms of direct colonisation largely came to an end. Colonialists had re-drawn the map of the world and had modelled it on the pattern of the nineteenth-century European nation states. Many of the administrative territories they carved out, particularly in Africa, bore little or no relation to the pre-colonial political divisions. It was these artificial constructs that became governmentally independent. For many of them a sort of nationalism, mimetic of Europe, was forged in fierce wars of independence. Few colonising powers left gracefully and none of them compensated their erstwhile fiefdoms for generations of rapacious extraction, or for the failure to permit the growth of indigenous social infrastructure. Newly independent states were, in general, impoverished and largely without the technological and managerial capacity to take command of such resources as they did possess. In any case, colonialism was almost entirely extractive and created little in the way of indigenous production and where some emerged, as in the case of the Indian steel industry, it was hedged about with Northern protectionist conditions. Companies, largely introduced by colonial regimes, continued to be the principal owners and managers of industrial plant and of industrial plantations. Mined resources, vegetable and mineral, were sold, of course, on the international commodity markets which were also controlled by the industrialised world. In substance this familiar story has changed little in the years since decolonisation.

There have, however, been some changes in the techniques of expatriate management; they are typified by the *maquila* industries of Mexico. In the recent industrial past, TNCs involved in manufacture or food production built their huge factories or their giant farms which were worked by what became powerful and well-organised workforces. Modern communications and processes have allowed these corporations to fragment production and, in the *maquila* system, numbers of different processes are subcontracted – some parts may be produced, others assembled and so on in different places. In each contract the TNC decides on the nature of the operations, dictates the processes by which they will be carried out, determines prices and delivery times. Final objects may be assembled under contract in one factory from parts also made under contract in others. Some parts of the process may even be carried out in factories owned directly by the TNC. Two major benefits accrue to TNCs adopting this method: they may substantially reduce their labour costs and they disempower their home-based and often unionised workforces (Browne et al., 1994).

The excellence of this arrangement from the point of view of the TNCs is obvious and the practice is being substantially extended. Plantation agriculture controlled, and often owned by TNCs is familiar enough, but it is normally monocultural, unwieldy in responding to TNC demand and, above all, allows for the development of an organised workforce. New investment in such enormous undertakings is rapidly being replaced, at least in part, by a more malleable system, one which adopts the principle of *maquila* industry. TNCs are increasingly offering production contracts to relatively small 'independent' 'family' farmers. Like so many other industrial processes, this has been pioneered in the US where, 'By 1980 nearly one third of US farm output by value was produced under some form of contract' (Watts, 1990, pp. 149 ff.). Watts remarks, a little caustically, that the system is known as 'vertical coordination' and now, in the US, far exceeds 'vertically integrated' or plantation agribusiness production. The end result bears little or no resemblance to what is usually conjured up by the phrase 'family farm'.

In one form or another, contract farming is being widely extended to the Third World, so much so that there are examples of agribusiness TNCs closing down their plantations in favour of some such arrangement (Watts, 1990). Agricultural contracts in the developing world, according to Watts, are principally arranged in three ways. In one of these, large suppliers offer direct contracts to small farmers, but negotiate the terms through their own organisations either with the state or with some more local institution; in another, small peasants are offered contracts either by local or by foreign merchants. The commonest version of the system is one operated by large processing and shipping organisations, often owned by the state, which give limited contracts, almost invariably of one year in duration, to innumerable small peasant growers. These contracts determine what is to be grown, the methods to be used and the price to be paid; those who issue them take absolute title to the crop.

In 1990 Watts claimed that 12 per cent of all sub-Saharan peasant farmers were growing sugar, tea, tobacco, fresh fruit and vegetables under contracts with either state or private suppliers to the international markets. Between them they accounted for 17 per cent of the total produced by all farms and for 30 per cent of everything marketed (Watts, 1990, p. 152). Diverting farmland to this purpose is in line with the World Bank's view of development, cash-crops are grown which will earn hard currency and so on. The Bank commonly urges the practice as a 'new agricultural policy' in tandem with its structural adjustment programmes. Women are overwhelmingly the main labourers on these farms (Mbilinyi, 1990), but it is the men who get paid and who then decide how much women will receive for household expenses. One Tanzanian woman, quoted by Mbilinyi, describes it as 'the big slavery'. It is certainly true that the system benefits a small coterie and that may well satisfy the Bretton Woods institutions which still seem to cling to that eccentric theory sometimes called 'trickle down'. All that has trickled down to most women is extra work in a world of escalating prices.

We have described here a policy of cost and risk reduction, often called 'runaway' agriculture, constructed in the interests of TNCs. It is in the light of this policy that we should consider, for example, Siad Barre's range enclosures which were such a significant factor in creating the crisis in Somalia (African Rights, October 1993), or the eviction of Kenyan Somalis from their rangelands (African Rights, September 1993) and the eviction of settled farmers (mainly Kikuyus) from their farms (Human Rights Watch/Africa, July 1994) to be replaced, in the last two instances, by followers of the President of Kenya, Daniel Arup Moi. Further examples are to be found everywhere; they are the enclosures of sixteenth- and seventeenth-century England writ large. Earlier in this chapter we touched on the collaboration of industrialised states, and their formation of customs and trading unions, with the objectives of TNCs. On the way we mentioned the issue of forbidding, through the mechanisms of the WTO, the sorts of protection Third World states might resort to for their fledgling industries and their own farming. We have considered how this process has been accelerated by the collapse of the Soviet Union. In our brief discussion of 'runaway' agriculture, we link these elements with the increased exploitation of, in particular, the rural populations of developing countries. We have also made the point that the World Bank adds to the difficulties by insisting on the objectives of the industrialised world, making them conditions of loans and attaching them to structural adjustment programmes.

Table 2.2 OECD official overseas development assistance as percentages of GNP

Country	1975	1985	1989	1990	1991	1992	1993	1993 (of which %age to ASPs†)
Denmark	0.58	0.80	0.93	0.94	0.96	1.02	1.03	27.2
Norway	0.66	1.01	1.05	1.17	1.13	1.16	1.01	19.8
Sweden	0.82	0.86	0.96	0.91	0.90	1.03	0.98	2
Netherlands	0.75	0.91	0.94	0.92	0.88	0.86	0.82	13.4
France	0.62	0.78	0.61	0.60	0.62	0.63	0.63	4.76
Finland	0.18	0.40	0.62	0.63	0.80	0.64	0.46	8.7
Canada	0.54	0.49	0.44	0.44	0.45	0.46	0.45	8.9
Belgium	0.59	0.55	0.46	0.46	0.41	0.39	0.39	2.6
Germany	0.40	0.47	0.41	0.42	0.40	0.39	0.37	2.7
Australia	0.65	0.48	0.38	0.34	0.38	0.37	0.35	11.4
Italy	0.11	0.26	0.42	0.31	0.30	0.34	0.31	0
UK	0.39	0.33	0.31	0.27	0.32	0.31	0.31	6.5
Austria	0.21	0.38	0.22	0.25	0.34	0.30	0.30	6.6
Japan	0.23	0.29	0.31	0.31	0.32	0.31	0.26	3.8
New Zealand	0.52	0.25	0.22	0.23	0.25	0.26	0.25	0
Ireland	0.09	0.24	0.17	0.16	0.19	0.16	0.20	0
USA	0.27	0.24	0.15	0.21	0.20	0.20	0.15	13.3

† Areas of Social Priority – programme designed to meet the need of the absolutely poor.
Source: World Bank, World Development Report 1995; Oxfam, The Oxfam Poverty Report, Oxford, 1995.

In this consideration of the political and economic background to humanitarian emergencies, we must list some other elements. With the exceptions of Portugal and Ireland, virtually all OECD states are reducing their development aid budgets. Few of them have ever achieved the 0.7 per cent of GNP recommended by the Brandt Commission in 1977; in 1993, only four did so (see Table 2.2 for a league table). Governmental cynicism plumbed new abysses when Margaret Thatcher cheerfully attached a 'sweetener', in the form of finance for a large and redundant dam, to an arms deal with Malaysia; her successor, John Major, or one of his satraps, made an equally grubby, if smaller, offer of aid to Dominica when Saudi Arabia, that bastion of democratic probity, asked him to deport one of its critics. Both incidents illustrate the way in which development aid budgets in many industrial states would, perhaps, be better seen as part either of their defence budgets or of their budgets for trade and industry.

What is happening now is the gradual replacement of development aid for the very poorest by funds for humanitarian assistance. This may be seen from some crude OECD figures published in a press release dated 20 June 1994 (quoted in UNICEF, 1995). They suggest that development aid from the industrialised nations has fallen to the lowest level for 20 years and now stands at an average of 0.29 per cent (we may contrast this with Denmark's 1.03 and The Netherlands' 0.82 per cent – see Table 2.2). On the other hand 'peace-keeping' operations in the five years preceding 1994 had risen in cost from US$ 0.3 billion to US$ 3.6 billion. The proportion of the UN's assistance budget given over to relief and emergency rose from 25 per cent in 1988 to 45 per cent in 1992. In the case of the US, the statistics for the Greater Horn of Africa are particularly telling (see Figure 2.1) since, as we have already remarked, countries within it were flooded with aid during the Cold War.

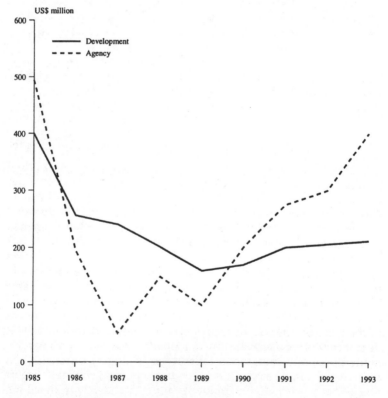

Figure 2.1 USAID expenditure (US$ m.): Greater Horn of Africa

Source: USAID, 1994.

Since our brief portrayal of the economic circumstances in which 'development', as well as humanitarian assistance, is supposed to take place is one of largely unregulated market exploitation, it may be a matter of some small relief that there is a common reduction in the budgets for 'overseas cooperation'. It is just possible, even if slightly improbable, that there will be fewer Pergau Dams, fewer instances of US and Commonwealth tergiversation in response to the Abachas of this world or fewer examples of a group like ASEAN welcoming the ruling thugs of soi-disant Myanmar into its club. Sadly, Malcolm Rifkind's pallid excuse for British arms sales to the Rwandan Hutu extremists[7] gives little ground for optimisim in this. What is certain is that as development expenditure gives way to humanitarian assistance, we are watching the unedifying spectacle of the rich world patching up the worst of the casualties its policies have created while pretending to a magnanimity.

The present authors feel that it is not an overstatement to see all this as a new Cold War, or possibly the old one in a new phase. In essence, particularly if we lean towards Hobsbawm's analysis of the economic aims and consequences of the 31 years of war, we may see the Cold War as being about trade and resources, conducted with the object of securing economic hegemony for Western capital. In the following chapters we shall consider seven recent catastrophes and the multiform elements which led to them. With the uncertain exception of Kenya, each one has involved continuous or spasmodic conflict, generally, but not always, confined within national borders. Commentators, particularly from the media, are inclined to refer to these wars as 'civil' or 'ethnic'; the former may be justified because the opposed forces are usually, but also not always, recruited within the country at issue, but war aims are often connected to international interests. Since 'ethnicity' is notoriously difficult to define, 'ethnic' is at best inaccurate and a product of laziness or, at worst, simply racialist (for an analysis of this question see Fukui and Markakis, 1994). For this reason we have been cautious in our use of either adjective; in each case where conflict has emerged we argue that, like the Cold War, it might reasonably be described as market-engendered. In each of them people are driven from their lands, die from the diseases of poverty and famine, become displaced or refugees or, at best, compelled to find alternative, but commonly more difficult, livelihoods in the interests of promoting a neo-liberal economic agenda. Almost without exception, these are the contemporary humanitarian disasters.

Part 2

Humanitarian Assistance in Action

CHAPTER 3

Somalia

Towards the end of the 1980s tensions in Somalia, largely a product of rapacious land-grabbing by Siad Barre and his associates, collapsed into a civil war in which clan loyalties governed, to a certain extent, its shifting alliances. Massive refugeeism and displacement, adding to the already huge numbers of those uprooted and driven from their homes by land-looting,[1] were a consequence of the fighting. In 1990–1 a severe drought added to the overwhelming difficulties experienced by the poor and vulnerable and a major famine ensued. During the years of drought the International Committee of the Red Cross (ICRC) and its associate, the Somali Red Crescent Society (SRCS) together with some NGOs, notably the Save the Children Fund-UK (SCF-UK), working as closely as possible with Somali professionals and volunteers, did their best to relieve those made destitute by war and rapine as well as drought. Their substantial success is unquestionably due, in large part, to working with, rather that in spite of, Somalis (MacRae and Zwi, 1994). Towards the end of the drought, these agencies, as well as other NGOs working intermittently in the country, finally achieved sufficient media coverage to persuade the UN and the richer nations to intervene. This story, including the notorious landing of the US Marines as the vanguard of the UN forces, is well enough known, but an understanding of the political nature of the disaster and its consequences calls for a slightly more detailed account of the events.

Somalia was part of one of the major battle grounds of the Cold War consisting of the Arabian Peninsula, the Horn of Africa and the Gulfs of Oman and Aden. While that war was, undoubtedly, one of ideologies as well as of market control, it was, in this region above all, a war about resources. For the US, whose domestic oil reserves were severely depleted, it was a struggle to ensure that the massive Middle-Eastern oilfields remained under its control or, at least, under the control of those TNCs based within US borders. In its later, hot, war against Iraq the US acted from much the same motive, though Halliday (1996), in his important discussion of the Gulf War, is inclined to put it more generously. Oil was a less pressing matter for the Soviet Union, but it was nonetheless a strategic asset that it would have preferred to see within its own ambit. The USSR was also alarmed by what it saw, probably correctly, as American encirclement and so was determined to undermine it wherever possible. Parallels may reasonably be drawn between the United States' drive for hegemony in the region and the earlier extensive annexation, by the British, of more and more territory in the interests of preserving its Indian Empire (Said, 1993). Following the collapse of Haile Selassie, Ethiopia had become the scene of intense jockeying between the Powers, a jockeying that spread very quickly to Ethiopia's neighbour, Somalia. The last act in that particular circus included the USA's backing for the corrupt regime of Siad Barre and even its financing of his gross expropriation of both settled and nomadic peasants (African Rights, October 1993).

Somalia's history as a political entity, separate from Ethiopian interests, began in the thirteenth century with the foundation of a state known as Ifat (Oliver and Fage, 1970). It was the largest of several Islamic settlements along the coast of what is now Somalia and ran from the port of Zeila east to Berbera and south towards Addis Ababa, it survived until the early fifteenth century when it was destroyed, and its King killed, in a battle with Ethiopia at Zeila in AD 1415. The survivors, principally Yemenite (ITeM, 1995), created a new realm further to the east which became the Sultanate of Adel and which rapidly reclaimed the lost territory. By the early sixteenth century, arms dealers from the Ottoman Empire had equipped it with sufficient firepower to pose what would have certainly been a fatal threat to Ethiopia. It was contained only by the intervention, in 1542, of a Portuguese Armada which razed Zeila, Berbera, Mogadishu and Brava. Portugal made no attempt to occupy the Sultanate, but simply resorted to pillage and destruction which eventually forced the decline of Adel into a series of smaller sultanates (Oliver and Fage, 1970; ITeM, 1995). Those in the north were largely clients of the Ottoman Empire, while the south, following the expulsion of the Portuguese in 1698, accepted the suzerainty of the Sultan of Zanzibar.

Portuguese adventures apart, serious European colonisation followed on the new importance given to the region by the building of the Suez Canal which opened in 1869. The French bought the port of Obok (this transaction led, finally, to the creation of Djibouti) which became their railhead for Addis Ababa. In 1885 the British, invading Zeila and Berbera, began to establish the northern colony of British Somaliland. Italy, compensating for its defeat at the hands of the Ethiopian Emperor, Menelik II, at the Battle of Aduwa in 1896, occupied the south and, in 1906, created the colony of Somalia. Ethiopia, in the course of the 1890s, also claimed a share of Somalian territory and incorporated the region of Ogaden.

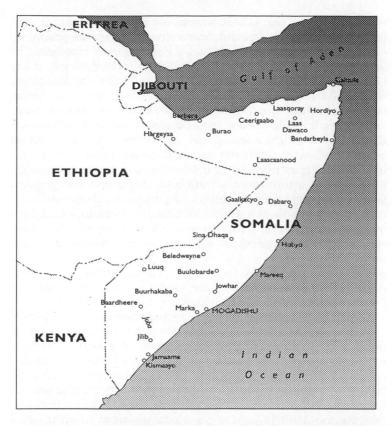

Opposition to British rule in the north was immediate and became the centre of opposition to colonial rule throughout the region. Its first and most resourceful leader was Sheik Muhammad bin Abdullah Hussein whose forces frequently defeated the British in the early years of the twentieth century and it was not until 1920 that Britain gained complete control of its colony (ITeM, 1995). Italy was removed from Somalia after its defeat in 1941 and Britain set up a temporary administration. Prompted, perhaps, by chrysalidian democratic ideals which would emerge in Britain after the war, it made some effort to encourage people to take part in District affairs and rescinded a ban on political campaigns (Issa-Salwe, 1994). This freedom led to the formation of the Somali Youth League, in 1947, which campaigned for the reunification of all Somali territories – Italian Somalia, British Somaliland, Djibouti, Ogaden and the North of Kenya (Davidson, 1994). In British Somaliland, a parallel movement, built from a coalition of political clubs, came into being in 1951 with virtually the same programme – it was called the Somali National League (Issa-Salwe, 1994).

Other political parties existed, but the importance of these two lay in their ability to transcend, not to ignore or deny, the potentially divisive clan structures which had, for so long, been exploited by invaders and colonisers alike. Britain, for example, during its shady negotiations with Ethiopia immediately before Somali independence, established a clan-based administration in the western Somalian territories of Ogaden and Haud, territories that it was about to return to Ethiopia. It would at least be in line with British colonial tradition that it did so in the hope, if not the knowledge, that such an administration would, under pressure, be fissiparous and so less of a threat. Elections in 1959, held under UN tutelage, led to the formation of a more or less non-clan based and independent government of this partitioned people, under which the territories of British Somaliland and Italian Somalia were united. It was formally instituted on 1 July 1960 and some commentators have remarked that a system so mimetic of the structures of the industrialised world was alien to Somali clan tradition (IOV, 1994, p. 57). While this may be so, it should be recognised that so, too, were the varying autocratic regimes under which Somalis had lived for so many centuries. At least they had voted for this one.

Somali clan structures spring from the nomadic pastoralism of its people and partition is peculiarly significant because it is among the first of the threats to their range-lands. International hostility to Somali demands for reunification, combined with the common effects of the abrupt withdrawal of the colonising interest, the failure of colonial regimes to lay the foundations of a serious infrastructure (particularly the case in the former British territory) and the problems in fashioning a new government all led to a difficult birth. Matters were made worse by an abortive military *coup d'état* in December 1961. Internecine squabbling, concentrating too much effort on reunification and too little on immediate problems led to a very shaky, corrupt and ineffectual government and planted yet more seeds of the ultimate collapse of the Somali state and the disaster of the early 1990s. Finally, in October 1969, following the assassination of President Shermake by a member of the police force, a military junta led by General Siad Barre seized power.

Barre was elected chair of the Supreme Revolutionary Council and began a programme of social and political reform designed, among other things, to end the power of the clans. Probably with an eye to help from the USSR he also allowed young, left-wing functionaries a substantial amount of power. He declared a government of 'scientific socialism' in which he equated the sharing of property with the ancient clan customs. Many of the policies advanced in the first years of the new regime might have been successful, but Barre and his Council swiftly became obsessed, like so many military regimes, with the problems of 'security' – by which, of course, they mean the consolidation of their own power. The left was driven out of office and a National Security Service was created to deal with any form of dissent, individual rights were suspended, and regional and district councils charged with rooting out opposition were created. Intellectuals were persecuted, clan divisions fostered, family members encouraged to spy on one another and a paramilitary force, the 'Victorious Pioneers' (*Guulwadayaal*), designed to terrorise people into submission came into being (Issa-Salwe, 1994). A personality cult built around Barre replaced serious policy.

In July 1977, vainly trying to conceal the real problems, Barre launched a war on Ethiopia to recover the alienated Somali territories. He almost succeeded, but was defeated by Cuban military intervention on behalf of Ethiopia and, by March 1978, retreated from the engagement. The war was a diplomatic disaster, since most other African states were opposed to redrawing the old colonial boundaries but, worse still, the adventure did irreparable damage to the Somali economy, causing substantial rises in fuel and grain prices which were increased yet further by the 1978–9 drought (ITeM, 1995). Barre, angered by Soviet support for both Cuba and the Mengistu regime in Ethiopia, ended Somalia's military agreements with the USSR, an act which rendered the Somali economy even more fragile. To deal with the consequent discontent he reinforced all his earlier machinery of oppression.

Somalia is a big country, about one-and-a-half times the size of France, with a small population – in the region of eight to nine million. Its climate is harsh, both arid and hot and it is subject to frequent and extended droughts. Some 70 per cent of its land is given over to pasture, traditionally grazed by the herds of the nomadic pastoralists, and about 2 per cent to arable farming – principally around the Juba and Shebele rivers. Landholding among settled farmers was customary, governed by a complex collectivity and a system of usufruct rights. These had, to some extent, been disturbed by the colonisers who introduced 'modern farming' and appropriated large tracts of land in the Lower Juba and Shebele for use as banana plantations. Not long after independence the ruling élite recommenced the process of expropriation. Using a mix of coercion and chicanery, they concentrated on the most fertile and accessible land. One consequence of this land-grabbing was a substantial increase in the numbers of landless peasants, but it was Barre's depredations, and those of his associates, following his abandonment of any semblance of progressive government, that turned that relatively slow increase into an exponential growth.

In 1975 a land reform act had been introduced which gave the ownership of all land to the state which would then regulate its disposal and use. It could have been a progressive and constructive piece of legislation, but it turned on making registration of land the means of establishing the ownership of leaseholds. This procedure failed, on the one hand, to recognise the complexities of customary land law and, on the other, discriminated against those who did not work within contemporary western patterns of 'ownership'. Clauses within the legislation and the failure properly to control it, allowed the powerful, both legally and by fraud, to register their ownership of huge amounts of land belonging, by customary law, to indigenous farmers. The process has been aptly described as 'land-looting' (African Rights, October 1993) and although the greatest and most damaging expropriations were in the agricultural regions of the Lower Juba and the Shebele, they were not confined to them. Water resources and pasture were enclosed in the north-west and, in 1988–9, an attempt was made to take over pasture in the Middle and Lower Juba. Successful and unsuccessful enclosures of range-lands led directly to the various, largely clan-based, armed oppositions to Barre's regime, which were further supported by the new landless peasantry and by those farmers still in situ.

Opposition to Barre was not, however, confined to dispossessed farmers and pastoralists, it included powerful figures who wanted to carve out their own fiefdoms – among them was General Mohammed Farah Aideed who came to control the military wing of the United Somali Congress – formed, in the late 1980s, by Aideed and other members of his Hawiye clan in exile in Rome (IOV, 1994). Barre was finally and bloodily defeated in January 1991 and the USC, which was the strongest group in the south, installed Mohammed Ali Mahdi as interim president. The most powerful movement in the north was the Somali National Movement; it seceded from a united Somalia to form the Somaliland Republic, covering the same area as the former British colony – it was proclaimed on 18 May 1991. In Somalia splits within the USC led to armed conflict between the adherents of Aideed and Mahdi which continued until the two sides signed a peace agreement in 1994. Other opponents of Siad Barre had, because they were excluded from the choice, rejected the appointment of Mahdi and subsequently either chose sides with one or other of the two main warring parties, or pursued their own agendas. Civil government came to an end in Somalia with the fall of Siad Barre and had been replaced by these factional wars and by opportunistic looting.

Farmers and pastoralists had, over countless generations, developed ways of dealing with major drought. Suffering and malnutrition were often acute, but societies, people, their herds and livelihoods commonly survived. Survival was based, obviously enough, on the management and conservation of limited resources and on a culture of sharing and mutual obligation. By the end of the 1980s land-looting had displaced huge numbers of people and yet more fled in the face of a mobile and violent war, so they were dispossessed of, or driven away from, precisely those resources which would have carried them through a time of drought. Smallholders in the Juba and Shebele Valleys were also defeated by the destruction or appropriation of the means of irrigation (IOV, 1994). African Rights[2] (October, 1993) makes a convincing case for the alienation of land as the principal cause of the famine of 1991–2. What is certain is that the horrifying death rate and the misery of enormous numbers of refugees and internally displaced people was a consequence of a complex of events of which drought was only one. Most of those events were political and social and may be traced back through the path we have summarised so briefly.

Before we consider the responses of the developed world to the crisis in Somalia, there are some other factors to take into account. Land-looters, whether creating privatised plantations and ranges or simply speculating, are, in effect, engineering a switch from a subsistence and trading economy to one heavily dependent on producing for the international market in cash-crops. Customary land rights were a bar, not merely to such a radical change in use, but also to the engagement in a world-wide neo-liberal market economy. Examples may be found everywhere; recent changes in the Indian State of Tamil Nadu is only one but may stand for many (Fatimson and Keshav Rao, 1996). Capitalism depends on the privatisation of all resources for the effective working of its principle of competition. This was spelt out, almost ad nauseam, in the results of the Uruguay deliberations – rules in every agreement limit the role of the state and of public policy in all matters of production and trade (GATT, 1994). Private ownership is also something that the 'aid' dispensing nations, particularly the US, understand; they are comfortable with it and it provides a context for the quaint proposals for national economic recovery, the *soi-disant* 'structural adjustment programmes', that they usually attach to their largesse.

Even before the final collapse of the state, Somalia was among the poorest countries in the world. All the terrifyingly usual conditions were present: life expectancy was 47 years; 72 per cent of the population had no access to health services; 63 per cent were without safe water; the average calorie intake was 17 per cent below normal requirements (UNDP, 1992). During the decade up to 1990 Somalia's per capita GNP had fallen to US$ 120, which the UNDP attributed to an average annual decline of 1.3 per cent (UNDP, 1992), its food production had diminished by 6 per cent and inflation had reached an annual average of 49.7 per cent. In 1970 external debt was somewhere in the region of US$ 77 million, by 1990 it had shot up to US$ 2.35 billion, which the World Bank estimates as 2576.2 per cent of its export of goods and services (World Bank, 1992). Somalia's dependence on aid may also be illustrated by the figures given in Table 3.1.

Table 3.1 Official OECD development assistance for Somalia 1984–90 (US$ m.)

1984	1985	1986	1987	1988	1989	1990	per capita US$ (1990)	%age of GNP (1990)
350	353	511	580	433	427	428	54.8	45.9

Source: World Bank, 1992.

We have already remarked on Somalia's climate, and the casual observer might be forgiven for thinking that it is not one in which crops dependent on large amounts of water could reasonably flourish. Nevertheless, Siad Barre's government decided in the late 1980s to launch a huge irrigated farm at Mogambo in the Lower Juba for the cultivation of rice. Land for the purpose, as well as control of scarce water resources, was seized, apparently even-handedly, from indigenous farmers, from some large new landowners and from the Somalfruit Corporation. Loans in aid for the purpose were negotiated through the Central Bank of Kuwait and compensation was given to the big landowners and to the fruit company, but not, of course, to the impoverished and dispossessed farmers (African Rights, October 1993). It is significant that the increased aid flows shown in table 3.1 coincide with the intensification of work on this and other major projects. The World Bank and the Italian ODA have been the largest investors in this kind of development[3] all of which has been founded on land privatisation and attempted integration into the free market economy. This aid was also instrumental in financing the programme of the private registration of looted land.

By the time of Barre's initial defeat in January 1991, the situation in Somalia was calamitous. Large numbers of people had been dispossessed by the land-looting and their number was augmented massively by those flying from the ravages of the civil war which had also caused huge loss of life. Food production had already been seriously affected by the drought of 1990, but the war caused yet more damage. Herds were raided, crops destroyed and people widely displaced. No more than 30 to 40 per cent of the normal production of cereals was achieved. Modest estimates from the UNHCR suggest that in the north the fighting drove approximately 426,000 refugees into Ethiopia and Djibouti, while in the South some 285,000 crossed into Kenya (UNHCR, 1993). Many more fled to the Kenyan border, part of an untold number remaining in Somalia, displaced from their homes. Using Watkins' comparative figures for refugees and internally displaced people (Watkins, 1995) as a rough guide we may assume that a minimum of 800,000 Somalis were displaced, though some well-founded estimates (for example, Kirkby et al., 1995) put the figure as high as 1.4 million. The UN estimated that more than 50 per cent of the population, some 4.5 million people, were affected by war, disease and drought. Health services, shelter, the provision of water, the distribution of food and clothing had all collapsed, not only in consequence of the war, but also in the face of an enormous rise in opportunistic banditry and looting (IOV, 1994).

Widespread famine ensued and with it came a vast increase in the diseases of poverty: measles, cholera, bacillic and amoebic dysentery, typhoid fever, pneumonia, tuberculosis, respiratory infections and malaria. These, and a few others, are major causes of death in all famines. Sen suggests that they are probably the principal killers and, in his case study of the Great Bengal Famine of 1943, makes the point that more than half the deaths caused by it occurred after that year (Sen, 1981). Much has been written academically, since Sen's pioneering work on poverty and vulnerability, which has eroded the view that hunger and, ultimately, famine and its consequent deaths are principally caused by food shortages. Issue has been taken with Sen over definitions of vulnerability (see, among others, Blaikie et al., 1994), but the socio-historical considerations that he insisted are paramount are not, in principle, in much dispute. Popular writing on the question has also taken the point; for example, Frances Moore Lappé and Joseph Collins list it as the first of twelve myths about world hunger (Lappé and Collins, 1986). Yet when we turn to the international response to the crisis in Somalia, it is as if this work had never been.

Throughout the civil war and during the drought, some relief agencies, the ICRC, SCF-UK and a few other NGOs, had carried on working. UNHCR had also sent observers as the numbers of refugees from the war mounted. Somalia has two rainy seasons each year, the long rains from April to June, called *Gu*, and the short rains from October to November, known as *Deyr* (IOV, 1994). The operations of the NGOs throughout 1991 had much to do with enabling farmers to prepare their land for planting in the *Deyr* rainy season, as well as administering relief paid for by UN specialised agencies. Continued fighting rendered much of this assistance useless and we have already remarked on the consequent decrease in production. Insecurity led to the evacuation of UN staff towards the end of 1991, though the ICRC and the NGOs remained in the country. Somalian agencies, particularly the Somali Red Crescent

Society (SRCS), had long appealed for international help for the displaced and destitute, but with little success. Their voices were added to by those of the NGOs and the ICRC and prolonged pressure combined with some successful television and press campaigning finally provoked a response. The UN launched its Consolidated Inter-Agency Appeal for Somalia in February 1992 (IOV, 1994).

Mahdi and Aideed had continued to fight for the control of the capital, Mogadishu, and, on 2 January 1992, the United Nations finally imposed an arms embargo on Somalia. This led to an interim agreement to a cease-fire which was signed by the warring parties at the beginning of March and the UN Security Council then announced a UN operation in Somalia. Its purpose was to monitor the cease-fire and to protect relief operations from attack and looting. Consisting of some 500 UN soldiers, it was to be known as United Nations Operations in Somalia (UNOSOM). Mohammed M. Sahnoun was appointed by the UN as its Special Representative working in the country. In theory, though the practice may sometimes be a little dubious, UN interventions are legal only when negotiated with the government of the country at issue. Little in the history of international law has prepared the legal ground for intervention in a state where no government exists, so the UN found itself negotiating with whomever it could find, principally the leaders of the various warring factions called, by the UN itself, the 'war-lords'. Not only did this take time, it rarely worked. Some commentators have generously described the early effects of this intervention as 'limited' (IOV, 1994).

Later in 1992 the first UN military observers, sent to monitor the cease-fire, arrived in Mogadishu, the Security Council authorised a large airlift for relief supplies and, in September, sent the first of a proposed contingent of 500 Pakistani soldiers to control the airfield and the port. This, too, ran into difficulty, since General Aideed's troops opposed the move, nonetheless it was finally successful and, from November, the UN controlled the airport. About a month later, it launched its '100-Day Action Programme for Accelerated Humanitarian Assistance for Somalia'. Its purpose was to bring together and to increase the work of the specialised UN agencies, the ICRC and the NGOs in feeding, medical care, varying forms of rehabilitation and the kinds of support which would limit, or even bring to an end, refugeeism and the further internal displacement of people (IOV, 1994). It was an ambitious and by no means an entirely inappropriate response to a complex emergency. It was, however, ill-designed to enable any long-lasting solutions since it was still ham-strung by the UN's need to negotiate with the very people who were instrumental in creating the problem.

UNOSOM's activities had demonstrated the futility of negotiating from a weak and indecisive position, so the UN Security Council, on 3 December 1992, called on the Secretary-General and the members of the UN to 'use all necessary means' (Resolution 794) to make humanitarian assistance possible in Somalia. A force of 40,000 troops (three-quarters of them from the US) to be provided by 20 countries and commanded by a US officer, was to be sent. Its purpose was to make secure the delivery of humanitarian supplies and relief activities. In a moment of unparalleled hubris, it was christened 'Operation Restore Hope'. The force itself was called the 'Unified Task-Force (UNITAF)' and could, with relative ease, have been delivered either to the port or to the airfield near Mogadishu. Instead, in a theatrical and warlike gesture, which proved only too apt (as well as pleasing the television programmers), the US commanders of UNITAF made its advance party wade ashore from landing craft, small arms held aloft, in a carefully choreographed, but entirely unopposed invasion.

Neither the port nor the airfield has ever been more than occasionally closed and the ICRC had rarely, if ever, been forced to suspend its monthly deliveries to Mogadishu. They had stabilised deliveries by making separate agreements with each of the two principal warring factions in the region led by Aideed and Mahdi. Agreements of this sort meant paying a 'tax' to the parties concerned, but it was certainly no higher than the landing fees common in all other parts of the world where humanitarian assistance is needed. Such an arrangement would have been open to the UN (African Rights, May 1993). While it might be thought to be disagreeable to deal with people widely seen by Somalis as war criminals, it would, in view of the UN's subsequent relations with them, have been disingenuous to plead such an excuse.

Public relations, responding to the simplicities of the mass media, of the US Congress and of European Parliaments, called the tune. Famine had struck in Somalia, people were dying for lack of food, war-lords were holding the 'victims' to ransom, the UN/US would ensure that the food got through. There is no doubt that along those routes that UNITAF was able to secure, food deliveries markedly improved. Nor is there any question that, as a consequence, the lives of many destitute people were saved. Both these results are, however, even less than the minimum that might have been expected and it is a matter of embarrassment that they should be offered in justification of a fiasco.

By the time that UNITAF had landed, the drought was over and normal food production was resuming. An indicator of this, widely accepted as the most reliable, is the movement in prices in the markets of South Mogadishu, given in Table 3.2.

Table 3.2 Cereal Prices in South Mogadishu[4] (Somali shillings per kg)

Month	Sorghum	Wheat	Maize
July 1992	3788	3233	4800
August	2349	2824	2674
September	1458	1858	1733
October	866	1100	1266
November	855	910	1199
December	791	824	1041
January 1993	720	745	891
February	661	657	763
mid-March	500	550	625

Source: CARE monetization programme, Mogadishu.

Providing food for vulnerable and destitute people is one essential and obvious element in famine relief, but, of course, it must be provided as part of a relief operation at a time when food supplies have, for whatever reason, broken down. It is particularly important to ensure that the most vulnerable, the malnourished children, the poorest of people and those prevented by conflict from functioning normally, have access to food. We have already remarked that most people affected by famine die of epidemic disease; feeding programmes are futile if they are not accompanied by effective measures in community health and curative medical care. All these efforts must be made with the object not only of saving lives, but of rehabilitating livelihoods. People recovering from the trauma of famine must be enabled to rebuild workable and sustainable economic communities. In a country where the main economic activities are in food production, it is less than completely productive to flood its markets with cheap food at the point at which local production begins to resume. Yet this is exactly what the UN operation achieved.

Food security and its politics and structures in any community lie on the margins of the subject of this book; it is enough here to remark that current free-market, international trade practice and law are inimical to it. In the case of Somalia any importation of food for relief purposes should have been geared to the increasing purchase, at local market prices, of food produced within the country. Imported supplies should then have correspondingly been phased out. Since relief food is purchased by the agencies either from international intervention stocks or from private supplies at the lowest possible international price, the massive deliveries to Somalia amounted to an immense dumping operation which, at the very least, did massive damage to an indigenous agriculture struggling to achieve some kind of normality. Just how damaging this was is well illustrated by the price of maize in one local market in the early months of 1993 when it fell to only 28 per cent of the local cost of production (African Rights, May 1993). In the cases of rice, beans and oil, figures provided by ICRC, Nairobi and CARE International Somalia show market prices falling in August and September 1992, then fluctuating dramatically until May to June 1993 when the prices steadied at less than 6 per cent of their high point in December 1992 (IOV, 1994). It was not the purpose of the IOV report to comment extensively on these figures, but it did point to the problem:

> The ICRC food-relief operation in Somalia effectively extended people's entitlement to basic food commodities .... The possible negative corollary of this is that too low a price will undermine the local farming economy ... it was not found possible to measure this relationship but anecdotal information suggests that at times food prices dropped below levels sustainable by Somali agriculture. (IOV, 1994, p. 142)

African Rights assembled impressive evidence, both from observation and anecdote, that 'It cannot be overstressed that the basic food supply problem underlying the famine was solved at least one month before the marines landed.' This does not mean, as its report points out, 'that the problem of famine and famine deaths was solved' (African Rights, May 1993, p. 11). Considerable numbers of very vulnerable people were still seriously affected by extensive fighting, and there were many others who were unable to get to centres of relief services, either because they were too far away or because they were too debilitated, or were faced with journeys too dangerous, to get to them. As we have already observed, diseases were the major killers and there is evidence that many of the later cases of under-nutrition, especially among children, were a result of attacks of disease (African Rights, May 1993, p. 16). What UNITAF achieved was the relative security of the food supply routes to major centres and towns in the southern part of the country, it paid little or no attention to the wider problems facing the Somali people, particularly those of health care. In this context it is worth noting that it, too, joined in the general habit among Northern agencies and NGOs in ignoring, often rejecting, Somali expertise and advice (honourable exceptions were the ICRC and SCF-UK) – a cautious reference to this abuse may be seen in the IOV report (IOV, 1994).

UNITAF was charged with the responsibility of securing a safe environment for humanitarian relief. Two obvious moves in fulfilling such a mandate would have been to enforce the arms embargo of

January 1992 and to engage in a vigorous programme of disarmament. In the case of the former, some consistency in policy might have been achieved had the UN leant on the government of Kenya to get it to make some attempt to stop the supply of arms across its border. So far as actual disarmament was concerned, the US, in the person of its envoy Robert Oakley, simply denied, at a press briefing in Mogadishu in January 1993, that it was part of the mandate.[5] In the event only the security guards hired by the relief agencies and NGOs and a few small shopkeepers who kept arms in self-defence against looters, bandits and the depredations of the 'war-lords' were actually disarmed.

UNOSOM and its mandate had been absorbed into Operation Restore Hope and it had originally been charged not only with coordinating the operations of the numerous UN organisations present in the country,[6] but also with taking responsibility for liaison between those bodies, the ICRC and the international NGOs. In effect it had been told to harmonise and coordinate their work. Popular international concern for Somalia was such that large numbers of international NGOs were present, each of them with differing objectives and mandates. Because they are responsible to their donors and because their continued funding depends on their ability to demonstrate effectiveness in their chosen field, territorial rivalry between them was common. Substantial UN funds were channelled through them which meant that their desire for complete independence from one another was, to a certain extent, compromised. Three major problems were, however, endemic in their work: competition for resources, varied and overlapping mandates and territoriality reduced their effectiveness; rapid staff turnover, a consequence of the stress under which volunteers worked, frequently resulted in the employment of inexperienced people who, while they might be qualified in their particular skill or profession, were unprepared for work in the field; a failure to realise that despite the overwhelming problems in Somalia, there was a population of well-qualified and capable Somalis who, with the exception of those agencies we have mentioned, no one saw fit either to consult or to enlist (IOV, 1994). UN attempts at harmonisation were, at the most, piecemeal and only partially successful, their most important result was the creation of an informal network of information and consultation. Little or no strategic planning emerged.

Operation Restore Hope was a standard UN peacekeeping mission. These are always and everywhere deeply flawed because the UN has separated peacekeeping from issues of human rights. It has long discovered that the easiest and cheapest way to reduce violent conflict to manageable proportions is to negotiate with the leaders of the combatants, principally with the ones who might win,

taking little or no account of the relationship of those leaders with
the people among whom they are fighting. It is for this reason that
the world watched, with some incredulity, the dismaying inactivity
of the UN in the face of war crimes and genocide in, for example,
Rwanda and Bosnia. In Somalia, apart from a poorly conceived
attempt at the arrest of Aideed, UNOSOM/UNITAF largely
confined itself to making deals with the leaders of the main factions
and so effectively engaged in a 'military approach to a humanitarian
problem' (HRW/A, April 1995). It made little or no attempt to
protect the poor and displaced from further attack and terrorisation
and certainly none to help them in their attempts to rebuild their
former livelihoods. Few things change – it is worth recalling that
the UN's Special Representative in Somalia, Mohammed Sahnoun,
was forced to resign in October 1992 because of his criticisms of
UN inactivity while countless Somalis were dying of disease or being
killed by warring factions.

In the north, where the UN did not intervene, the Republic of
Somaliland, which has never achieved international recognition,
has largely become a client state of Ethiopia. In the south, a
precarious mix of clan elders, business people, professionals,
women's organisations and religious representatives have been
meeting to find ways of resolving the problem of the war-leaders
and of the breakdown of the state. They received no support from
the UN presence in Somalia and now that the UN forces have
withdrawn, they are facing renewed intimidation from the various
factions. The factions themselves continue their battles for supremacy
and not only are they concentrating on the nascent civil organisations,
which they see as a threat to their power, but they are also continuing
to attack, and to add to, the huge numbers of displaced people. In
February 1995, an estimated 150,000 to 200,000 displaced people
were camped around Mogadishu alone (HRW/A, April 1995).
Since then repeated attacks on the villages (for example, on
Haraawe, Osman Moto and Malenda) have worsened the situation.
Matters have not improved since the death, from heart failure, of
Mohammed Farah Aideed – his son's succession has led to bloody
internecine power struggles.

We are left with the question of whose hope was restored by
Operation Restore Hope. Some commentators, particularly among
the more sanguine of the NGOs, cling to the unquestionable fact
that some lives were saved by the UN's protection of the food supply
routes. They might, perhaps, consider the cost of those lives. Many
of the troops behaved like an invading army, displaying the customary
contempt of white men for people of another colour and abusing
their civil rights. Some also murdered and tortured Somali citizens.[7]
Random shooting by UN troops on the frequently dubious ground
that they felt themselves to be under attack was also common, so,

too, were strong-arm tactics and theft (African Rights, May 1993). At no point did the UN, its forces or, with the two great exceptions to which we have referred, the NGOs and agencies working with it consult Somalis about their activities. In practice, between them, they reached an uneasy accommodation with the principal warring factions, thus indirectly legitimising them, while establishing a patchy system of support for the dispossessed.

We may speculate on the future. Despite the struggle to rebuild civil society carried on by that complex of interests to which we have referred, the most probable outcome is the ultimate victory of one of the factions, or an alliance between two of them, followed by the reestablishment of a military government. This time, however, it will be a state in which the landed interests of the powerful will have been consolidated at the expense of a large but powerless population of the dispossessed, a not uncommon phenomenon. In such an event, the new state may rely (so long as it conceals the worst of its abuses) on the support of the Bretton Woods institutions for its integration into the market economy; multilateral and bilateral agreements will certainly follow. Cynics might feel that the history of continuous stumbling error in the UN's interventions in Somalia have speeded the destruction of peasant ways and the incorporation of the country into modernity and that in some ways the errors were, therefore, far from egregious. For the WTO, the TNCs and the banks, a Somalia producing for the world's commodity markets is a more comfortable proposition than one dominated by differing forms of peasantry. The burgeoning industry of humanitarian assistance will take care of the casualties.

CHAPTER 4

Kenya

From the beginning of 1992 until 1995 a humanitarian emergency was declared in northern Kenya. Parts of the region are considerably populated by ethnic Somalis and, indeed, from 1960 until 1963 they waged what was finally an unsuccessful struggle to reunite their region with Somalia. Some of the difficulties facing people in the area in the 1990s were caused by Somalia's collapse and the spread of violence across a border never much recognised by nomadic pastoralists. Difficulties produced by growing violence were further compounded, in 1991 and 1992, by the influx of some 285,000 refugees from Somalia, which almost quadrupled Kenya's total refugee population (UNHCR, 1993). Matters were made worse by the long-standing hostility of the Kenyan government to refugees from any quarter, but particularly from Somalia and, therefore, the failure to protect them. Somalis became prey both to bandits from either side of the border and to corrupt and racialist security forces which equated 'Somali' with 'shifta' or 'crook' (African Rights, September 1993). Since pastoralism has, for countless generations, been the predominant form of production in the Ogaden region of Ethiopia, Somalia, north-east Kenya and the east of Sudan, violence, coupled with the intransigence of the more southerly settled people's executive and bureaucracies, has become a massive onslaught on livelihoods.

Kenya, unlike Somalia before the 1990s, is relatively well known to the public in the industrialised world, particularly the British. The history of the region and its people, like all other African histories, is ancient but was ignored by its nineteenth-century conquerors. Davidson (1964) mentions both its earliest known, iron-age, civilisation and its culture; Oliver and Fage (1970) write of the organised states in East Africa of the thirteenth and fourteenth centuries. For our purposes we must follow the colonisers and look briefly only at events around, and since, the time when the borders of modern Kenya were established.

Towards the end of the eighteenth century a wave of evangelists and explorers, especially from the United Kingdom, swept over Africa. Largely philanthropic in nature (H.M. Stanley, when in the service of Leopold II of the Belgians, was instrumental in changing that), it mapped Africa with the object of saving souls. Once the slave trade had been outlawed in Europe, other forms of commercial activity began to grow, but in the mid-1870s very little of Africa was under European rule. Leopold's creation, with Stanley's help, of a vast personal empire in the Congo stimulated the other European powers to scramble for the rest of the continent (Oliver and Fage, 1970). In 1885, Bismarck, no doubt recalling his diplomatic successes in the Congress of Berlin of 1878, convened, with the support of France, an international conference to consider a common response to the ambitions of Leopold. Now known as the Berlin Conference, it was the gathering at which the European powers agreed among themselves on the partitioning and control of Africa. Several of them, most notably Germany, had already begun to annex substantial territory and, by the beginning of the twentieth century, European states claimed sovereignty over virtually the entire continent. Exercising that sovereignty was another matter. The long, bloody war waged by Britain in the Sudan or the frequent clashes between differing European invaders that marked the closing years of the nineteenth century are testimony to the difficulty – we have remarked on Britain's problems with Sheik Muhammad bin Abdullah Hussein in the previous chapter. No significant change to the Berlin arrangement was made until the end of the 1914–18 war, when Germany's 'possessions' in Africa were redistributed among the victors.

At the Berlin Conference Kenya was ceded to Britain together with an unclear agreement about Uganda and an understanding that the Sudan could also fall to it. Salisbury was the British prime minister at the time and he lacked the resources with which effectively to govern the region. In a move which would, in a later age, have delighted his Tory successor Thatcher, he gave over the administration of the Protectorate to a private chartered company, the Imperial British East Africa Company. It was not until around the turn of the century, with the construction of the railway line from Uganda to the coast, that white settlement really took hold after nearly half the indigenous population in the regions surrounding the railway had died as a result of a smallpox epidemic, a disease introduced by the Indian labourers employed in building that line (ITeM, 1995). Their lands, conveniently underpopulated, were appropriated by white settlers in a process which also drove out most of those who had survived the disease. By the end of the 1939–45 war, fewer than 3000 white farmers controlled 2.6 million hectares of Kenya's best land (Davidson, 1994). No compensation was ever offered for this 'act of theft' (ITeM, 1995).

The rise of Kenyan opposition, the Kenya African Union, whose first president was the renowned Harry Thuku and whose third was Jomo Kenyatta, Tom Mboya's Kenya African National Union (KANU) and the party of the north and north-east, the Kenya African Democratic Union first presided over by Ronald Ngala (Hodgkin, 1961), and their final merger as KANU led by Kenyatta, has frequently been told elsewhere (see, *inter alia*, Barratt Brown, 1995; Davidson, 1971, 1994; Hodgkin, 1956, 1961; Kariuki, 1963). What the fight for independence meant has most movingly been portrayed by Ngũgĩ (1967/1987). It is a history of opposition to colonial misrule which commonly exploited linguistic, cultural and ethnic differences in a country artificially created for an alien commercial agenda. These differences were exacerbated during the struggle by the inevitable consequences of a long guerrilla war in which armed opposition was frequently organised, for its own protection, along community lines. Independence, in 1961, produced a fragile unity which could have blossomed into something much greater with the institution of 'Harambee', a movement of local cooperation and management of resources (thought, by some contemporary NGOs, to be their own invention). Unfortunately central government, like so many elsewhere, saw the immense popularity of this movement as a threat to its own hegemony and gradually took control of it.

Jomo Kenyatta notoriously moved from leading a party of liberation to creating, out of his extended family, his friends and supporters, a ruling bourgeoisie and to building a neo-colonialist state and perhaps the most obvious moment of his identification with Western agendas was in allowing the Israelis to use his military installations for their infamous raid on Entebbe in Uganda. A study produced by the ILO in 1972 commented that 'the power of the centre over the periphery may well be greater today that it was before [independence]' (ILO, 1972). When, in 1978, Kenyatta died, the last remaining vestiges of democracy died with him as his vice-president, Daniel Arap Moi, took interim power. Elections were held a few weeks later, but since KANU was the only party allowed to contest them, Moi's presidency was confirmed. It is against the background of national disunity and of corrupting power among ruling élites that we must examine the extraordinary events in Kenya between 1992 and 1995.

In what Davidson (1994) has described as 'a "no holds barred" system of free enterprise', Kenya, during Kenyatta's presidency, substantially increased the colonial pattern of production for the international market. Tea, which makes up 22 per cent of Kenya's exports, and coffee, 19 per cent (ITeM, 1995), account for substantial parts of that production, but vegetables, fresh and dried fruit and even flowers for the developed world's luxury market (up to 18 per cent of exports) are rapidly catching up. North American and British firms invested heavily in the new Kenya and, on the way, enriched a number of urban businessmen and rural tribal leaders. To begin with, this investment was confined to financing, sometimes consolidating, the plantations created from land stolen from its indigenous inhabitants in the colonial period. In passing we should recall that, unlike the people from whom they stole, the white settlers who left at independence were compensated for the loss of 'their' lands. Big plantations call for large workforces and for heavy machinery, and they need also to be supported by some infrastructure and by accessible processing plant. Not only do they call for large capital investment, but they can also, as we pointed out in Chapter 2, become centres for the organisations of the workforce.

In the mid-1970s North American TNCs began to withdraw from plantation ownership in Africa in favour of giving contracts, mainly to women growers, for fruit and vegetables (for a more detailed account of this change see Bernstein et al., 1990). Under these contracts, which are now common among all TNCs, what is produced, the methods employed and the prices paid are all decided by the contractor. Increasingly, intermediaries are used, either private or state, between the TNCs and the farmers, a phenomenon which adds to the opportunities of a relatively small élite. Although contract farming in Africa began during Kenyatta's lifetime, its rapid growth in Kenya has taken place during the Moi regime. Watts (in Bernstein et al., 1990) estimated that '17 per cent of total farm output and 30 per cent of total marketed output' was produced by contract farmers. The importance of this for our discussion lies in the extent to which it encourages inter- and intra-communal competition for productive land, and to which it engenders a clientalist politics. Moi inherited a corrupt state, indeed as vice-president he obviously played a substantial part in making it so. It was one in which the state's client, urban bourgeoisie, taking increasing advantage of TNC finance, aggravated economic and social distinctions. Parastatal organisations, originally created to facilitate development and the integration of the rural and urban economies, largely became the means of social control through bribery. Such a state of affairs can only be maintained by increasing repression; as an example we may recall that European capital gave rise to an even more depressing, brutal and internationally catastrophic state built on corruption in Hitler's Germany (Grunberger, 1971, see Chapter 6); organisationally it had much in common with contemporary Kenya. Resolving this mess proved to be beyond Moi's ability. He began his presidency with a campaign against ethnically-based power blocs, the most important of which was GEMA (Gikuyu, Embu and Meru Association), an organisation dominated by tribal leaders and businessmen who had grown rich from TNC pickings and which was dissolved following its involvement in a violent conspiracy against the government (ITeM, 1995). It was a short-lived effort: Moi re-joined the kleptocracy and has, for some considerable time now, also resorted to playing the ethnic 'card' in maintaining his power and enriching his clients.

Domestic food production declined between 1979 and 1993 by an average of 0.4 per cent (World Bank, 1995). This decline, consequent on the increase in plantation and contract farming combined with drought, led the Kenyan government to import substantial quantities of cereals. From 1980 to 1993, annual cereal imports increased from 387,000 metric tonnes to 569,000 metric tonnes. Simultaneously, the value added to agriculture declined from just over US$ 2 billion to under US$ 1.4 billion, in part this is another consequence of the rise in contract farming. Both of these elements are significant in the increase, at the same time, of Kenya's external debt from US$ 3.4 billion to US$ 7 billion (World Bank, 1995). In 1992, when external debt stood at US$ 6.4 billion, the cost of servicing it was 27 per cent of the value of all exports of goods and services (UNDP, 1995).

Despite the increasing wealth of the new bourgeoisie, most people remain poor and many live in acute poverty. For some of the common indicators see Table 4.1 which, of course, expresses them in percentages, somehow sanitising the picture; it is worth reminding ourselves of the brute numbers. In 1992 Kenya's population was estimated at 25.4 million of whom some 25 per cent were urban (UNDP, 1995). We may see, then, that nearly eleven-

and-a-half million people in rural Kenya have no access to health services; one million seven hundred thousand town dwellers and nearly eleven million people in rural areas have no safe water; almost two million townspeople and nearly twelve-and-a-half million rural people do not have adequate sanitation. Even expressing the figures in this way obviously conceals marked differences in levels of both possession and deprivation, but putting them together with the unanalysable percentage of calorie intake makes it scarcely surprising that Kenyan lives are, on average, shorter by 20 or more years than lives in most industrialised countries.

Table 4.1 Some poverty indicators in Kenya

| Life expectancy (years) | %age of population with access to | | | | | | Calorie supply %age of need |
| | Health services | | Safe water | | Adequate sanitation | | |
	urban	rural	urban	rural	urban	rural	
55.7	n/a	40	74	43	69	35	89

n/a – not available
Source: UNICEF, 1995.

Early on these trends persuaded Moi to abandon the moderately progressive beginnings to his presidency and first to make peace with his former opponents, then, finally, as in the case of Oginga Odinga, to crush them. He increased the power of the executive and reduced that of parliament, and he also made membership of KANU compulsory for all civil servants (ITeM, 1995). Torturing and murdering opponents became the norm together with violent attacks on the offices and property of all those Moi and his ruling élite chose to think of as threats to stability, including women's groups, human rights activists and indigenous NGOs (Jennings, 1995). Paranoid responses from rulers to the protests of a deprived people are common enough, particularly when, as in this case, repression is directed to the preservation of an extremely profitable empire. Watkins, commenting on the frequency with which Third World rulers see national wealth as personal fortunes largely to be transferred to overseas bank accounts, remarks that:

> In Kenya, financial fraud involving the falsification of export and import invoices in connection with structural adjustment loans, cost the country an estimated $430m between 1991 and 1993; more than the combined health and education budgets. (Watkins, 1995)

Enthusiastic plundering by TNCs and by government and its officials on the one hand, and its external debt and falling productivity for home consumption on the other, has reduced Kenya to a fiscal ruin. In 1993 its gross international reserves were US$ 437 million, little more than the amount spirited away in the invoice fraud described by Watkins and a sum which would cover imports for roughly two weeks. The country is heavily dependent on aid and from 1991 to 1993 this was running a little below US$ 900 million each year; in 1993 aid formed 16.1 per cent of its GNP (World Bank, 1995). Attempts were made by the World Bank, the IMF and the Club of Paris to persuade Moi's government to move towards their kind of financial orthodoxy, but agreement was slow. The Club of Paris tried to attach clear conditions to further aid. These were the acceptance of the World Bank's proposals for economic reform, including the IMF's demand for a huge increase in rates of interest, acceptance of the World Bank's demand for reform in agricultural marketing, agreement to USAID's proposal that the parastatal market institutions be dismantled (ETC UK, Fellows International, ACTS, Kenya Pastoralists Forum, October 1995; ITeM, 1995). Other changes were also called for – an end to the grossest abuses of human rights, including the right of organised political opposition, and the holding of free elections.

The Club of Paris, together with USAID and the multilateral organisations, acted in this case as a consortium of donors. First among the principles of action for such a body is consistency and a group made up of bilateral as well as multilateral donors cannot easily achieve this. Norway, for example, taking the consortium at its word, actively intervened to promote the Club's democratic aims (ITeM, 1995), but got little support from the other members who largely contented themselves with rhetoric. Since Norway is a small donor, the government of Kenya could happily ignore it, particularly as Moi did at first show some signs of democratic reform. Multiparty elections were held in December 1992, but they were notorious for widespread intimidation, bribery and fraud and for a hopelessly divided opposition (HRW/A, July 1994). Moi won with 36 per cent of the vote and there is now 'serious doubt whether the first steps have been or ever will be followed by effective structural reforms' (Stolz, 1996). Conditionality, as the practice of attaching conditions to aid programmes has become known, is rarely successful in those cases where donors (perhaps we should rename them 'investors') have a considerable economic interest in the recipient country. It suffers, too, from the refusal of investing states or the multilateral organisations to take responsibility for the consequences of their conditions; glaring examples may be found in the structural adjustment programmes (Stolz, 1996).

Kenya's government, whether or not by design, found a bizarre solution to its increasing difficulty in fending off the more uncomfortable conditions loosely attached to aid packages.[1] In 1991, Moi, while attending the National Ploughing Championships, met the representative of the Food and Agriculture Organisation (FAO) and mentioned to him that he was worried about a looming shortage of maize and the effect of a drought in the North-Eastern Province of Kenya. His interlocutor suggested an application for assistance to the World Food Programme (WFP) and a survey, with which the FAO would help, of what cereals were available and of what might be needed in the course of 1992, a suggestion which Moi seems to have accepted.

In November an application to the WFP was made by letter from Kenya's Secretary to the Cabinet and Head of the Public Service in which he mentioned three districts as in particular need. Two weeks later he sent another letter listing eight such districts, but in which he made no mention of one of the first three. Four days later he wrote again increasing the number of districts to 17, including all those that he had given in the first two letters. This uncertainty seems to have had less to do with fast moving events in remote areas and more to do with tailoring a request to meet the donors' well-known interest in drought. Real needs can only be met by building long-term food security which has to do with support for livelihoods, both in the production of indigenous food supplies and in other surrounding trades and industries. Aid donors and recipient governments, however, whatever expert advice they may seek, are, as we observed in our discussion of Somalia, influenced by the simplicities of mass communication: famines are caused by drought, if drought can be foreseen then emergency food supplies provided in good time will save the day. The Kenyan government, at the time of its appeal, was preparing a drought contingency plan, which it released in March 1992, for the distribution of emergency relief. Combined with the approach to the WFP made on the advice of the FAO and which involved UNICEF on the way, this plan completed the picture of a growing humanitarian crisis, even if its location was a trifle uncertain.

In their report, ETC UK and its associated evaluators make the point that FAO and UNICEF were central to putting the UN system into motion 'frequently acting for the United Nations Development Programme (UNDP) which should have been the lead coordinator of a United Nations Disaster Management Team (UNDMT)'. With a fine sense of caution, if not irony, the evaluators go on to remark that 'it has proved difficult to obtain any record of UNDMT's operation' (ETC UK et al., 1995, p. 4). Undeterred by any fear of innovation in UN humanitarian practice, WFP went ahead to appoint the charitable organisation CARE to arrange for the delivery of supplies and, not to be outdone, a number of bilateral donors, including Britain, organised separate deliveries through their own national NGOs. International humanitarian assistance had arrived in Kenya in search of an acute crisis. Two lesser crises were, of course, solved immediately: pressure on Moi for reform was submerged in the face of more urgent demands and donor states were able to provide aid under another guise, discreetly putting aside their earlier attempts at conditionality.

Seventeen of Kenya's 39 districts (we exclude Nairobi from the total and Makueni District had not been created at the time of the appeal) had been listed, but the main problems were thought to exist in the north and north-east of the country. North-Eastern, Eastern and the northern part of Rift Valley Provinces are all substantially inhabited by nomadic, or, in some instances, semi-nomadic pastoralists, many of them, particularly in North-Eastern Province, ethnic Somalis. Like Somalia, these are arid lands, though they, too, have pockets of settled agriculture, particularly in what is now Makueni (formerly part of Machakos District). Both forms of rural production are constantly affected by the vagaries of the climate and, just as in Somalia, drought is an ever present concern. It is not, however, an absolute; rains vary in intensity from flood to complete failure in these regions as they do everywhere else. Extended and seriously damaging drought is periodic, not permanent, and we may take the history of the Turkana district in the Rift Valley Province, where all major droughts seem to have been given names, as an example (summarised in Table 4.2).

It may be seen that, in Turkana district at least, there were eleven droughts, or famines in which drought played a part, in the 67 years between 1925 and 1992. While Turkana was not uniquely affected and other districts suffered equally, it would be rash to extrapolate too widely from this list because conditions at any one time can vary considerably over the huge arid areas in the 17 districts for which Kenya sought help. Consistent statistics are hard to find which makes comparison difficult, but a crude indication of these variations is given in Table 4.3 in which the available rainfall figures for Turkana in the north-west are compared with those for the district of Mandera in the north-east. Figures for the entire rainfall for a substantial area (Turkana is 77,000 sq. km., two-and-a-half times the size of Belgium, Mandera is about the same size as Belgium) can mislead since the actual distribution of rain makes a huge difference to everyone living in it. As an illustration, Table 4.4 shows substantial variations between the local divisions of Turkana. Similarly, annual statistics can disguise important differences. There are two rainy seasons each year, the long rains from March to April and the short rains from October to December, and growing seasons are, obviously, closely linked to the pattern. Table 4.5 gives examples of seasonal variations in two divisions within Turkana.

Table 4.2 Summary of Drought/Famine Years of Turkana District

Year	Turkana name	Description
1925	Ekwakoit	Year of white bones: bones of dead animals scattered throughout the district
1943	Ekwam Lonyang	Year of dust: dust storms throughout the district
1947	Ata Nachoke	Year the cattle wept: many animals died of a disease which affected their lacrimal glands
1949	Ekaru A Ngilowi	Year of hides and skins: in which pastoralists survived on the sale of hides and skins salvaged from animals which died in the drought
1952	Lotira/Karoi	Year that was not moving: a longer than usual dry season
1953–4	Lokulit	Year when hunger beat people like a whip: animals died because of the lack of rain and people went hungry
1960	Namotor	Year of emaciated animals: long rains lasted only for a month so animals had insufficient fodder
1971	Kimududu	Year of the very hot sun
1971	Lolewo	Year of cholera: many people died or were too weak to look after their animals
1979	Loukoi	Year of CBPP/CCPP diseases which killed many animals
1980–1	Lochuu/Lopiar	Year of maize: following the 1979 drought relief food was distributed
1991–2	Karoi/Lobolbolio	Year of white bones: animals affected by throat disease; long rains were short; an earthquake before the long rains seen as a bad omen

Source: ETC UK et al., October 1995.

Table 4.3 Annual rainfall in Turkana and Mandera districts (mm.)

District	1991	1992	1993	1994	LTM†
Turkana	925.80	551.30	1083.00	423.50	945.1
Mandera	286.00	227.00	497.50	265.00	266.00

† LTM= Long-term mean
Source: compiled from ETC UK et al., October, 1995.

Table 4.4 Annual rainfall in five divisions of Turkana (mm.)

Division	1991	1992	1993	21994	LTM
Turkwel	81.0	126.0	198.0	134.5	222.8
Kakuma	385.0	141.0	532.0	379.0	288.8
Lodwar	149.5	61.3	117.4	130.8	163.7
Lokori	195.7	177.5	157.6	273.0	269.8
Kalokol	114.6	45.5	78.1	150.5	170.4

Source: ETC UK et al., October, 1995.

Table 4.5 Monthly rainfall in the Turkwel and Lodwar divisions of Turkana (mm.)

Y/M	1991 Turk	Lod	1992 Turk	Lod	1993 Turk	Lod	1994 Turk	Lod	LTM Turk	Lod
Jan.	11.0	14.0	0.0	0.0	42.0	9.0	00.0	0.0	5.7	6.0
Feb.	0.0	0.0	0.0	3.6	42.0	8.5	00.0	1.0	11.6	6.3
Mar.	20.0	46.0	54.0	14.4	2.0	2.6	10.0	18.9	26.7	17.3
Apr.	2.0	8.3	28.0	20.8	0.0	5.6	82.0	50.8	68.1	40.6
May.	10.0	38.0	0.0	10.6	112.0	77.3	22.0	7.5	38.3	22.2
Jun.	0.0	0.0	0.0	0.8	0.0	10.4	0.0	1.4	9.2	7.0
Jul.	18.0	4.9	0.0	0.0	0.0	0.0	0.0	4.5	14.9	14.8
Aug.	6.0	27.6	0.0	0.0	0.0	0.0	0.0	10.7	5.6	8.9
Sept.	0.0	0.0	32.0	0.0	0.0	0.0	0.0	0.0	10.5	3.8
Oct.	14.0	8.6	12.0	3.0	0.0	0.0	12.0	8.5	5.3	8.3
Nov.	0.0	1.1	0.0	6.1	0.0	4.0	12.0	27.6	14.0	16.9
Dec.	0.0	1.0	0.0	2.0	0.0	0.0	0.0	0.4	12.9	11.6

Source: Turkana Drought Contingency Planning Unit.

Although these tables are illustrations only, they are, at least in pattern, representative of conditions throughout all 17 of the apparently stricken districts. Drought in 1991–2 was patchy and intermittent, circumstances with which nomadic pastoralists have been familiar from the night of time. Indeed this is largely why they are nomadic; living in arid territory they move their animals to those places which have had rain and in which, therefore, the grass has grown. An official of the WFP in a Back to Office Report following his visit to four districts remarked:

> Few districts are experiencing drought stress at present, for example in West Pokot conditions are much better than last year, they have had adequate rainfall, their animals are healthy and

their harvest is on a par with a normal year ... local NGOs, bilateral donors and GOK [Government of Kenya] appear to be capable of meeting current levels of demand. (quoted in ETC UK, October 1995)

Even though there plainly were some places in which people needed help (the report refers to them as 'pockets'), this report, together with detailed records of the kind that we have quoted above (Tables 4.3–4.5), might, perhaps, have been expected to give pause to Northern agencies rushing to relieve the problems of drought and its effects on pastoral production. The declaration of this acute emergency was, however, also based on a fear that national stocks of maize might be inadequate and here the picture becomes even murkier.

While watching the ploughmen at that encounter with Moi, the representative of the FAO in Kenya had volunteered help with a survey of the country's cereal needs. An investigative team was sent to Kenya in February 1992 and it estimated that 300,000 tonnes of cereal, chiefly maize, would be needed to make up the shortfall. A year later a further estimate suggested that the shortfall called for 1.44 million tonnes of which about half would have to come in the form of food aid. By the end of the emergency FAO was still predicting that Kenya would suffer from famine unless another 600,000 tonnes of cereal were sent in aid. Crops did decline seriously: production was relatively low in 1992 and very poor following the failure of the short rains in 1993, but the ETC UK et al. evaluators point out that the FAO assessments take as their baseline Kenya's own forecasts for cereal production – these are invariably optimistic. They add that 'the FAO statistics, while not covering the pastoral areas adequately, remain the only constant base of information about food production throughout the emergency areas and were used, therefore, for calculating what was needed to make up the shortfall' (ETC UK et al., 1995, p. 6). Humanitarian assistance calls for substantial investment from donors. Even though the famous 'donor fatigue' was probably invented by the mass media in search of a story, donor nations and organisations, nonetheless, not unreasonably prefer to dig no deeper than they have to. FAO's conclusions were 'strenuously questioned', particularly by USAID.

The FAO may well have been mistaken about the size of the real need, if any, in Kenya but it was not alone. Altogether five inter-agency assessments of the situation were made between 1992 and 1994. WFP, among others, pointed out that they all came to quite different conclusions which, since the government of Kenya repeatedly exaggerated the numbers of people in need, even the sizes of populations, so as to increase the amount of aid, is scarcely surprising. No matter how dubious, these incessant predictions achieved the continued supply of aid to Kenya in the wake of the Club of Paris's decision, in November 1991, to suspend it. The WFP, even though its contribution was substantial, was only one of several donors. Setting out the size and value of its supplies (see Table 4.6) gives an inkling of the scale of the indirect support given to Moi's regime in the two years following the Club's sanction, a point not lost on the ETC evaluators:

> The need to maintain development budgets, despite official requests through the Paris Club to end aid to Kenya until its Government implemented agreed reforms, was a major consideration for European donors, but it was difficult to address at the time. Transferring development aid to humanitarian assistance rather neatly resolved this problem .... In retrospect, it does seem unusual that Kenya, for the first time since Independence, should declare an international appeal and that ... donors and multilateral agencies should support such an appeal without adequate evidence of famine. (ETC UK et al., 1995, p. 12)

Table 4.6 WFP commitments

Date of approval	Cereals (tonnes)	Pulses (tonnes)	Vegetable Oil (tonnes)	Total	Total Cost US$ m.
20/05/92	25,200	–	–	25,200	8.4
13/07/92	25,000	5000	1500	31,500	15.1
04/09/92	25,056	3758.	1253	30,067	14.0
23/12/92	99,800	1733	1920	103,453	36.6
11/01/94	42,620	10,368	1556	54,544	25.7
12/05/94	46,290	6940	2310	55,540	21.4
Totals	263,966	27,799	8539	300,304	121.2

Source: WFP, quoted in ETC UK et al., October 1995.

Drought-induced and widespread famine by which acute emergencies tend to be judged could not, early in 1992, easily be found in Kenya. Nevertheless vulnerable people, principally, but not exclusively, in the northern and north-eastern pastoral regions, were in trouble. Before discussing their problems we must first attend to another phenomenon engendered by declarations of emergency – a statistical myopia. WFP, UNICEF, the Red Cross and NGOs, particularly those like MSF, all, quite reasonably, need not only to ensure that they are sufficiently supplied to achieve their aims but also to be able to calculate the effects of what they do. Part of the investigation into the numbers in need consists of gauging their degree of want and the commonest measure is the amount of malnutrition among children aged between 6 and 60 months. There are two widely used methods for determining this, they tend to produce different answers and neither seems to be particularly reliable.

In 1992, UNICEF, using one method, discovered that in three districts an average of 40.5 per cent of the children were stunted, 25.2 per cent were wasted and 58.3 per cent were underweight (percentages do not add up because each category calls for a different measure). These are, of course, very serious figures which should cause alarm and which demand a response. UNICEF and others did respond to what they saw as an acute emergency, but seem not to have noticed that their measurements were taken at the end of the dry season when malnutrition among all nomadic pastoralists is common. By 1995, once the emergency was deemed to be over, the comparable figures in the same districts were, respectively, 28 per cent, 16.9 per cent and 39.5 per cent. While it would be churlish to discount the value of the efforts made by the agencies and the NGOs towards achieving this reduction, the second measurement was taken at the end of the long rains when food is far more plentiful and the incidence of malnutrition or under-nutrition, of both children and adults, is correspondingly reduced. Many agencies active in Kenya for the duration of the emergency justified their intervention on the basis of improvements like these, but by any standard the 1995 figures, if any confidence can be placed in them at all, are still outrageously high and scarcely cause for satisfaction.

Both before and during the years of the emergency there were large numbers of vulnerable and hungry people in north and north-eastern Kenya. There were many reasons for this, among them the time it takes for pasture and, in the case of poor settled farmers, fragile cultivable land, to recover from earlier droughts. We have referred at the beginning of this chapter to civil war and banditry spilling over from both Somalia and Sudan, often involving large-scale cattle theft. Evaluators from ETC UK et al. were among the few, if not the only, enquirers actually to ask vulnerable people where they thought the causes of their difficulties lay and in what proportion. In Mandera district, where most of the Somali refugees were to be found, the answer was given as 50 per cent insecurity consequent on events in Somalia (elements were the collapse of trade and the impossibility of crossing the border for grazing, cattle raids, competition from refugees), 30 per cent the lack of local services and 20 per cent drought. In every district where the question was asked drought was always felt to be the least of the problems, security was always the greatest. It is, of course, important to recognise that where political and social events inhibit livelihoods, drought can be disastrous.

Two parastatal organisations figured largely in the lives of all rural people; they were the National Cereals and Produce Board (NCPB) and the Livestock Market Division. Both were deeply corrupt, but still commonly intervened, up to a point, to steady prices and to facilitate food distribution and the recovery of herds after periods of drought. High among the World Bank's demands was the reform, more or less to the point of extinction, of these two bodies, particularly of the NCPB. The World Bank was supported in this by USAID whose representative at a food aid meeting in March 1992 insisted that USAID would not use 'food as a weapon in our cereals market liberalisation dialogue' (quoted in ETC UK et al., 1995), a promise somewhat undercut by another view expressed in one of USAID's e-mail communications:

> We should indicate that we do not find weather to be the principal cause of the shortage (the causes are not in our stars but in our food policy [sic]). We should then go through the litany of central policy problems that have discouraged production by farmers and raised prices to consumers. We should then indicate that principal policy reforms required removals of price controls, movement controls and prices to mills. (ETC UK et al., 1995)

In those sentences we may easily detect the finger of the monetarist free-marketeers who seem to dominate the Bretton Woods institutions.

Throughout the emergency the main agencies, some donor states and an assortment of NGOs laboured to get basic food, some necessary dietary supplements and a modicum of medical care, both curative and preventative, to the growing numbers of people unable effectively to support themselves. These efforts, carried out with devotion and often considerable courage by the field workers, were successful. Few, if any, people starved to death, the toll taken by disease was kept remarkably low and several valuable initiatives, largely to do with health care and veterinary services, were begun. All the agencies involved monitored progress, but unfortunately the terms of reference given to the monitors were entirely to do with the effectiveness of the mechanisms of delivery. One other major area of concern to the donors was the danger of making people so dependent on relief that they would be reluctant to make their own efforts. This theory has even been dignified with the title of 'dependency syndrome'. The world changes little, exactly the same worry was offered by the British government as one of its reasons for not intervening effectively in the Irish Famine, especially over the winter of 1846–7, and has been offered ever since by right-wing apologists for governmental inaction in the face of poverty and inequality everywhere (Hutton, 1996). Various forms of 'workfare' were introduced in Kenya, as in Ireland, some of them useful, but many of them seem not seriously to have been directed towards recreating livelihoods.

Food was delivered and, at first, quite a lot of it was appropriated for private gain, but that was swiftly brought under reasonable control. The NCPB found a new temporary role as a necessary part of the chain of distribution. Just as in Somalia, relief supplies distorted local producer prices, but, for a variety of reasons, not quite so straightforwardly. From time to time and from place to place, there were instances of local produce bought in preference to relief food, but the evidence is thought to have been confused by the number of relief workers possessed of ample funds buying for themselves in the same markets. Eventually, in 1995, following a judgement based on about as much evidence as the one that brought them in, the major donors decided that they had done enough, the emergency was over and they could leave. Because there has long been a working division between development and humanitarian assistance (now being addressed by some development analysts) any initiatives begun during the relief programme were abandoned either to make their own way, or in the distant hope that developmental programmes might take them over.

What none of the agencies seem to have considered was why, since there was no absolute drought, the numbers of those in need were so large and growing. They did not ask the question put to people by the evaluators from ETC UK et al., but since they live in the expectation that the poor will always take advantage and slide into 'dependency', they hardly could. In practice there is little evidence of any serious exploration of events in the region by the agencies' senior bureaucrats. It is not necessary to attribute positive bad faith in the matter, it is enough to recognise the climate in which these bureaucracies worked; they had, at least in part, as we have already observed, grasped at humanitarian assistance as a decent alternative to development aid to a corrupt and oppressive government. Belief in good faith is, however, severely strained when we recognise that development aid for Kenya, with no conditions attached (HRW/A, July 1995) was resumed in December 1994 and that in less than six months the humanitarian programme was closed abruptly and without notice or explanation to the people among whom it had worked or even, in many cases, to the workers and NGOs in the field.

Events in Somalia account for much of the insecurity in the region, and to a lesser extent so does the war in Sudan (see Chapter 5), but there are other factors within Kenya which shed an altogether more dismaying light on matters. Moi, in resisting external pressure for democratic, multiparty elections, had pleaded in excuse that the parties would only form along ethnic lines and that elections involving them would lead to ethnic conflict. His prophecy seemed to be justified by substantial clashes, particularly in Rift Valley Province, but all the evidence points to KANU incitement (HRW, 1995). A report from Human Rights Watch/Africa provides evidence of police involvement in such battles. Government transport and military equipment have also been used in the fighting. The report goes on to point out that Moi, rarely missing a chance to shift blame, accused the Kenyan Catholic bishops of stirring up civil war when they protested at his violent and ethnically divisive tactics (HRW/A, July 1994). Much of this is designed to keep the president and his KANU cohorts in power, but it is significant that most of these clashes have ended with the displacement of people (often in very large numbers – see HRW/A, July 1994) and the occupation of their land. In some districts this has been confined to the appropriation of the farms of sedentary farmers, in others pastoralists have been driven from their ranges. As in Somalia, land-looting has become a considerable force in creating a displaced, landless and vulnerable population.

The Kenyan government's interest in those of its people beyond the ambit of profitable agribusiness has rarely been more than minimal, so while its failure to provide even the most basic of services either for pastoralists or subsistence farmers may be reprehensible, it is not surprising. Insecurity consequent on neighbouring civil wars could, with a willing government, have been contained; instead it was added to in the prosecution of a venal élite's own agenda. In place of serious international pressure on Kenya, justifiable under international human rights legislation (Stolz, 1996), the international community effectively offered a temporary and minimal welfare state for the displaced. A chronic emergency caused by national and international events, made worse by venality and by free-market ideology, was treated as if it were a sudden and acute emergency. Chronic emergencies call for investment and the painstaking building or rebuilding of livelihoods and of all kinds of security, including that of food. Acute emergencies may sometimes call for radical rescue operations. To use the techniques of the latter to solve an instance of the former is simply to make the last case far worse than the first. Responses to acute emergencies commonly concentrate people in particular areas, distort markets by large imports of cheap food, undermine local production and so further destroy the base for sustainable livelihoods. In the case of these years in Kenya, it is difficult to ignore the doubts raised by the extraordinary convenience of this emergency for so many of the powerful parties involved.

Moi has, yet again, secured his power, aid has resumed, USAID, the World Bank, the IMF and the WTO have got their way over the parastatals and the destruction of what vestigial price protection remains for indigenous producers. In April 1996 the IMF announced a new 3-year loan for Kenya from its Enhanced Structural Adjustment Facility.[2] Its 'background' briefing remarks: 'Direct controls on domestic prices, internal marketing, external trade, and the exchange system have been eliminated, and the exchange rate and interest rates are now fully market determined.' In setting out what it calls the 'Medium-Term Strategy for 1996–98' it proposes the 'privatisation and restructuring of the parastatal sector' and 'further development of outward-looking competitive markets'. Kenya Airways is to be privatised, the NCPB is to be 'commercialized' and management of the Port Authority is to be 'contracted out'. Camdessus'[3] comrades are not lacking in social concern; they propose shifting funds from hospitals to 'preventative and primary health care' and from universities to primary and secondary education. The badly needed increase in expenditure in both sectors in each of these areas would not, of course, conform to the central purpose of an ESAF loan, the 'consolidation of the fiscal adjustment'. It would be difficult to find a set of conditions better adapted to the exploitation of Kenya and its resources by TNCs and foreign capital. Legalised land-looting will bring yet more Kenyan farming into its web and nothing in the package is designed to address the problems of the chronic crisis in the north or, come to that of the increasing numbers of poor and marginalised people throughout the country.

Moi remains in power, adopting yet more *outré* methods of survival,[4] and continues to resist political reform. His assaults on human rights persist and the brief flurry of aid conditionality has subsided, victim to those interests on which Stolz (1996) commented. In Kenya we may see an outstanding example not just of a humanitarian emergency created by easily identifiable political and economic forces, but one created for clearly political ends. That act of creation suited the interests of Kenya's partners in 'development cooperation' as much as those of Moi and his associates, but its effect on ordinary people within its ambit was simply to deepen a chronic exigency and so hasten the demise of a culture unwelcome in a predatory free-market world.

CHAPTER 5

Sudan

Convention has ensured that the literature covering humanitarian disasters and their relief deals almost exclusively with those which include among their causes some major natural event, usually drought, flood or earthquake (see, for example, Sen 1981; Wijkman and Timberlake, 1984; Walker, 1989; Blaikie et al., 1994). All these authors, and many more, make the point that social, political and economic events are crucial elements among the causes, and Wijkman and Timberlake go a little further in questioning the 'naturalness' of most disasters. Much of this work was pioneering, to do with challenging entrenched and comfortable opinion, and it would be ungenerous to complain that it failed to draw one important conclusion – that the physical event, natural or not, may not only be one among several other important causes, but might even be among the least important. Sen is the exception among these writers, he made the point by implication, but did not then pursue all its consequences. All the same this revisionist literature has exposed the mistake lying at the heart of the tradition it was trying to reform and which may be seen in the subtitle Blaikie et al. gave to their book – *Natural Hazards, People's Vulnerability, and Disasters*. Natural hazard is not the place from which to start since our argument is that humanitarian emergencies themselves are primarily political events. Much depends on how they are defined, international reactions to them and their relationship to national and international politics, all of which was amply illustrated by the cases of Somalia and Kenya. In both those, despite the political and historically chronic nature of the events, a natural hazard, drought, was invoked as the primary cause of a specific disaster.

For this reason we shall look, in this chapter, not at the drought from 1983 to 1985 which affected ten million people (Peters, 1996) and 'claimed the lives of perhaps 100,000 in the Sudan' and which is discussed by Blaikie et al. (1994, pp. 200–4), but the war which has caused the deaths of approximately 1.3 million people (HRW/A, November, 1994b) and has displaced, or forced to become refugees, a further million-and-a-half to three million (UNHCR, 1993; HRW, 1995, US Department of State, 1997[1]). Astonishingly Blaikie and his fellows, although they head the relevant section of their book 'Sudan 1983–92', seem not to have noticed this event, but then the military dictatorship headed by President Omar al-Bashir and Sheikh Hassan el-Tourabi, the leader of the National Islamic Front (NIF) and who may be even more powerful,[2] are not exactly natural hazards.

At 2,376,000 sq. km., Sudan is the largest state in Africa, and its Arabic name once referred to an even greater area. Mamelukes from Egypt had begun incursions into the region in the fourteenth century, in the course of which they destroyed the Christian Nubian state of Dongola on the Nile, but it was not until the nineteenth century, when they relinquished power to Muhammad Ali (1769–1849), that what is now Sudan was brought under Egyptian control. Egyptian forces, under Muhammad Ali's command, first invaded Sudan in 1820 and, by the 1850s, were replaced by a civil administration (Oliver and Fage, 1970) which survived until the British occupation of Egypt in 1882. In 1881 Muhammad Ahmad led a revolt which ousted the Egyptians and took the title 'Mahdi' ('Saviour', it was he who led his forces to victory over the British, who had intervened, at Khartoum in 1885) and began a campaign

for the restoration of Islam (ITeM, 1995). We may reasonably extend Halliday's (1996) analysis of contemporary Islam in the Middle East in which he argues that 'Islam' as a religion cannot simply be identified with the social and political systems created in its name because these are not in any way homogeneous, even though many of them insist on extremes in elements of the *Shari'a* (Islamic law) to justify their Draconian regimes. Albert Hourani also provides an interesting explanation of the process (Hourani, 1991). In any case justifying the state on a model of some mythical past is a device often resorted to by 'charismatic', if oppressive, leaders. Muhammad Ahmed al Mahdi, by 'Islamicising' the state, not only created a northern Arab establishment but, since the greater part of the south was Christian or animist and racially not Arab, effectively split the country and marginalised the people of the south.

Between 1896 and 1898, Britain, supported by Egypt in its expansionist ventures, gradually defeated the Mahdi, culminating in the battle of Omdurman and, a year later in 1899, an Anglo-Egyptian administration took over. It was an uneasy relationship since Egypt, with its not entirely unreasonable ambition to control the waters of the upper Nile Valley, was hoping to re-establish its hegemony over Khartoum. Britain, in return, threatened to allow the people of the south a 'federal independence' (ITeM, 1995). Governors General were British, but were appointed by the Egyptians; Britain used the assassination of one of them, Sir Lee Stack, in 1924, as the excuse for ending the arrangement and excluding Egypt from power (Oliver and Fage, 1970). The customary British colonial administration was then put in place, making Khartoum its centre, and Sudanese Arabs were employed in most of the junior bureaucratic posts (Hourani, 1991). Dividing in order to rule is one of the oldest tactics, Machiavelli gives an excellent description of it in his brief account of the Roman Empire in *The Prince* (Machiavelli, 1961), and the British, whose personnel were overstretched in keeping their empire together, embraced the method with enthusiasm. They made frequent attempts to 'preserve' the south by declaring much of it a 'closed area', a device which further divided the country and added to the northern Sudanese sense that the south was peopled by an alien race.

Britain's inability to maintain its empire following World War II (Hobsbawm, 1994) led to a protracted quarrel with Egypt which was only resolved when Egypt reached its own agreement with the Arab leaders in Khartoum. This seems wonderfully to have concentrated even British diplomatic minds and, in 1953, it led to Egypt, in association with Britain, offering Sudan a self-governing mandate followed by an agreement to a peaceful independence, one of the few unbloody decolonisations (Hourani, 1991). Elections took place in 1955 and independence was declared in 1956. British and Egyptian interests in Sudan have differed: Britain was anxious to preserve its huge cotton and strategic interests, the latter in relation to the Suez Canal, while Egypt was more interested in controlling the Nile and in establishing a wide Arab alliance or federation. Both objectives led to an arrangement in which power was concentrated in the hands of the people most likely to serve them, the Arab leaders in Khartoum. Because the northern Arabs are the majority this was likely to happen anyway, but there are ways of securing the interests of large minorities which seem not to have been explored.

Southern Sudan, largely inhabited by people who are neither Arabs nor, for the greater part, Islamic, had not been party to the agreement between Khartoum, Cairo and Westminster and were frightened by the prospect of Arab rule (Hourani, 1991). A few months before the elections, an armed and separatist struggle was launched which rapidly developed into civil war, ending only in 1972. At independence, Sudanese elections produced a government beset by Egyptian pressure to the north and by a growing civil war in the south; it survived only until 1958 when it was deposed by a military *coup d'état* (Oliver and Fage, 1970). Civilian rule was eventually restored and a moderately progressive and secular government briefly held power, even though the army continued to occupy the south. This constitutional government was overthrown in 1969 in yet another *coup* led by Ja'far al-Numayri who abandoned secularism for a very conservative form of Islam (Hourani, 1991). His rule was chequered, involving increasing dependence on the World Bank and an alliance with Saudi Arabia. He aroused opposition by accepting the structural adjustment measures of the IMF but, reinforced by dubious elections in 1983, resorted to even greater terror by formally incorporating the *Shari'a* into Sudanese law (ITeM, 1995); this included mutilation as a legal punishment. Apostasy from Islam, which came to mean public disagreement with Numayri's singularly eccentric theocratic views, attracted the death penalty; Numayri had an Islamic opponent, Mahmoud Mohamed Taha, an eminent liberal and humanistic Islamicist, hanged for it in January 1985 (HRW/A, November 1994a).

Numayri was deposed in 1985 by his military chief-of-staff Abdul Rahman Suwar al-Dahab who in turn lost power, in 1989, to the present regime headed by General Omar al-Bashir in an uncertain alliance with the NIF which was led by Sheikh Hassan el-Tourabi. All three regimes simply regarded the south as a region to be contained by whatever means, its largely unmeasured resources to be used for the purposes of the northern state; none of them made the slightest attempt to develop the south or to alleviate the poverty of its inhabitants. Cotton, principally grown in the region between the White and Blue Niles, has been the mainstay of the Sudanese economy and accounts for 40 per cent of its exports (ITeM, 1995). Sudan has been and, to a certain extent, still is a major producer of wheat, but the IMF, in addition to its structural adjustment programmes, insisted on the concentration on cotton (Peters, 1996).

In prosecuting its development, first by building the Roseires Dam on the Blue Nile, then the ill-fated Jonglei Canal on the White Nile and by colonising Nuban land for cotton production, successive governments had borrowed heavily. Military expenditure, the price of repression, was also high – by 1992 it was running at US$ 532 million, equal to 44 per cent of the combined health and education budgets. Both these sets of costs, together with the collapse of cotton prices in the 1970s and the inexorable rise in the costs of the oil used to support cash-crop production, were instrumental in bringing Sudan to its 1992 level of indebtedness, US$ 16.2 billion (UNDP, 1995). Consistent failure to service its debts led, in 1993, to Sudan's suspension by the IMF. In the decades before suspension, the Bretton Woods organisations had demanded the adoption of their usual structural adjustment programmes, the most notorious of them, in 1979 and 1984, led to popular, but unsuccessful, rebellion (ITeM, 1995). Recently, the debt having grown to US$ 17 billion, Sudan and the IMF have reopened negotiations and have agreed a formula for repayment.[3] Since then the debt has increased to around US$ 19 billion[4] and, on 13 February 1997, the IMF issued a press release renewing its threat to expel Sudan if it failed to toe the line and going on to say that the rate at which 'Sudan implements the program (of economic and financial adjustment) satisfactorily in the judgement of the Executive Board' will be reviewed 'on a monthly basis'.

Some time before the price of cotton collapsed the Khartoum government had begun to introduce mechanised farming into the Nuba Mountains and the nearby plains, some of Sudan's most fertile land, occupied by Nuban smallholders.[5] A semi-state company, the Mechanised Farming Corporation (MFC), was in charge of the process and it first established a fairly large network of cotton growing holdings at Habila. Two hundred were created, of which 191 were leased to absentee landlords. This was followed by nine other smaller projects, but, even more importantly, the Corporation began giving leases to private speculators for parcels of land between 400 and 600 hectares. Few, if any, of these new landlords were local Nuban farmers or, indeed, farmers at all. As in so many other instances (see, for example, Chapters 3 and 4), landholding in Nuba was customary, but a 1925 colonial land act, amended in 1961, had vested all unregistered land in the state excepting only customary title recognised by the Registrar of Lands – a charter for land theft of which the MFC made extensive use. The finance needed for these

deals and for the MFC's programme of expropriation on its own
behalf came as a loan from the World Bank. In 1974 the criminal
law was amended to make entering property for any purpose
deemed to be injurious to the landlord a matter of criminal trespass.
Nubans attempting to re-enter their expropriated farms, even when
they were not being used, were thus criminalised. When the new
leaseholders do put their land to use it will be, as in so many other
parts of Africa, for the mechanised production of cash-crops for
the commodity market.

Khartoum's depredations have not been confined to the south
and to Kordofan, the province in which Jibāl an Nūbah lies. For
example, pastoralists near Sudan's Red Sea coast had been forced
by three major droughts between 1980 and 1990 drastically to reduce
their herds, and they then watched as their traditional range lands
disappeared, enclosed by the state and sold into the privatising hands
of commercial interests. Peters (1996) maintains that successive
droughts so diminished their livestock that the pastoralists largely
gave up in favour of labour in the docks of Port Sudan or in the
new agricultural enclosures and that once the droughts had ended,
few people wanted to return to nomadic pastoralism. Certainly, in
place of the camels they once owned, many of them now herd goats
or have opted for sedentary smallholding (Watkins, 1995). Peters
makes no direct mention of their exclusion from parts of their
traditional rangelands, nor does he comment on the fact that many
of them are not Arab but Nuer.

In the south, resistance to the regime has been fairly continuous
even though between 1972 and 1983 there was relative peace.
Fighting broke out again in 1983; this time the southern force, called
the Sudan People's Liberation Army (SPLA), fought not for
separation but for a united, equal and secular Sudan. By 1991 it
had, however, split into two factions, the SPLA-Mainstream and
the SPLA-United (African Rights, December 1995), subsequently
renamed the South Sudanese Independence Movement, which is
separatist. Both forces have an easy relationship with Ethiopia and
with Eritrea each of which allows them more or less free passage.[6]
Peters may be right in asserting that many of the Nuer pastoralists
have voluntarily abandoned nomadic life, but they are also voluntarily
joining the guerrillas in the war against Khartoum.[7] Before the split
the SPLA had extended its recruitment northwards into the Nuba
Mountains, an area largely peopled by non-Arab Christians and
animists and also persecuted by the religious right in power in
Khartoum. They had long coexisted, particularly in the plains
immediately around the mountains, with the pastoralist 'Baggara'
Arabs, trading with each other in the staples they produced. As part
of its defence against the SPLA, Khartoum armed the Arabs who,
using the SPLA's recruitment drive as an excuse and with

encouragement from Khartoum, began to attack and pillage the Nubans. Nonetheless, as African Rights points out, Nubans, particularly the intellectuals, see themselves culturally and politically as part of Sudan and are largely unwilling to support southern separatist aspirations.

Racialism, usually an exercise in power, will flourish without help, but the venomous mix of class and racial distinction, perfected by British imperialists and decked out in the meretricious trappings of the Victorian court (the British like to call it 'tradition'), taught profound and vicious lessons. The Arabs of northern Sudan, in the past themselves the object of British racialism, have perfected their own version. 'Nuba', the name given to a large part of the south, is a racialist word referring to the black inhabitants, but northern Arabs also gave their own names to the Nuban tribes, thus the Legalege became the *Kawalib*, or 'dogs'; another group was called the *Ghulfan*, or 'uncircumcised'; two others were distinguished by the Arabs as the *Mesakin Tuwal* and the *Mesakin Qisar*, the tall and the short Mesakin – 'Mesakin' itself means, variously, 'poor', 'harmless' or 'miserable' (African Rights, July 1995).

Khartoum's aggression against the Nubans had its obvious economic motive, but in many ways it has also become the focus for its unsuccessful war against the south, even though Nuba is part of Kordofan and geographically northern. The story of the war is told brilliantly and in disturbing detail by African Rights (July 1995), it includes all the expected horrors – air, artillery and mass troop attacks on civilians, murder, rape and torture used as normal weapons of state terror, armed militias recruited from other deprived groups but who can be relied on to accept racialist cant, the censorship and persecution of all opposition and so on. By 1994, war in Nuba and the south, together with disastrous agricultural and general economic policies, had produced around Khartoum alone a displaced population of about 800,000 squatters (HRW, 1995). The government has reacted by doing its utmost to relocate as many as possible to distant concentration camps or, in the case of young men, to indoctrination centres; against the majority it has launched repeated armed attacks, demolishing, wherever possible, their squatter housing. Social engineering (encapsulated in that revolting phrase 'ethnic cleansing') is being carried out in Sudan in the interest of securing the economic power of an élite which has not hesitated to harness religion, racialism and war against its own fellow nationals to its cause. If final proof of its racialism were required, it is only necessary to look at the refusal of the NIF to recognise non-Arabs as Muslim, at its slaughter of them and at the destruction of their mosques and holy books (African Rights, July 1995). In short, Omar al-Bashir, the NIF and their accomplices and their predecessors have created a huge humanitarian disaster.

Blaikie et al. may, perhaps, be excused for ignoring this disaster in their potted account of events in Sudan; it has, after all, gone relatively unnoticed by newspapers and television. We can only suppose that because, since the war began 13 years ago, the average daily death toll has been a paltry 281, it is seen as 'Small Disturbance in Sudan, Not Many Dead'. Even so, there has been an international response of sorts and it may best be described as etiolated.[8] Not much of it has come from the World Bank and the IMF both of which have concentrated on protecting the interests of their shareholders and clients by using their only sanctions in the interest of debt repayment. Now the IMF, in return for an agreement by Sudan at least to pay back something, has restored its normal service to the regime.

During the famine of 1988–9, so well covered by Blaikie et al., the UN had established a moderately successful relief programme called 'Operation Lifeline Sudan' (OLS), it has kept this open in a reduced form in southern Sudan and is working partly out of Khartoum and partly from its logistical base on the Sudanese border with Kenya. Shortcomings in OLS and, come to that, in nearly all international programmes of humanitarian relief are discussed by African Rights (December 1995; for a wider international analysis, see Sogge et al., 1996) and we point to some of them below but, despite these, it has been successful in helping numbers of people. Its latest appeal for international support, launched in 1996, has not been markedly fruitful which means that the future is unclear (Peters, 1996).

Another UN initiative was the appointment of a special rapporteur for Sudan, Dr Gáspár Biró, who visited the country twice in 1993. Khartoum was so incensed by suggestions in his report that its interpretation of *Shari'a* was a violation of human rights that they forbade his return, a situation to which the UN seems resigned. In October 1996, a new regulation segregating women from men in public gatherings and on public transport was added, with little or no international protest, to Sudanese law, though it seems, so far, not to have taken effect.[9] In the US a condemnation of Sudan's human rights record has been published in the State Department's *Country Reports on Human Rights Practices for 1993*, but the US has excluded human rights from the brief given to another special envoy it sent to Sudan; its Ambassador does visit the southern war zones. All this needs to be seen in the light of the US conviction that Sudan is one of those countries nurturing 'international terrorism'; we may recall US support for the dubious Egyptian claims that Sudan was harbouring those responsible for the attempt, in June 1995, on President Hosni Mubarak's life. The EU condemned the bombing by the Sudanese airforce, early in 1994, of displaced civilians camped in Equatoria, which killed many and led large numbers of the survivors to become refugees in Uganda. It has also protested at the government's use of violence against demonstrators trying to protect their squatted homes, in the gigantic shanty town around Khartoum, from destruction and has called on Sudan to end its violent campaign against the squatters.

OLS's mandate is to provide relief in all war zones and in areas controlled both by the government and the movements of rebellion. WFP and UNICEF are the two principal UN agencies administering it and at no time has it challenged the government's refusal to let the agencies operate outside specific areas; they are not, for example, allowed into Nuba. This is because UNICEF believes that any challenge from OLS would provoke the Sudanese into forbidding its operations elsewhere. With one exception, more principled responses have come from international and indigenous NGOs and from churches. That exception is CARE, which has been UNICEF's principal NGO partner in OLS; it has joined UNICEF in a plea to other international NGOs to assist in their efforts, fortunately without response since further collaboration with Sudanese blackmail can only worsen the situation (African Rights, July 1995).

A continuous stream of information and analysis, otherwise virtually unobtainable, has been provided by African Rights and Human Rights Watch/Africa. They have lobbied and made constant recommendations to the relevant parts of the UN and the governments of the industrialised world. African Rights has also succeeded in sending an important fact-finding mission to the Nuban mountains which resulted in its report on genocide (July 1995). Oxfam has worked extensively with the displaced, particularly with women who are among the most vulnerable, to help rebuild livelihoods, an ambition constantly frustrated by further state violence (Watkins, 1995) and, recently, has produced an accessible 'profile' of the country (Peters, 1996). Many other NGOs have also made substantial efforts to help those in need and it is the view of some commentators that they would do more, but are inhibited by the agreements that most of them have made with UNICEF/OLS (African Rights, December 1995).

NGOs enjoy several advantages under these agreements: they are enabled to apply to the large donors for funds to support their work on both sides of the conflict; cheap or free transport and logistical support are provided through OLS facilities; the means of communication and assistance in training matters are made available to them; OLS arranges security clearance for them with the government of Sudan. In return UNICEF/OLS has effective control over NGO activity. As African Rights has remarked (December 1995), all this is very much in the interest of the Sudanese government since it makes any sanctions that the UN or particular governments might like to impose on the ground of its human rights record almost impossible. The SPLA tried to organise an alternative system of relief for the areas under its control. Constructed on the Eritrean and Tigrayan models it was compelled to work in a far larger region than either of its exemplars, it lacked their political and social base and its organisation was poor. African Rights (December 1995) makes the point that this is particularly to be regretted because indigenous social structures which could transcend the ethnic and cultural divisions of the south are thin on the ground.

Sudan's disaster is exacerbated by a difficult climate and environmentally destructive economic choices. An estimated 60 per cent of its territory is desert or affected by desertification and much of its surface water is badly polluted (ITeM, 1995), but none of this has done more than add peripherally to an enormous loss of life and of livelihoods, nor has it been responsible for massive displacement and refugeeism. This humanitarian crisis has been created by the political, social and economic choices of a ruthless and racialist élite which has commandeered a suitably tailored account of religion in its support. Its 'Islamic' state has excluded non-Muslims from positions of any importance in government, the armed forces and the judiciary. Although there are exceptions they are too few to make any significant difference to the systematic discrimination against, and oppression of, all non-Muslims (HRW/A, November 1994). Arbitrary arrest and detention are common and although the courts are said no longer to apply the *Shari'a* penalties of stoning or amputation,[10] flogging continues and torture, particularly of political suspects, is normal. Since even 'Islam' has been redefined to exclude non-Arabs, Sudan has, in effect, become a state in which apartheid and genocide are instruments of control. Khartoum's abuse of human rights is summed up bleakly in the US Department of State's Human Rights Report (30 January 1997):

> Government forces were responsible for extrajudicial killings, disappearances, forced labor, slavery, and forced conscription of children. Government security forces regularly harassed, arbitrarily arrested and detained, tortured, and beat opponents or suspected opponents of the Government with impunity. Prison conditions are harsh, and the judiciary is largely subservient to the Government. The authorities do not ensure due process, and the military forces summarily tried and punished citizens.

That huge numbers of people are in great need of help is beyond question. The Famine Early Warning System bulletin of 25 April 1997, for example, pointed out that 'Sudan's food security situation remains bad: more people need food assistance this year than at the same time last year'. UNICEF and others are treating the situation as a full-blown humanitarian disaster, but it is another instance in which the moral dilemmas become acute. Neither the World Bank nor the IMF have shown much inclination to push the Khartoum government into acting in accord with international law on human rights, but then, as Stolz (1996) has observed, where economic imperatives are at stake, conditionality is rarely more than discussed. Both financial institutions are required first to protect their shareholders' interests and justice must take its place in the queue. Some of those shareholders have considerable economic interests in Sudan in addition to their shares in the Bank and the Fund, but desultory diplomatic complaint is about as far as any of them have gone. Even more problematic is the role of UNICEF/OLS and the NGOs; in working with the Sudanese state they have, in many areas, taken on its responsibility to care for its own citizens and have, therefore, effectively if unintentionally, legitimised its actions. One consequence of UNICEF's need always to negotiate with the government for access to those affected by disaster is that it is unable seriously to take into account what affected populations, its 'clients', might see to be their best political and material interests. An OLS Weekly Report, dated 7 January 1997, offers a good illustration of Sudanese governmental control of UN operations and is worth quoting in full:

> The Government of Sudan (GOS) has approved the OLS flight schedule from Lokichokio for January 1997 into southern Sudan, with the following restrictions:
>
> Malualkon, Nimule, Akak, Boma, Chukudum, Ikotos, Labone, Nyamlell, Pariang and Yomciir.
>
> Flights to areas south of the lines Juba-Torit-Kapoeta and Juba-Kajo Keji.
>
> Yei can be supplied from Juba by air or road and not from Lokichokio or Uganda.
>
> Lietnhom and Mayen Abun in Bahr el Ghazal are not approved from Lokichokio, but can be supplied from the north with specific approval.
>
> GOS rejects flights to Abuong, Akoc, Ayein, Gorwhy, Kandak, Midel, Pakok and Palang.

This example is chosen at random and could be matched by numbers of others. NGOs, by working under the shelter of the UNICEF umbrella, must also follow UN practice and much of their work is conducted in short-term bursts. 'Parachuting' into a region is scarcely the way either to win trust or to engage in the methodology of participatory development. A patchy welfare state is not only no substitute for locally engendered institutions, but, by being imposed from without by experts from other cultures, successfully undermines their creation. There are important exceptions, for example, Oxfam working in Western Equatoria is specifically doing so with 'cooperatives and local women's groups' (Peters, 1966), but they remain the exceptions.

Halliday (1996) makes an impressive case for first examining the political, economic and social problems in any state which resorts to its own version of Islam for ideological justification – Sudan is no exception. Land-looting by a brutal and venal urban bourgeoisie, reinforced by the financial policies of the Bretton Woods circus and outside economic interests, seem not so much to be justified by the NIF's brand of Islam but, rather, Islamicisation is offered as an alternative spectacle. It becomes a sleight of hand concealing the economic and social realities behind what is, like the problems we have outlined in the cases of Somalia and Kenya, a chronic humanitarian disaster. Yet the techniques of humanitarian relief employed by UNICEF/OLS and the NGOs are, once more, designed to deal with sudden catastrophe and not with long-term and structural deficiency; conceptually they are techniques developed for, as it were, the road disaster or rail crash and writ large. Since UNICEF and its associated agencies as well as the majority of NGOs are all committed to the view that programmes in development should always be designed with, managed by, 'owned' by the people for whom they are intended, the need to see programmes of humanitarian assistance as exceptional must become important. Determining that the need to bring 'relief' to the suffering is paramount seems to be characteristic of those who design these programmes and by this token they are artificially lifted out of the context in which they must operate and the people revert to being subjects. Harrell-Bond (1986), although she was dealing solely with the question of refugees, was among the first brilliantly to analyse this issue, and it is one to which we must return in our final section. In the meantime Operation Lifeline Sudan is condemned to supporting the insupportable until there are dramatic changes in the Sudanese government or until the UN fails economically to be able to sustain it.

That the agencies are acting as if what is happening in Sudan is a sudden and immediate crisis, rather than a long-term and chronic emergency, is not really just a perverse misunderstanding. Both the OLS and the NGOs are, of course, compelled to manoeuvre around a series of war zones to achieve their ends, which ensures that many of their responses are characteristic of humanitarian intervention. Few possibilities for assisting in sustainable and continuous projects for development exist in a mobile war, particularly one conducted against the people for whom projects are designed by the state with which project designers are cooperating. One surreal element in the situation is the pressure from the Bretton Woods organisations for the 'rationalisation' of the economy which precisely supports the long-term war aims of the Khartoum government. Since the IMF is an agency of the United Nations, there can be few better examples of incoherent policy than the spectacle of its engagement with Khartoum while the OLS struggles to support Khartoum's victims.

Be that as it may, the solution to this most obviously political of disasters will lie in both national and international political processes. Surrounding states, members of the Intergovernmental Agency for Drought and Development (IGADD), have long tried to act as brokers for a peace. In 1995, UNESCO brought the warring parties together at a conference in Barcelona and the OAU has also worried at the problem – neither has come any closer to resolving the matter. On 21 April 1997 President Omar al-Bashir signed a peace treaty with the southern leaders, but the opposition in exile is reported to have rejected it[11] and the war continues with, at the time of writing, increasing success for the southern forces. Hassan el-Tourabi is negotiating separately with the southern military, offering independence as part of a strategy to consolidate his own, northern, power.[12] In the recent past, Khartoum had allied itself with the terrorist groups in northern Uganda who are attempting the overthrow of the Musaveni government. These groups also joined forces with the Hutu extremists allied to Mobutu. Khartoum's support for them has led both Uganda and the Democratic Republic of the Congo to feel that they would be safer, and Central Africa as a whole more secure, if the repressive Sudanese oligarchy were replaced. They are likely to continue support for the SPLA in any future confrontation. It should, of course, be obvious, that so long as the World Bank and the IMF continue to find ways of shoring up a repressive and bloody regime in the interests of securing their own phantasm of economic stability, then Khartoum will continue to wage a war against its own people and books about diaster in the region will continue to concentrate on droughts. Coherent and principled international policy could bring the worst of this suffering to an end; there is now a hope, no matter how slender, that the major changes being wrought throughout Central Africa and the Great Lakes Region may produce that policy.

CHAPTER 6

Mozambique

In the last three chapters, arguing that humanitarian disasters are largely politically and economically engendered events, we have concentrated on the ways in which humanitarian assistance has, to a substantial degree, fitted into the pattern of contemporary developments in international capital. We have taken the view that modern capital is, by its nature, impelled towards homogeneity and because it is founded on a dubious principle of perpetual growth through competition between very limited economic and social forms of enterprise, cannot deal either with other cultures and their forms of trading or with people and societies too poor to compete. In the early nineteenth century William Blake came, for different reasons, to a similar conclusion about capital and industry (Ackroyd, 1995). Since humanitarian assistance involves huge sums of money, usually dispensed by the states most nearly interested in the institutions of capital, it is scarcely surprising that it, too, has generated a culture in conformity with its origins. Nonetheless, in fairness we must point out that in each of the cases we have so far considered, there were remarkable examples of successful humanitarian intervention.

In Somalia, for example, UNHCR in partnership with several local NGOs (with the exception of the ICRC, cooperation with INGOs was less fruitful) established, by means of what it called 'Quick Impact Projects' (QIPs), a number of successful social projects. These were to do with water, sanitation, agriculture, market buildings and so on; some 28 small income engendering enterprises were also helped to begin work. Many of these QIPs successfully provided alternatives to refugeeism for numbers of people in areas fairly near the border with Kenya (IOV, 1994). Until 1993 and the General Assembly Resolution 48/116, UNHCR dealt only with refugees and was not permitted by its mandate to work with displaced people who remain in their country of origin. To legitimise its operation within Somalia, it created a fiction, uncomfortably mimetic of earlier international interventions in Africa and known as the 'Cross Border' and 'Cross Mandate Operation' (IOV, 1994), in which Kenya's border had temporarily 'moved' 300 kilometres into Somalia and maintained it until the QIPs were established. The consequent expansion of the UNHCR mandate, following the action in Somalia, is hedged about with major restrictions. It may work with displaced people only when there is a 'link' with a refugee problem, only with the consent of the state concerned or, where appropriate, with one or more parties to the conflict producing the situation, and its involvement must be called for by the General Assembly or the Secretary-General of the United Nations, or even by the Security Council.[1]

Other success stories were also to be found in the 'emergency' in Kenya since many of the 'workfare' programmes proved to be socially valuable, though there is little evidence of job creation for those driven out of pastoralism (ETC et al., 1995). Operation Lifeline Sudan, in its opening stages, was positively welcomed by the Sudanese and worked very successfully, until its lack of engagement with the process of building local institutions and capacity consequent on its agreement with the government, became a serious problem (African Rights, December 1995). To underline the point that not all humanitarian interventions are doomed to failure, even when they involve insensitive and high-handed action, we will consider one of UNHCR's success stories.

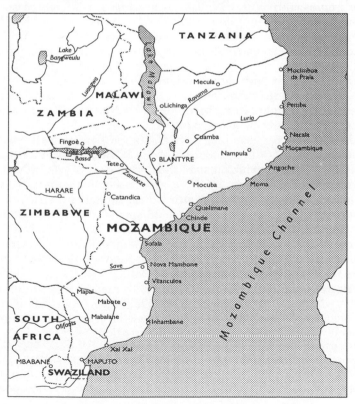

Mozambique should not, by nature, be a poor country. Moyo et al. (1993) suggest that it is exceptional in possessing 'a relatively rich but only partly explored and developed resource base' and 'an overall lack of population pressure on resources'. They add that such environmental problems as it does suffer from are local and largely a consequence of war and they illustrate this with a very telling table (6.1). That war led to an immense displacement of people and to large-scale refugeeism and it is reasonably clear that most of the local problems listed in Table 6.1 spring from the enforced movement of people.

Table 6.1 Environmental problems and issues characteristic of many sub-Saharan countries as they occur in Mozambique

Problem/issue	Significant nationally	Locally relevant
Population pressure on resources	No	Yes
Resource overuse	No	Yes
Overcultivation	No	Yes
Overgrazing	No	Yes
Overfishing	No	Yes
Conflict between pastoralists and cultivators	No	No
Agriculture and pastoral extension to erosion-prone environments	No	Yes
Perennial drought lasting many years	No	Yes
'Drought' caused by massive soil degradation	No	No
Deforestation	No	Yes
Excessive commercial logging	No	No
Extreme fuelwood scarcity	No	Yes
Limited water availability, poor water quality	No	Yes
International conflict over water use	No	No
Transfrontier pollution	No	Yes
Industrial pollution	No	Yes
Use of Third World countries as dumps for industrial waste	No	No

Source: Moyo et al., 1993.

Parts of the UN, if not all of it, continue to label the war in Mozambique as a 'civil war'; for example, a UNDP newsflash, dated 27 November 1995, commented that 'multi-party elections ... put Mozambique on path to peace and democracy and ended one of

Africa's *bloodiest civil wars*' (our emphasis). It was, of course, a destabilising war of intervention waged by South Africa through the medium of mercenaries and disaffected Mozambicans, many of whom were former adherents of Salazar. South Africa was supported by Britain, France, the US and Italy (Davidson, 1994; ACAS, 1978), Mozambique's government was helped, intermittently, by the USSR; embedded in Cold War rhetoric, it was also, in a real sense, a neo-colonial war. The interest of the industrialised nations, in particular the US, in the region was relatively straightforward and remains so. Transnational capital had invested heavily in South Africa; Southern Africa as a whole was of strategic and material interest in the Cold War; it was important that 'friendly' governments were kept in power and Mozambique had begun independence by nationalising some of its hitherto expropriated assets. Despite a voluntary arms embargo suggested by the UN in 1963, Western states supplied South Africa with a formidable armoury. In November 1977, two months after the death of Steve Biko, the UN imposed a full embargo with the exception, insisted on by the US, of certain nuclear military equipment. It made little difference, the quadrumvirate continued to supply South Africa with all the heavy equipment a modern army and airforce usually demands, including delivery systems for nuclear missiles (ACAS, 1978).[2] Extensive military training was also provided covertly.

South Africa trained, armed and supplied the RENAMO forces, while the West, by means of its own agencies and of mercenaries, provided intelligence and military assistance in the field (ACAS, 1978).[3] It was a war which, although it dragged on in a desultory way, ended only with the collapse of apartheid in the Republic of South Africa, but it had, by that time, rendered Mozambique economically one of the poorest countries in the world (see Table 6.2), had involved the death of its president and had resulted in the destruction of many of the hopes formed in the struggle for independence. Above all it had destroyed the lives and livelihoods of millions of Mozambicans.[4] Table 6.2 also points at one of the country's most intractable social problems, the extremely rapid rate of urbanisation, much of it fuelled by refugees from the war.

In practice Britain, the US and the apartheid Republic of South Africa have, despite the change in the latter, achieved their war aims. South Africa has become a member of the SADC and, since development is equated with participation in the TNC trading network, is likely to become the engine of 'development' at least throughout the Community. This prospect is added to as Mozambique, together with the other 'front-line' states, is clasped firmly in the embrace of Northern interests in the form of the World Bank and the IMF. If a report in the *Guardian*[5] is to be believed, then the governing élite is showing signs that it might follow the customary pattern of driving for commodity farming. Meldrum reports a Mozambican functionary as saying 'Why should we reserve 20 million hectares for poor people who don't even pay taxes?' RENAMO leaders, instead of being arraigned as war criminals, have become a 'respectable' opposition to FRELIMO, as has its splinter, the National Union of Mozambique (UNAMO). The future remains uncertain – RENAMO has not been comprehensively disarmed and, from time to time, attempts the establishment of an autonomous regime. In 1993 it demanded that half the country should be ceded to its control, a move which caused the UN, which had intervened to achieve the peace deal in 1992, to delay elections until the matter was resolved.

Table 6.2 Some indicators of the economic effects of the war of intervention in Mozambique†

Total external debt	US$ 4.9 billion
Current account balance	US$ –881 million
Military expenditure as %age of health and education budgets	121
Annual growth rate per capita GNP, 1980–92 – %age	–3.6
GDP per capita	US$ 64
Life expectancy	47.5 years
Mortality rate under 5 years of age	273 per 1000 live births
Population without access to safe water	78%
Population without access to adequate sanitation	81%
Proportion of households headed by women	22%
Urban population (as %age of total), 1970–92	1970: 6% 1992: 30%

† Figures refer to 1992, the end of the war.
Source: derived from UNDP; 1995, World Bank, 1995 and UNHCR draft working paper on Reintegration Strategy (December 1994).

The huge and rapid growth of urbanisation is largely a reflection of the size of the population displaced by war, for which figures are generally not given in World Bank or UN statistics. Estimates put it at well over four million, at least three times the number of returning refugees (ETC International, 1994). There were over 1.5 million refugees, the distribution of most of them is set out in Table 6.3 and it is of some importance, in the light of general difficulties in the region, that the majority fled to surrounding but almost equally impoverished states. Just as in the case of Sudan, Mozambique has been the scene of a human disaster directly caused by war even though, unlike Sudan, its enemy was largely external. At a conservative estimate, one-third of the population lost their homes and their livelihoods, and the real proportion is probably greater. Included in the peace agreement, signed in October 1992, was an undertaking by the UN to provide humanitarian assistance to the value of US$ 560 million which was to become part of a larger, US$ 1.0 billion, UN programme in Mozambique (ETC International, November 1994). This was, in effect, the declaration of a humanitarian disaster. 'Complex', the fashionable adjective for contemporary disasters, is designed to make clear that there is no one simple cause and may, we feel tempted to argue, be inappropriate in this case. Solutions are certainly complex, but the principal cause was simple aggression promoted by a foreign state and its allies.

Table 6.3 Principal host countries for Mozambican refugees

Malawi	1,058,500
South Africa	120,000
Swaziland	48,100
Tanzania	75,200
Zambia	26,300
Zimbabwe	136,000
Total	1,464,100

Source: derived from UNHCR, 1993 and 1994.

This would not immediately be apparent if we were to take as our guides two agreements reached by UNHCR with UNDP and UNICEF in Mozambique, both signed on 2 March 1994, setting out the areas of competence for each agency in the enormous business of repatriating and reintegrating most of the refugees and displaced people. As in the case of the UNDP newsflash on which we have already commented, the first paragraph of the preamble to both agreements commits each signatory to 'support, within their respective mandates, the reintegration of returning refugees and internally displaced persons into the recovery process of Mozambique following sixteen years of *destructive civil war* [our emphasis], compounded by drought'. This is not a mere cavil – characterising the war thus prevents the awkward questions about the complicity of powerful members of the UN, including at least three members of the Security Council, from arising. We may ask if it is possible that the UN agencies would not have exerted themselves to the same degree had they been unable to shift the blame in this fashion on to warring Mozambicans. Perhaps it is some small relief that the war was not described as 'tribal conflict'. RENAMO is given, by this description of the war, a legitimacy which everyone, but particularly the people of Mozambique, may come to rue.

Inter-agency agreements of this kind are customary and unremarkable; another example was 'The Memorandum of Understanding between UNHCR and the WFP', of roughly the same date and covering food supplies for returning people. But these two contain one significant departure from received wisdom. Humanitarian assistance has usually been seen as an extraordinary intervention, hugely expensive and to be brought to an end as soon as normal development activities can resume. The agreement with UNDP-Mozambique specifically sets out the need to 'integrate humanitarian aid with longer-term development endeavours in order to achieve self-reliance and sustainability of sectoral interventions' (paragraph 1.7). A similar clause, also 1.7, makes much the same point in the agreement with UNICEF: 'coherent [sic] and complementarity in external support for the reintegration and recovery process of Mozambique will be conductive [sic] to its effective use and avoidance of a disruptive effect in the transition from short-term humanitarian assistance to longer-term development programme'. There are ways in which this represents a welcome conceptual shift from the UN's responses in Somalia. In place of a media directed and ill-considered supply campaign, lacking clear goals and coordination, but vaguely and largely inefficiently directed towards snatching 'victims' from death by starvation, we have here a statement of intent to knit together the work of the Mozambicans and their government, the development agencies and the humanitarian effort.

According to a 'Final Project Monitoring Report' (UNHCR, 1994), 'By the end of 1994 some 1,651,971 refugees were reported to have returned from the six neighbouring countries of asylum.' Published numbers do not agree (see Table 6.3) and surveys were rough and ready – for example, it was first thought that 250,000 refugees were in South Africa, but in the course of assisting their return the estimate was revised to 120,000 (some of this difference may be accounted for by the 100,000 or so refugees who had found employment in South Africa). Even so, it is clear that well over 1.5 million refugees had returned to Mozambique by the end of 1994, and others have been returning since. This massive migration was a mix of people who made use of the routes organised by the agencies and of those who found their own way home. Small-scale spontaneous return, mainly from Malawi, had begun in 1986, but large-scale return took off in 1993 with a UNHCR programme of organised voluntary repatriation. In that year before the massive operation of 1994, an estimated 109,000 refugees returned from Zimbabwe and Malawi (UNHCR, 1994). It would not be too large a claim to suggest that getting the relationship between humanitarian action and development right was, to a considerable degree, responsible for the overall success of UNHCR's intervention. Other elements also helped. Despite its war-engendered difficulties, the government of Mozambique was still effective; the evaluation reports list no less than 95 government agencies, departments and ministries involved, in varying degrees, in the operation. Of these the most important was *Nucleo do Apoio aos Refugiados* (NAR), since it became UNHCR's counterpart within the government. Because the UN is happiest when it has a government to deal with, the NAR's role as the coordinating body for all the activities to do with the reintegration of the refugees was central. Apart from state agencies, well over 40 indigenous NGOs were also involved even though, in terms of investment and organisation, they may have been overshadowed by the international non-governmental organisations. Unlike the cases of Somalia, Kenya and Sudan the involvement of indigenous NGOs seems to have been an organisational principle and, of course, the existence of a government prepared to be democratic and not enmired in corruption is a transforming condition. The most important element in this success was the desire of the overwhelming majority of the refugees to return to their homes.

Although the programme was a response to a humanitarian disaster, it was very carefully planned and at every stage, from the country of asylum through the varying means of transport to the transit camps and the final destinations, it was adequately monitored. Some sense of the scale of what was involved can be had by listing the main elements of the operation in tabular form (Table 6.4). For each phase or part of the programme extensive planning, surveying, research and evaluation is claimed and there seems every reason to suppose that much of this preparation actually took place. Table 6.4 is not intended as any more than a general survey and is certainly not exhaustive, its purpose is to give an indication of the scope of the programme.

Herculean though the labour of securing the return of so many refugees and displaced people may have been, even with their collaboration, it was only half the operation; reintegration was also necessary. Apart from the killing, maiming and all the other human horrors, the war had left a legacy of appalling destruction; UNHCR, in its 'Reintegration Strategy' (RS, 1 December, 1994) gives some indication of its scale. Commercial networks were almost all destroyed, transport had been very badly damaged, some 4000 primary schools and 1100 rural health posts had been destroyed or abandoned and land-mines had been planted on a massive scale in roads and in fields. Mozambique shares with Angola the doubtful distinction of being the most mined country in Southern Africa

Table 6.4 List of elements in UNHCR's programme of refugee repatriation in Mozambique (1994)

Type of Assistance	Details	Assisting Agency
Food	Food supplements for returners.	Caritas
Transport and logistics	Hiring engineering and logistics consultants; providing and maintaining transport (25 trucks, 5 tractor/trailers, 9 pick-ups, 16 4WD vehicles, 7 station wagons, 15 light vehicles, 16 motor-bikes, 3 aircraft charters); funding transport hire, agency and NGO fuel, maintenance and administration, regional transport costs, transport for crossing River Limpopo, funding right-of-way fees, taxes, handling/storage fees, warehousing, transport for refugees from border-crossing to internal transit points, costs for NAR's own trucks, salaries for indigenous workers.	CARE, CVM, MAR, NAR, RRR, SCF
Domestic needs	73,000 jerry cans, 1600 cooking pots, 128,000 blankets provided.	STS
Potable water	Approx. 130 boreholes constructed or rehabilitated commonly by QIPs involving local cooperation; water storage tanks and distribution points (unnumbered) built.	AMRU, CEAR, MSF-Fr, MSF-Sw, RRR, WRI
Sanitation	Latrines constructed in transit camps; 194 additional and improved latrines constructed to protect water supplies. Sewage systems reconstructed. Funds for MSF-Sw to cover light vehicles. Salaries of national project staff paid.	AMRU, CEAR, MSF-Sw, RRR, SCF
Health and nutrition	Evaluation and supervisory consultancies; training in water and sanitation; QIP construction, rehabilitation and stocking of 24 health posts (stocking delayed to 1995); technical assistance and training for local staff; pick-ups, light vehicles, bicycles and a generator purchased for health centres.	AMDA, MSF-Es, MSF-Fr, MSF-Sw, RRR, SCF-US,
Shelter and other infrastructure	8 transit facilities constructed; 328 km. of road improvements; 2250 tents provided; light vehicles funded.	Caritas, CVM, ECMEP, MSF-Sw, RRR, SCF
Community services	Social services provided in communities and transit facilities; trained staff helped local *activistas* (community workers) in giving information, referral services for family reunification, help and counsel for vulnerable returners; 150 *activistas* given training in helping vulnerable groups – 120 went on to receive and help them; office supplies, fees, communications, transport and salaries funded.	CEMIRDE, NAR, SCF, SEAS, STS
Education	Funds for office costs, equipment, supplies and communications; 'Mine Awareness Campaign' provided training for 130 people who would disseminate information about land-mines; mine awareness material (T-shirts, stickers, posters etc. for schools and communities; teachers' salaries funded during repatriation project; KULIMA salaries, equipment, supplies, rents and communications funded for project.	AMRU, CEAR, KULIMA, RRR, SCF
Agriculture	Seeds and tools distributed through WRI; 176,000 agri-tool kits distributed by UNHCR sub-offices.	CARE, CVM, NRC. RRR, WRI
Legal aid/protection	2 station wagons and 3 pick-ups provided; costs of regional registration workshops, seminars with authorities of asylum countries and Mozambique; translation of protection material and guidelines into Portuguese.	STS
Agency operational support	Funds for operational and management support for implementing partners, i.e. running costs, consumables, utilities, furniture, equipment, maintenance, incidental costs; funds for 16 light vehicles, 70 telephones etc.	MSF-Sw, CARE

Source: Compiled from *Final Project Monitoring Report 1994*, Part II (UNHCR, 1994).

(Macrae and Zwi, 1994). The RS values the damage to the economy wrought by the war at US$ 15 billion. Inevitably in such circumstances, reintegration is virtually a process of re-creation. Quick Impact Projects, small-scale, short-term and low-cost projects designed to get basic social and economic structures going and which need only limited and short-term support to succeed, are the linchpin in UNHCR's strategy for moving from humanitarian relief to development. One of the best descriptions of them is given in *Humanitarian Aid to Somalia* (IOV, 1994, p. 266):

> QIPs are intended to help local communities to resume a normal life after years of disruption. Essentially they are rehabilitative and aim to serve the most pressing human needs of the target communities ... . There is normally a funding ceiling of US$ 50,000 per QIP though many cost considerably less than this ... . They are designed to be sustainable ....

'Sustainable' here means that they must be financially self-supporting or, for example, as in the case of educational projects, have secure financing from sources other than UNHCR. In Somalia QIPs had a chequered history and a survey of people working in the field 'suggested that possibly a quarter could be described as good, and about a quarter as poor or worse' (IOV, 1994, p. 280); presumably the other 50 per cent were middling. As the QIP programme was designed to attract refugees back to Somalia it was impossible to evaluate it as a whole because there are no means of telling what would have happened without it. However, there was little difficulty in recognising that extreme insecurity and the general lack of the most rudimentary state institutions rendered the prospects of survival for most QIPs, at the very best, speculative.

Whether from its experience in Somalia or from other sources, UNHCR seems to have learnt valuable lessons. Its programme of QIPs in Mozambique, many of which are included in the list of its activities in Table 6.4, were infrastructural, necessary for the support both of basic human needs and to allow for the development of income-generating activities; Table 6.5 summarises the statistics. The subsequent administration of a high proportion of them was handed over to national or local authorities which gives them a far greater chance of survival, even in a desperately poor country, than otherwise would have been the case. The considerable variations in the numbers of QIPs in any given province are, obviously enough, reflections of the numbers of people returning to it and of the degree of rebuilding needed. There is a little grumbling in the evaluation reports about the quality of some of the road repairs, but, apart from a few projects which failed, usually for extraneous reasons, no comment is offered about the rest and we are left to assume that they were largely successful; yet there were very serious organisational shortcomings.

Table 6.5 QIPs summary statistics 1993–6

Province	Sector						Totals
	Health	Education	Water	Roads	Productive	Other	
Niassa	22	36	89	23	5	0	175
Cabo Delgado	2	0	0	2	0	0	4
Zambezia	18	56	92	6	1	4	177
Tete	46	139	318	36	0	0	539
Manica	30	57	80	37	20	4	228
Sofala	10	27	24	0	4	4	69
Gaza	24	25	65	3	6	1	124
Inhambane	2	0	1	0	0	0	3
Maputo	27	18	36	0	1	0	82
Totals	181	358	705	107	37	13	1401

Source: 'Quick Impact Project Database Overview' in UNHCR Evaluation Report, July 1996.

Eighty per cent of the refugees were women and children and it follows that they constituted at least 80 per cent, or thereabouts, of those returning (WCRWC, 1995). Estimates suggest that between 30 and 40 per cent of returning households were headed by women and these estimates are borne out by the very high proportion of such households in Mozambique as a whole (see Table 6.2). Even though UNHCR publishes its policy on gender issues (UNHCR, 1990) and its own *vade mecum* for its staff (UNHCR, 1991), few, if any, QIPs were designed with or for women. For example, the delegation from the Women's Commission for Refugee Women and Children (WCRWC) specifically asked the women in two of the villages they visited about their involvement in QIPs, only to be told 'that they had not been involved in any aspect of these programs' (WCRWC, 1995, p. 7). It is not altogether surprising that the delegation discovered that the QIPs failed to 'address the community-level needs of women, especially heads of household' (WCRWC, 1995, p. 3). What is odd is that members of the staff of UNHCR, citing the need to see 'people' rather than 'refugees', seem not to have felt that their *Guidelines* applied to their own planning and programme execution. USAID personnel in Mozambique held the view that matters of gender were best left to the NGOs.

Men everywhere, particularly rural men, are conservative, not the least because maintaining control, particularly of the means of production, pays. This is not the place to argue for a more rational relationship between the sexes and within families and we merely observe that earnest male development experts, particularly from the major UN agencies, returning from work in 'the field', are often wont to offer the hardness of women's lives as a reason for not expecting too much. They have been known to suggest, possibly even with some substance, that throughout the developing world men will not allow women to take up responsibilities beyond the household. Yet the literature is filled with examples of women who, given the smallest opportunity, seize the initiative and take over the development of their own lives and communities (see, for example, Dankelman and Davidson, 1988; Sontheimer, 1991); there are even examples of men coming round to the view that this is a good thing (WCRWC, 1995). Plainly there is a long way to go before oppressive gender relations largely become things of the past and possibly even further to go before it is recognised that 'many long term economic processes have been harmful to the needs of poor people in general ... [and that] the emphasis on private property and commercialization has often reduced women's access to resources' (Sen and Grown, 1988).

Nonetheless, women can obviously be helped by encouragement from others, but leaving this encouragement to NGOs, as some people in USAID have suggested, is a questionable policy. While many NGOs have their hearts in more or less the right place, few of them have adequate experience or training in implementing serious gender policies. Most NGOs, particularly the INGOs, are run by men, doubtless well meaning, for whom gender policies may be worthy but come well down the pecking order from politicking with their own or other governments, fundraising, policy control and image. That personnel from UNHCR and USAID should also feel that gender issues were not their concern tempts the present authors to feel that remarks about the conservatism of rural men in the developing world and their desire to retain control would surely be just as well applied to the men of the UN and US agencies and, indeed, of the NGOs.

Failure seriously to address gender issues in the QIPs programme may have led to the major imbalance, shown in Table 6.5, between infrastructural and 'productive' projects – of the 1401 QIPs, only 37 (2.6 per cent) were to do with production. Yet income-generating QIPs must clearly be integral to any programme intended to fit smoothly with the resumed process of development. UNHCR had clearly recognised this in Somalia where a far higher proportion, 28 out of 320 (8.7 per cent), of the projects were entrepreneurial, and if agricultural and livestock QIPs are added to the income-generating projects, then the Somalian total becomes 122 (38 per cent – IOV, 1994). One important difference between Somalia and Mozambique, which may go some way to explaining this disparity, is that in the former, entrepreneurial production and pastoralism are all principally occupations dominated by men. Even much of agriculture, particularly where it is concerned with commodity farming, is at least controlled by men. In Mozambique international agencies and the NGOs were dealing with a predominantly female population, so we are consequently left with the suspicion that income-generating projects were felt to be less important because women's work was seen mainly to be within the household and its, largely subsistence, farm.

We do not need to suppose a conscious policy, a sort of male conspiracy to keep women in their place. Rather the automatic assumption that support for household and farm is enough to make women secure springs naturally from the culture and tradition within which many of these organisations were founded and which belong to the people who work for them. It is the tribal culture of the Northern bourgeoisie and it is so pervasive that they are commonly unaware of its influence on them. But women in the Third World, or anywhere else for that matter, do not live in some idyllic space where honest toil on the land will meet all basic needs; they live in the same world as men where few people can manage without money. In Mozambique, pressed on all sides to 'liberalise' and 'modernise' its production and trading, this is increasingly the case. Thus the women's desire, recorded by the delegation from WCRWC (1995, p. 7), for 'opportunities to earn money' is certainly something which should have been addressed by UNHCR in its QIPs programme.

It would be foolish not to recognise that many of the QIPs not specifically directed towards women nonetheless helped them. Indeed, apart from facilitating women's entrepreneurship, it is frequently the case that the projects most likely to benefit them are those generally directed towards the alleviation of poverty and economic self-sufficiency and in which particular efforts are made to help women (IOV, 1997). A 'Briefing Note' (UNHCR, March 1996) produced by the final evaluating mission and dated 28 March 1996 makes the point. Water projects obviously help those women who would otherwise be compelled to spend substantial amounts of time and energy on water collection. Seeds and tools programmes, food distribution, the creation of health facilities and the building of schools also help them, and so, too, does the provision of mills for cereals. UNHCR also set up some extremely valuable and productive seminars in the Districts on 'gender activities'. One very important activity was the rehabilitation and construction of around 5000 kilometres of road and the building or repair of 65 bridges (UNHCR, July 1996). These have been invaluable in enabling producers, particularly women, to reach markets. All these are very important, but they stop short of one

of the decisively effective moves – income-generating activities specifically designed for women.
A few projects of this sort were started by NGOs funded by UNHCR. For example, the Jesuit Refugee Service helped to organise a comprehensive training programme, in three centres in the Angonia district, which included sewing lessons and instruction on adequate marketing and pricing of the final products. Another project run by a Mozambican NGO, *Amai A Pa Bandam*, but originally funded by UNHCR, helped to create 31 groups numbering 1516 women in total, engaging in horticulture, sewing, pottery and in small-scale animal husbandry. It is hoped that these ventures will survive the end of UNHCR funding and there is reasonable expectation that they will do so (UNHCR, 1994).

In many ways, since development is not directly the agency's business, it is obviously a better thing for projects which must survive beyond the resolution of any immediate crisis to be encouraged by NGOs rather than directly by UNHCR. In the case of the agency's infrastructural projects continuation was ensured by handing them over largely to state or semi-state organisations or to NGOs, and much the same process could have taken place had UNHCR been more active in promoting projects designed to help women earn a living. Dare we suggest that had such promotion happened on a large scale, quite a number of projects might even have been handed over to the women themselves? That this did not happen constitutes a major failing illuminated, perhaps, by the success of the very few women's projects that were begun. It is instructive to set this against the intention expressed in paragraph 19 of UNHCR's Reintegration Strategy:

> An important component of the reintegration programme is the temporary community employment that can be generated through the implementation of QIPs. Consideration will be given to the reintegration of returners who have received vocational training in the country of asylum. Given the fact that women play a major role in agricultural production, the daily collection of water, the processing of grain and the cooking of the meals, and that the main areas of return tend to have very high numbers of female-headed households, serious attempts will be made to ensure that a representative number of female heads of household are included as beneficiaries of QIPs. Through the micro-projects community participation is promoted in all stages of the project cycle.

'A representative number' would have been large indeed, we have already pointed out that 80 per cent of those who returned were women and children. The RS, in its 'Sector Objectives', once it has dealt with food security, water, sanitation and health projects, many of which were QIPs, turns to 'micro-projects', community QIPs and becomes filled with might-have-beens. These were to be implemented in 'districts with at least 10,000 returners or in communities where returners represent 10% or more of the population' and it was intended to:

> Promote participation of beneficiaries:
> The population, particularly women, should be involved in the different stages of the project cycle, from identification of needs to project completion and follow-up. (RS, paragraph 32)

Implementing partners, either NGOs or INGOs, would be required to include a 'local capacity-building component' in their bids for UNHCR work:

> Implementing partners must improve the local capacity to maintain and follow-up on the projects by encouraging the participation of community members, particularly women, in all stages of the project cycle. (RS, paragraph 38)

In its comment on the outcome, the Evaluation Mission concludes that:

> In summary, while it is untrue to state that the issue of gender has been totally ignored in the course of this operation, it has not consisted in a clear and mainstream policy issue. More women-orientated activities could have been implemented and field offices and NGOs could have been required to report systematically on such activities ... . It has been remarked that even those activities which do target and/or benefit women are not necessarily carried out as a result of a conscious effort to implement UNHCR's policy on refugee (returner) women, but are merely the result of an 'opportunity which came along'. (paragraph 24, UNHCR, 1994)

The mission's report is solely concerned with 'Activities Targeting Women and Community Participation' and not with the overall objectives of reintegration. For that we must turn to another evaluation, that of ETC International dated November 1994, undertaken on behalf of the government of The Netherlands. UNHCR's objectives were the return and reintegration of the refugees and ETC International, looking at the achievement of movement and the satisfactory creation of essential infrastructure, concluded that UNHCR had been overwhelmingly successful in reaching its objectives. Since it is plainly true that nearly all the refugees have come back to Mozambique and have been resettled, the ETC mission could hardly have concluded otherwise.

UNHCR's success was palpable and admirable. However, it was not a success in a vacuum; people, principally women and children, have been helped to return to a society which is in the throes of major change and we have already remarked on the extent to which that change is, at least in part, dictated by the priorities of the Bretton Woods organisations. Later in this book we shall consider the political implications of the UN practice of working principally through INGOs or the nearest thing to them available in any given country. In Mozambique, where change includes a substantial *de facto* shift in gender relations consequent on an extraordinarily high number of households headed by women, it is something of a tragedy that UNHCR was unable to launch far more income-generating QIPs for women. Sustainability would probably have depended on establishing systems of micro-credit comparable to the beginnings of the Grameen Bank in Bangladesh, but these are now, at least in principle, scarcely unusual. Projects of this kind swiftly become developmental and outside UNHCR's remit, but it was, after all, working together with development agencies like the UNDP and UNICEF which might reasonably have supported such moves. This failure, probably unconsciously, reproduces the wider political failure to which we have repeatedly pointed in the earlier chapters.

CHAPTER 7

Rwanda

That the greater part of a million women, men and children, 14 per cent of the population, were slaughtered in Rwanda in the three months following 6 April 1994 (Joint Evaluation of Emergency Assistance to Rwanda (JEEAR), 1996, Vol. 1) has been said so often that there is a danger of becoming insensitive to its horror. Many others were maimed, raped, traumatised, one million people became internally displaced and two million fled to nearby countries. It was a carefully planned and well-organised campaign. Two major and remarkable reports provide an account packed with historical detail and political analysis of the terrible events of that genocide: *Rwanda: Death, Despair and Defiance* comes from African Rights (September 1994) and *The International Response to Conflict and Genocide: Lessons from the Rwanda Experience* has been published by the Steering Committee of the JEEAR (March 1996). We consider them both to be essential reading. Rakiya Omaar, principal author of the African Rights report, determined to record the truth before it could be sanitised, and who was an early visitor to Rwanda once the killing was stopped, wrote in her preface:

> Nothing can prepare one for the experience of genocide and the murderous campaign to eliminate political opposition in Rwanda. There are no words that can do justice to the anguish of the survivors and the cruelty of the killers.

This was a humanitarian crisis which took place in the presence of the international community's forces and much of it was recorded by the cameras of the developed world's television services. Drought, earthquake and flood played no part in this disaster; it was a political and economic event and the international response to it was also, and continues to be, political. Few people outside the wilfully uninformed and the Neanderthal right continue with the outrageous and racialist suggestion that it was a product of 'tensions between the tribes',[1] but many still seem unprepared to acknowledge the degree to which the developed world was, and continues to be, complicit in the disaster. There are others on the right offering a more sophisticated version of the 'tribal tension' version of events; they see it as the product of an internecine 'struggle for scarce resources'.[2] Resources in Rwanda are scarce, though less so than

in several neighbouring countries, but our purpose in this chapter
is to point to the essentially political and economic causes of this
'complex' humanitarian crisis and to the political nature of the
international response, neither of which had much to do with the
availability of resources. For this purpose, events before and after
the genocide must be taken into account.

When ethnic distinctions are invoked as explanations for major
divisions, particularly in cases where culture and language are the
same or closely related, they are, unlike political differences, as we
pointed out in Chapter 2, always and everywhere suspect. We may
instance the pathological determination of some Irish people in the
partitioned north-east of their island, where cultural differences seem
infinitesimal to the outsider, to distance themselves ethnically from
the remainder of their fellow inhabitants. It might be argued that
since these people have rejected a national self-definition in favour
of an entirely politically constructed non-nationality – Britishness
– they, unlike the English, the Welsh and the Scots, could be ahead
of their time. 'Ethnic' division within Rwanda is equally suspect,
though, as in Ireland, or in any number of other European countries,
it is possible to discern different lineages. Farmers are 'Hutu',
pastoralists are 'Tutsi', hunter-gatherers and potters are Twa, and
are all people of the region. If the pastoralists were, as some still
maintain, of another cultural group and did come after the farmers,
they were, as in so many other and similar histories (that of England
springs to mind), swiftly assimilated by the Hutu. They 'took over

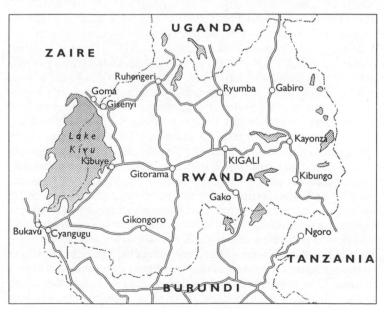

the language spoken by Hutu and Twa (*Kinyarwanda*) and incorporated Hutu traditions and cults ... they shared the same hills – there was no segregation of people – and they intermarried and bore the same names' (African Rights, May 1994, September 1994; JEEAR, Vol. 1, p. 22). Since the history is so clouded, we can at least make a working supposition that any distinction between Hutu and Tutsi was originally occupational or class rather than linguistic, cultural, tribal or ethnic. Patrick D. Gaffney of the University of Notre Dame makes the same point:

> Described by ethnographers as analogous to a feudal or a caste system, the hierarchical relationship between the cattle tending Tutsis ... and the Hutu agriculturalists ... involved an elaborate web of economic contracts and ritual exchanges which also provided for fluid movement between these status categories.
>
> Thus some who had been regarded as Tutsi ... could slip down and be reclassified as Hutu. Likewise, Hutus ... could advance into the class of Tutsis. The clan system overlapped and crosscut both groups ... . (Gaffney, 1994)

Until well into the nineteenth century parts of what is now Rwanda's northern and its south-western territory were autonomous and the rest of the state, although monarchical, was divided into a number of locally administered regions. With the uneasy exception of some small Hutu enclaves in the north, the country was effectively united and brought under central and autocratic control by a Tutsi king, Rwabugiri, who reigned from 1860 to 1895. He seized the lands of both Tutsi and Hutu and introduced a system of labour in which settled farmers (Hutu) were given access to land in return for work, a system from which pastoralists (Tutsi) were exempt; not the least, one might suppose, because to include them would have been impractical. Tutsi who had previously held power were removed from office and replaced by others whose loyalty to the King could be relied upon. Thus Rwabugiri, also known as Kigeri IV, effectively transformed Rwanda into a modern centralised, monarchical state and with centralisation came the increased hier-archalisation of the largely traditional social distinction between the farming Hutu and pastoralist Tutsi Rwandans. 'Traditional' because by this time, although pastoralism continued many Tutsi had become, like their Hutu neighbours, peasant farmers. Under Rwabugiri's rule each district was administered by a tripartite chieftainship in which the two senior posts went to Tutsi chiefs and a junior post to a Hutu chief. Military command, law-making and giving and tax collecting were Tutsi domains, agricultural affairs and the setting of land taxes, both lower down the scale of authority, were looked after by Hutu appointees. The King's objectives were simply to secure power, but the effect of this structure was to sow the seeds of a society which could begin, like the Irish after partition, to see itself as 'ethnically' divided.

Following the Berlin Conference of 1885, Germany created a series of protectorates, many of which were based on agreements with existing African states (other colonisers took the same course wherever they could), among them, in 1899, were Rwanda and Burundi. Rwanda's centralised system was perfectly tailored for indirect colonial rule, a clear advantage since Germany lacked the resources for anything else. When, after the 1914–18 war, Belgium took over the administration of both countries it, too, made use of the Rwandan ruling structure. As colonialism continued, so its abuses began to emerge more clearly. Rwabugiri had centralised the state and concentrated power in his own hands and in those of his supporters, but he did so in a manner sufficiently relaxed to defuse major overall discontent. Belgian colonisers, on the other hand, rapidly rigidified the pattern, removed political power from indigenous administrators thus reducing them to cyphers and thus, while maintaining a puppet monarchy with a few distorted trappings, they destroyed the fabric of Rwandese society.

Among their worst and most devastating crimes, that of virtually all European colonisers, was the construction of the widely accepted racialist myth. It postulated the existence of a pale skinned, northern race related to the 'Caucasians' and supposed to incorporate the allegedly Caucasian virtues of intelligence, creativity and the ability to command. Known to their inventors as the 'Hamitic Race' they were assumed to have moved south, generally conquering the lesser breeds or occupying 'empty' land. This curious and nastily romantic account is exemplified in the near pornographic writing of H. Rider Haggard, particularly, of course, *She*, published in 1886, in which the eponymous anti-heroine embodies the Hamitic myth; not only is the novel imperialist propaganda, it is also deeply misogynous. Hamites became, by dint of some supposed racial superiority, the 'natural aristocrats' among African 'tribes'. For the Belgians the pastoralists were Hamitic quasi-Europeans and could be transformed into an 'ethnically' justified intermediary ruling élite. 'Hamitic' survives among philologists and linguists as the name of a group of languages, but the racial theory is now completely discredited; unfortunately, as the JEEAR discreetly points out, with the use of an illustrative quotation from a work published as late as 1983, it still has a few adherents (Vol. 1, p. 27).

As Belgium introduced forced labour, land appropriation, commodity farming and all the other colonial horrors, they used Tutsi as their agents to the point where it became an ideological imperative to prefer Tutsi over the supposedly inferior 'race' of Hutu. During the 1930s, particularly following a demand from one Leon-Paul Classe, Vicar Apostolic to Rwanda, who threatened the emergence of 'a viciously anti-European communism' (quoted in JEEAR) if the authorities failed to act, all Hutu were removed from their positions in the tripartite chieftaincies and were replaced by Tutsi – the English were not alone in adopting a policy of divide and rule.

What had developed into class distinction during nineteenth-century centralisation was transformed by the Belgian state and its church into a racialist 'ethnicity', in essence indistinguishable from the theories of Johann Gottlieb Fichte, grandfather of Nazi anti-Semitism. In Rwanda, as in Germany, genocide has been the worst and most disastrous of the consequences of this transformation, but we may see others in what the exercise of a Christian charity might lead us to call the 'confusion' of those Western commentators, like James McCabe of the World Bank (see note 1), who insisted on describing the Rwandan conflict as 'tribal'.

Throughout the world direct colonialism had always been opposed by some of its subjects and their struggles famously bore fruit after the great Northern war of 1939–45. During the late 1950s and early 1960s the revolutionary tide of decolonisation swept Africa and by 1965 34 states had achieved independence, among them Rwanda (Davidson, 1994). Belgium could scarcely avoid the storm, particularly as its infamous record in the Congo became common knowledge. Its response was to abandon its Tutsi minions and give support to a Hutu revolution (1959–61) which abolished the monarchy and got rid of the Tutsi control of political structures. Belgium supported the revolution by helping a new administration, controlled by Hutu, to replace all Tutsi with Hutu chiefs. It also created an indigenous military force of whom 85 per cent were Hutu and 15 per cent Tutsi, roughly reflecting the national proportions. The Roman church, in what is one of Africa's most Catholic countries, changed its mind too and lent its authority to the new Hutu ascendency. Thus in just under a century, from the accession of King Rwabugiri in 1860 to the beginning of the Hutu revolution, Hutu and Tutsi Rwandans had been brought to see themselves largely as opposed factions. Many of them, particularly ambitious Tutsi (African Rights, September 1994), had even internalised the Belgian propagandist account of them as separate races.

Large numbers of Tutsi were compelled to become refugees in the course of the 1959–61 revolution and other refugees, both Tutsi and Hutu flying from oppressive government, followed in successive years. Subsequently these refugees were neither allowed to return to Rwanda nor made welcome in the countries to which they had fled. Their difficulties led, more or less directly, to the formation of the *Front Patriotique Rwandaise* (FPR – RPF in English) which, in 1990, launched a military campaign – its military wing was the *Armée Patriotique Rwandaise* (APR – RPA in English) – to compel a change in government and enforce their right to return.

Behind all this lay yet another distinction, that between differing Hutu, which had, to a great extent, been submerged in the course of the revolution. Those Hutu, chiefly around Ruhengeri in the north, who had remained independent of Rwabugiri's kingdom were finally defeated and annexed, at the beginning of the twentieth century, by a force led by Germans and Tutsi. Memories of this defeat led them particularly to detest Tutsi, but also equally to be hostile to most other Hutu who favoured a *rapprochement* with their Tutsi neighbours. President Habyarimana and his immediate supporters were all immediate descendants of these northern conservatives.

Since this is not a history either of Africa or Rwanda, we can only pick on those salient features of the past which bear on our thesis. For this reason we have neglected to discuss Burundi. Also colonised first by Germany and then by Belgium, its history is intimately linked with that of Rwanda; it is also geographically, culturally, linguistically and genealogically allied to its neighbour. There were Hutu and Tutsi in both countries who would have been happier to see them united and this position was strongly supported by the General Assembly of the United Nations. In the two years before independence, the UN repeatedly urged the Belgians to broker a peace between Hutu and Tutsi opponents and to unite the countries. Belgium ignored the pleas and, on 2 July 1962, granted independence to the two separate states – a *fait accompli* the UN was compelled to recognise. This was effectively partition and is also playing its part in the subsequent terrible history, particularly as, following their defeat in Eastern Zaïre, extremist Rwandan Hutu attempt to consolidate a power base in association with their Burundian counterparts so as to renew their genocidal war.

Describing colonial administration compels a view of the divisions in Rwandese society which conceals another reality. Rwanda is mainland Africa's most densely populated country and in 1991 there were thought to be 6.5 million Hutu, 600,000 Tutsi and about 30,000 Twa living there, giving a population density roughly equivalent to that of The Netherlands. These figures are taken from a census and while they may not be completely reliable are largely thought to reflect the proportions at the time that it was taken (JEEAR, Vol. 1). It is also important to remember, however, that between 1959 and 1964, well before this census was taken, as many as 60 per cent of the Tutsi population had become refugees (ITeM, 1995). Only 5.4 per cent of the people of Rwanda lived in urban settlements, of whom two-thirds were in Kigali. Villages on the European pattern do not exist and rural settlement is in the form of groups of households or compounds on the land which they farm. Since the farming is carried out almost entirely in the hills, these groups are simply referred to as 'hills': 'Every hill consists of several *ingo* ... where Hutu and Tutsi traditionally live side by side on the same slopes' (JEEAR, Vol. 1). In *Kinyarwanda*, Rwanda's principal African language, hills are *musozi*; enclosure, compound and household are all *rugo* – of which the plural is *ingo* (JEEAR, Vol. 1). Bureaucracy, administration, could be divided along spuriously conceived 'ethnic' lines, but it was not a perception with much immediate resonance in the day-to-day life of the hills where Hutu and Tutsi lived together, intermarried and farmed together. Until recently pastoralists and settled farmers lived lives of mutual accommodation, but land-hunger, a consequence of increased farming for the commodity market, had produced friction.

Apart from the colonial administrative history other elements in Rwanda's descent into violence are depressingly familiar and also bear comparison with so many Third World states. Land-hunger is one; only two-thirds of the country's land area is available for arable agriculture which means that each square kilometre must support an average of 406 people, and in some areas the density is more than twice that number. Despite popular belief, akin to that in fairies at the bottom of the garden, large populations are not a serious factor in the creation of poverty but, on the contrary, are a resource (Lappé and Collins, 1986; Sen, 1994). It is a resource crying out for policies for creating jobs off the farm. Since hydro-electricity has yet to be extensively developed, Rwanda's main, non-human, resource is its land. Belgium had used it extensively for the production of coffee but did so by compelling small farmers to devote a certain proportion of their land to coffee bushes, a practice continued by governments since independence. Tea was also grown for export, but on plantations and on a very much smaller scale. JEEAR suggests that its production occupied only 1 per cent of the arable land; nonetheless, by 1992, it accounted for 30 per cent of the country's exports. The Evaluation also remarks that only one plantation has been created on land formerly settled by small farmers; it is in Ruhengiri, home to the most conservative of Hutu. What, in the longer run, may be very significant is that about one-third of Rwanda's forest cover has been removed to make way for plantations.

JEEAR, quoting the World Bank, says that from 1970 to 1979 Rwanda's GDP increased by an annual average of 4.7 per cent and although growth continued in the first years of the 1980s, it soon came to an end. Table 7.1 gives the figures. Part of the decline is a consequence of the worldwide fall in coffee prices which came to a head with the ending of the International Coffee Agreement in 1989. Because all land in Rwanda is the property of the state and the farmers have only the right of use and because law regulates coffee production, the state became the sole dealer between the coffee growers and the market. By fixing the price paid to the producers at well below the international producer level the government was able to make substantial profits in the years of growth. Not, perhaps, surprisingly, little of this money seems to have been used as a hedge for the peasant producers against fluctuations in international prices.

Table 7.1 Rwanda: Gross Domestic Product – 1980–92

Year	GDP Rw.fr. bn	%age growth (nominal terms)	%age growth (real terms)
1980	108.0	–	–
1981	122.6	13.5	2.8
1982	130.9	6.8	4.1
1983	142.1	8.6	6.2
1984	159.1	12.0	–5.0
1985	173.6	9.1	4.6
1986	168.9	–2.7	5.1
1987	171.9	1.8	–0.6
1988	177.9	3.5	0.5
1989	174.2	–2.1	–6.0
1990	176.5	1.3	–0.1
1991	193.8	9.8	–3.3
1992	207.2	6.9	–1.3

Source: *International Financial Statistics Yearbook*, quoted in JEEAR.

Problems arising from collapsing coffee prices were not the only ones besetting the Rwandese government. Ever since the Hutu revolution Tutsi refugees, well before the RPF launched its campaign in 1990, had mounted sporadic attacks on Rwanda in response to the government's refusal to let them return. The government frequently responded by discriminating yet further against Tutsi remaining in the country. In 1973 a violent incident, almost certainly provoked by the army, became the excuse for a military *coup d'état* led by Juvenal Habyarimana who was, at the time, both an officer in the army and Minister of Defence. Like most military rulers, he and his followers moved swiftly from their early rhetoric to thoroughgoing corruption and tyrannical government which they entrenched by continuing to favour the cause of those northern and annexed Hutu in order to ensure their support (HRW/A, June 1993). In the list of economic woes facing Habyarimana's state the RPA's attack added the immense cost of a military operation to falling coffee prices. Further difficulties were caused by drought in the south and centre of the country which led to yet more economic problems and to substantial local discontent at government incompetence.

Economic and political difficulties grew rapidly throughout the 1980s and so, as a consequence, did the national debt. Table 7.2 illustrates the point. In 1989 Rwanda's total external debt had declined from its high point in the previous year, but in the following three years it increased by 36 per cent to US$ 873.3 million, over four-and-a-half times its 1980 level. Increasing indebtedness accompanied by governmental corruption produced, as usual, the further impoverishment of ordinary people, both Hutu and Tutsi and this, in turn, was exacerbated by drought. By 1991 the IMF, rarely prepared seriously to undermine even the most corrupt of 'liberalising' governments, imposed instead a structural adjustment programme (SAP) designed to stabilise the economy, make Rwanda 'internationally competitive', reduce the role of the state in the economy and to make some kind of provision for the most vulnerable.

Devaluation, the reduction of guaranteed prices for the small coffee growers, the relaxing of price controls prior to their ultimate abolition and the privatisation of parastatal enterprises were all familiar elements in the programme. The IMF is nothing if not quaint in its notion of social provision for the vulnerable, and the chief elements in that part of the package included the well-tried nineteenth-century remedies for poverty: workfare and redeployment. Whether, as the Fund would probably claim, it was because the Rwandese government failed immediately to implement some of the SAP provisions, or because it failed to bring its military expenditure under control, the budget deficit actually rose in 1992–3 from 12 per cent to 19 per cent of GDP and subsequent SAP credit was suspended (JEEAR, Vol. 1). Before the Rwandan economy could be reorganised to the satisfaction of the World Bank and the IMF the calamity of April 1994 had begun.

Externally, in the course of his attempted construction of a neo-liberal market economy, Habyarimana and his single party *Mouvement Révolutionnaire National pour le Développment* (MRND – National Revolutionary Movement for Development) government had established close economic ties with both Zaïre and France and, indeed, enlisted their military support against the 1990 incursion of the RPA (ITeM, 1995). Critics of these alliances and of MRND repression, some of whom had been party members, were also forced into exile. Among them were several prominent Hutu who joined the RPF. Internal repression leading to substantial refugeeism also created serious instability in neighbouring states already beset by their own problems. Towards the end of the 1980s, they, together with the principal sources of aid, pushed the Rwandan government into a modest package of reforms in which other political parties would be established and power at least shared. These proposals were unpopular with the ultras in the MRND and Habyarimana used the move by the RPF in 1990 as an excuse to abandon them.

Table 7.2 Rwanda's external debt (US$ millions)

	1987	1988	1989	1990	1991	1992
Total external debt	606.1	654.5	644.3	736.2	833.1	873.3
Long-term debt	559.8	609.3	598.9	687.8	768.7	804.3
Short-term debt	39.3	41.5	44.5	48.3	51.9	56.9
of which:						
interest arrears on						
long-term debt	0.3	0.7	0.9	2.8	4.5	7.6
Use of IMF credit	6.9	3.7	0.9	0.1	12.5	12.0
Public & publicly guaranteed						
long-term debt	559.8	609.3	598.9	687.8	768.7	804.3
Official creditors	548.5	601.9	593.9	684.1	766.1	802.8
Multilateral	390.6	436.3	478.2	542.2	612.6	646.5
Bilateral	157.9	165.6	115.7	142.0	153.5	156.3
Private creditors	11.3	7.4	5.0	3.7	2.6	1.5
Total debt service	23.8	22.7	29.0	21.6	25.3	24.4
Ratios (%ages)						
Total external debt/GNP	29.8	30.8	27.2	33.2	51.4	55.4
Debt service ratio†	13.3	12.9	18.4	14.4	17.7	n/a

†Debt service as a %age of exports of goods and services.
Source: World Bank, World Debt Tables. Quoted in JEEAR, Vol. 1.

Coffee prices would not remain forever depressed, indeed crop failures in the early 1990s, especially in Brazil, have caused a substantial rise. Tea had continued to be a valuable export commodity. Rwanda had been drawn into the net of liberalised economies producing for a commodity market and measured by the standards of the World Bank was, despite the difficulties of the 1980s, in a relatively healthy condition. It was ruled by a malleable, if corrupt, government which was prepared to cooperate with the economic interests of its aid investors. France in particular, in consequence of its intense interest in Zaïre, was doubly anxious that the Central African boat should not be rocked. Despite this, discontent among Rwandans with the MRND's repression combined with the attacks of the RPA certainly made Habyarimana's regime look shaky and it may have been this which led the MRND ultras to form the *Coalition pour la Défence de la République* (CDR), a new and influential party of the far right.

There is, perhaps, a sense in which the description of this neoplasm as 'far right' gives it a political identity and suggests, no

matter how unpleasant, a politically coherent agenda. In practice
there is little evidence that CDR had (or has, since it still exists)
any aim other than securing power and resources for its extremist
Hutu leadership and even if it was not merely a thin political
disguise for a planned military *coup*, it certainly has had the closest
links with the military and its intelligence services (African Rights,
September 1994). It had clearly existed as a faction within MRND,
its views had been advocated by the newspaper *Kangura* at least
since 1989, but it came into being publicly in March 1992. By 1993
it dominated *Radio Télévision Libre des Milles Collines* (JEEAR,
Vol. 1).

A mixture of pressures had forced Habyarimana to compromise
with the RPF in an agreement reached at Arusha in Tanzania late
in 1992. The Arusha process and the accords and protocols that
arose from it were the last and, at the time, a major hope for a
peaceful settlement and a transition to democracy. A summary of
the agreements may be found in JEEAR (Vol. 1, pp. 42–6). Once
again, other political parties would be formed and power-sharing
was proposed (HRWAP, January 1994) and, once again,
Habyarimana swiftly reneged on his undertaking. Human rights
for any Rwandese were, at best, severely compromised throughout
this dreary record, but Tutsi, in particular, were the permanent
objects of MRND oppression; massacres were frequent,
displacement and refugeeism grew constantly. These abuses,
together with Habyarimana's rejection of the Arusha accords and
protocols, forced further military interventions by the RPA during
1993. In August 1993 Tanzania acted as broker for yet another peace
agreement which had, as part of its terms, a return to the Arusha
accords. This agreement, unacceptable to CDR, its military allies
and the extremists within its own ranks and in MRND produced
Habyarimana's assassination, which was the signal for the irruption
of the carefully prepared genocidal assault against all Rwandese
opposition.

A necessary and unequalled history of that crime against humanity
is contained in *Rwanda: Death, Despair and Defiance* (African
Rights, September 1994), and our purpose is not to attempt a
synoptic account of it, but to consider international responses to
what was possibly the most conspicuously presaged humanitarian
disaster in this century. Belgium and France are the two largest and
most important bilateral donor-investors in Rwanda, and Belgium
– possibly with some confused sense of repairing the damage
caused by its colonising past – had brought considerable pressure
for democratisation and peace to bear on the MRND government.
At the outset of the 1990 engagement, Belgium stopped all military
support for the government. Following the August 1993 agreement,
the UN sent 2700 soldiers in a mission called UNAMIR to oversee

the re-establishment of peace – Belgian troops formed the largest contingent. However, when ten of its soldiers were killed in April 1994, it immediately withdrew its support and was thus instrumental in the failure of the UN intervention. There were other significant elements in that failure to which we shall return.

France played a much less ambiguous role; it had done much to help the survival of the MRND government and it scarcely bothered to conceal its support for the interim government set up following the assassination of Habyarimana and for the Hutu extremists. Its military support, which began with an agreement signed as early as 1974, consisted of troops, advisors, training and armaments as well as the financial credit with which to pay for them. In the 1990s French officials repeatedly claimed that their troops were present simply to ensure the safety of French nationals and other expatriates. This activity seems to have involved French batteries in giving artillery support to the Rwandan army (FAR) against the RPA and also deploying troops near RPA occupied areas where no expatriates were to be found (HRWAP, January 1994). French tactical advisors were active with the FAR throughout the offensive launched by the RPF in 1993. Between 1990 and 1994 this military support was also backed by a programme of arms supply which, in terms of a country the size of Rwanda, can only be called massive.

The Human Rights Watch Arms Project has documented this supply, a large part of which took the form of a US$ 6 million contract with the Egyptian government financed by France through its semi-state bank the Crédit Lyonnais. It covered:

- 70 mortars armed with 10,000 high explosive shells;
- 6 long-range artillery guns armed with 3000 high explosive shells;
- more than 6000 shells for larger mortars already possessed by the FAR;
- 2000 rocket propelled grenades;
- 2000 anti-personnel landmines;
- 200 kg of plastic explosive;
- 450 Kalashnikov rifles;
- over 3 million rounds of ammunition.

At the time that the contract was arranged, Boutros Boutros Ghali was Egyptian Minister of Defence. Quite aside from the disgraceful record of the UN in Rwanda, this may just possibly have been a factor in the present Rwandan government's objection to his second term as Secretary-General to the UN.

Previously, following the commencement of the 1990 RPA campaign, France had already supplied substantial armaments more directly. These included:

60mm, 81mm, and 120mm mortars, as well as 105mm LG1 light artillery guns. The 120mm mortars and the 105mm guns require a wheeled carriage, and have a range of over 5,700 meters and 11,500 meters respectively. France also provided the spare parts and technical assistance to maintain dozens of French-made armoured vehicles, including Panhard Light Armoured Cars ... equipped with turret mounted cannons and 7.62 machine guns. France also kept operational French-made Panhard M3 Armoured Personnel Carriers, as well as six French-made Gazelle helicopters. (HRWAP, January 1994, p. 16)

French fiscal generosity (mightily encouraged by Rwanda's pledge of its future tea crops as collateral) seems also to have made possible the purchase of weaponry from South Africa to the value of a further US$ 5.9 million. This deal was largely for light weapons, rifles which are also capable of launching rifle grenades, light and heavy machine guns, grenade launchers, 60 mm mortars, fragmentation grenades, ammunition and so on. Obviously the FAR used these arms against the RPA, but they were also the equipment used in its military support for the Rwandese militias (*interahamwe*) and by the *interahamwe* themselves. Some six to seven weeks *after* the genocide had begun and while it was being widely reported throughout the world, a shipment of arms destined for the Hutu extremist government arrived in Goma – it had been despatched by France (African Rights, September 1994, pp. 671–2). It is not clear to the present authors whether direct financial support was given to the government's purchase from China of the machetes it distributed throughout the nation for use by the foot soldiers of the *interahamwe* – they were possibly cheap enough not to need it.

Evidence that the slaughter of Tutsi and Hutu opponents had been carefully planned, both by the MRND and the CDR, is offered by African Rights (September 1994) and is largely accepted by JEEAR (Vol. 1, pp. 51–2) and by many others.[3] What has, perhaps, been less widely canvassed is the suggestion that 'UNAMIR and some foreign embassies had seen [detailed written plans] before the massacres took place' (JEEAR, Vol. 1, p. 53).[4] Past massacres, their frequency and scale, had entered into common knowledge so that if these plans were seen by UN officials or forces and by embassy staff there can have been no possible ground for dismissing them as incredible. That apart the UN was given ample warning by Rwandan opposition politicians and by human rights activists who lobbied the UN Secretary-General's Special Representative, Jacques Roger Booh-Booh, on the matter (African Rights, September 1994). It may not be too charitable to assume that UN and embassy personnel warned their respective employers

of what was about to happen and, if so, then the dereliction of the
UN is even more culpable than its miserable performance in
Somalia. We can take little comfort from the UN forces', including
the remaining Belgians, desultory efforts to look after white
expatriates as it abandoned black Rwandans to the slaughterers.
France had been a powerful ally of the MRND government and
a personal friendship seems to have developed between the Presidents
Mitterrand and Habyarimana. The aeroplane in which Habyarimana
was shot down was a present from Mitterrand's son.[5] African
Rights (September 1994) makes a strong case for seeing the
widespread and uncritical association of France with Francophone
states in Africa as a means of retaining consequence as a permanent
member of the Security Council and, in support of this thesis, quotes
Mitterrand: 'Without Africa France will have no history in the 21st
century.'[6] However, the authors of *Rwanda: Death, Despair and
Defiance* go on to consider the complexity of the relationships.
France included former Belgian as well as French colonies in this
post-colonial network, hence its alliance with Zaïre and its President,
Mobutu Sese Seko. We accept the view put forward by African
Rights, but are also inclined to believe that since Zaïre is rich in
resources (ITeM, 1995), prestige within the Security Council may
not be the sole motive behind French meddling in Central Africa.

Rwanda's government, with its lengthy history of murder,
oppression and authoritarian rule, lost any last shreds of legitimacy
it may have had by launching into genocide in 1994. It was facing
an increasingly determined and successful onslaught from the RPA
and was obviously in danger of losing that war. The UN's failure
to provide even minimal protection for Rwandese people from the
government's armed forces and *interahamwe* is, of course, only one
element in its dereliction. Booh-Booh, the special representative of
the UN Secretary-General, and his successor, Shaharyar Khan, both
worked hard, presumably with Boutros Ghali's authorisation, to
achieve a cease-fire between the RPA and the FAR. Had they
succeeded they would have effectively conferred a new legitimacy
on the Hutu extremist government as one of two equal belligerents.
It was into this situation that France launched its *Opération Turquoise*,
immediately and disastrously endorsed by the Security Council of
the UN. France invaded the south-west of Rwanda, occupying
roughly 20 per cent of the national territory just as the Hutu
extremist government was about to fall (HRWAP, May 1995). It
has been claimed that this operation saved the lives of many who
would have been killed by the *interahamwe*, and this may even be
true. It is equally true that lives would also have been saved by the
success of the RPA. What is certain is that the timely French military
control of the south-west protected the retreat of the Hutu extremist
army, ensuring its safe arrival in Zaïre. JEEAR remarks that 'Force

Commander General Lafourcade sharpened the partisan edge of the intervention by declaring ... that members of the "interim government" – who were directly linked to the genocide – would be allowed to seek asylum in the French zone' (Vol. 2, p. 55).

In June, the Security Council had finally decided that some response to genocide might not be beyond it and it mounted UNAMIR II which was charged with disarming the *interahamwe* and, when its forces bumped into them, they did so. No attempt to seek out the militias was made and, far more importantly, UNAMIR II was not asked to disarm the retreating FAR which retired to Zaïre with its armaments intact. A second, minor but symbolically important, effect of the French operation was to allow the creation of camps within Rwandan borders for the internally displaced which were entirely controlled by Hutu extremists. These were effectively guerrilla enclaves, but they presented less of a threat to a new Rwandan government and its people than the army billeted in camps outside Rwanda. RPA forces succeeded in closing most of these guerrilla centres without much bloodshed. An exception was Kibeho in April 1995 where extremist resistance to closure led to 'both sniper fire and machete attacks among IDPs ... evacuation ... deteriorated into a full-scale battle using innocent victims as expendable tools of war' (JEEAR, Vol. 2, p. 64) and around two thousand people are believed to have been killed (estimates have varied from 300 to 8000; 2000 is the official UN figure). Some of the responsibility for the deaths of the innocent, particularly for those who were summarily executed at the end of the engagement, lies at the door of inexperienced RPA soldiers out of reach of the government's limited means of communication. But despite routine reactions from the developed world anxious to discredit any apparently anti-authoritarian movement, JEEAR (Vol. 2) adds that 'The deaths were caused by gunfire, machetes and trampling ... many of the dead had machete wounds. Since the RPA did not have machetes, this suggests that the hard core elements in the camps were responsible.'

Zaïre had also forged a close alliance with the MRND and the CDR governments and many Zairean Hutu became recruits to the *interahamwe* (African Rights, September 1994). But its chief role in the genocide was to act for French interests, both diplomatic and logistical, and it was, of course, from Zaïre that France launched its initial invasion and subsequently supplied its troops. More importantly, following the genocide, Mobutu's government allowed the creation of camps controlled by the FAR and the *interahamwe* and facilitated the command of these forces by an extremist government in exile. Following the end of the open fighting Zaïre allowed the delivery by France of yet more arms to the FAR, including artillery pieces, machine guns, rifles and ammunition, which made possible its re-formation and its extensive re-training. China, Zaïre and at least one US arms dealer have also supplied weaponry, the French continued to provide training at their bases, Bangui and Bouar in the Central African Republic, and Zaïre maintained storage facilities (HRWAP, May 1995). The report of the Joint Evaluation, partly relying on evidence from the Human Rights Watch Arms Project, remarks:

> Currently the Rwandese army in exile has an estimated troop strength of 50,000 ... and [has] brought the Hutu militias under its control .... [In these camps there is] an army that is rebuilt, where military ranks are recognised, military discipline observed, an extensive communications network has been set up, and the weaponry and logistics well built up. Finally, the army in exile has aligned itself with Hutu militia from Burundi, inflaming the already tense situation inside Burundi and threatening to regionalize the conflict. (JEEAR, Vol. 1, p. 69)

Zaïre was among those countries whose activities have ensured that this particular humanitarian crisis reached a hiatus rather than an end. It, too, has a Tutsi population, resident near its eastern border for at least four centuries and known as the Banyarwanda. Failure to find the funds to pay its army together with its subservience to French policy led to the Zairean government's attempt to dispossess the Tutsi and to use their land to reward its soldiers.

With or without the support of the RPF, Zairean Tutsi had clearly organised themselves in advance against this final escalation of the Franco-Zairean support for the extremists. They easily repelled the notoriously ill-trained and unpaid Zairean army and immediately established an alliance with the principle Zairean opposition group led by Laurent Kabila. This alliance is one of unlikely partners: Kabila's own group is largely a left-wing secessionist party from the province of Shaba, but he drew in anti-Mobutu guerrillas, also secessionists, from the province of Kasai whose leader is André Kissasse Ngandu and who, far more than anyone from Kigali, is likely to have influenced the military tactics of the alliance. There is a creakiness in this coalition not only because of each party's special interests, but also because of recent and violent hostility between Shaba and Kasai.[7] Nonetheless it is this alliance, simply described as the 'rebels' by an indolent Western press, which routed the Hutu extremists from their entrenched camps in Eastern Zaïre and finally overthrew Mobutu; we have yet to see how it will survive in government. In the course of that war, Hutu extremists, in addition to allying themselves with Mobutu, attempted to establish new bases and alliances in Burundi, supported in both endeavours by the French attempt to rescue Mobutu's regime by means of a mercenary intervention.[8] At the time of writing the effect of Kabila's success, in the re-creation of the Democratic Republic of the Congo, on Burundi's fortunes is unclear.

Unquestionably Rwanda itself, in 1994 and since, has the dubious distinction of being numbered among the greatest humanitarian disasters of the twentieth century. It is not thus because of the numbers involved. After all in the great Bengal Famine of 1943, for example, estimates suggest that over three and a half million people died (Sen, 1981), but because, like the genocides of World War II, Bosnia and East Timor, it was entirely politically engendered. In each case the perpetrators were not isolated megalomaniac tyrants; they all received substantial international and domestic support. Detailed analyses of this phenomenon exist for World War II; they largely remain to be written for Third World examples.

From the beginning of the genocide and the intensification of the RPA response it was unquestionably dangerous to attempt any humanitarian intervention in FAR controlled areas, though the ICRC, the WFP, CRS/Caritas and some others made courageous and partly successful efforts. Some evidence exists that matters were easier in the RPA areas (JEEAR, Vol. 3). The notorious failure of the wealthy world to come to the aid of the fledgling RPF government – the only legitimate government of Rwanda, formed in July 1994 following the RPA victory – was to a considerable degree emulated by the failure of the INGOs, at least at first, to work seriously within the borders of the state. A senior representative of one INGO explained that his organisation was actively discouraged from doing so by UN agencies.[9] Whatever the reasons, humanitarian assistance, badly needed in Rwanda, was chiefly concentrated on the refugee camps. The world chose to ignore the genocide and the attempts of the survivors to rebuild their lives.

Large numbers of moderate Hutu as well as Tutsi survivors had fled the country either in terror of the *interahamwe* or because they did not want to remain in a war zone, but, as African Rights points out:

> The huge exodus was not wholly spontaneous ... [it] was also organised by the *interahamwe* ... a large minority were killers, many of them professional *interahamwe*. Unfortunately, from the start the professional humanitarian response prevailed ... [camps were] organised along the lines of the administrative structures that had previously existed in Rwanda. Power was handed straight back to those responsible for the massacres. (African Rights, September 1994, p. 652)

This comment was made specifically about a camp in Tanzania, but African Rights goes on to say of the camps in Zaïre that 'The same dilemmas as in Tanzania were repeated on a larger scale' (ibid., p. 655). Military refugees had their own camps, but the civilians included the *interahamwe* and a huge range of officials and others who perpetrated the genocide; it was they who formed the Rwandan administration of the camps.

Camps, particularly in the Goma area, had been swiftly organised into those for the wealthy, others for the army and yet more for the majority. In those camps holding the majority the authority of the militias backed by military support was rapidly put into place. Large numbers of those herded into the less privileged camps were unquestionably innocent refugees, many of them in great need. JEEAR's report records the levels of malnutrition in the Goma camps; in August 1994 that ran from 17–23 per cent only declining to 2.5–5 per cent in January 1995 (Vol. 3, p. 96). It seemed to the agencies that the sheer size of the influx meant that the organisation of food and medical supplies could only be through the acceptance of the communal structures that the extremists brought with them. It is very uncertain that this was the case and the appalling consequences are clear: those most in need were the last to benefit, effectively the international supplies propped up the extremist regime at precisely the most important moment. When it was at its most vulnerable and might possibly have been contained by international action, the genocidal regime was buttressed by UN agency and INGO feeding programmes and, during a crucial phase of their development, took the decisions about who was to be fed and when.

The UNHCR and many INGOs tried hard to persuade innocent refugees that it was safe to return, that reports to the contrary were simply extremist propaganda, and they also refused to provide food for men in uniform. At first there was a considerable degree of international opposition to the re-arming of the Hutu extremists and serious attempts were made to persuade the UN and some Western states to make aid conditional on the killers being rooted out (African Rights, September 1994). This plea was ignored and CARE articulated the developed world's response: 'Our remit is to provide humanitarian assistance. That is what we have to do.'[10] The organisation agreed that this would mean feeding those who were responsible for genocide. It was a position reinforced at a meeting of ECOSOC on 19 July 1996 by Yasushi Akashi, Under-Secretary General for Humanitarian Affairs, when he said that 'the foremost responsibility of the international community was to save lives'.

It is an attitude which developed in tandem with the gradual loss of interest in the genocide on the part of UN and other observers within Rwanda and their increasing preoccupation with what they saw as the new government's infringements of human rights. An example of this change of focus may be seen when Kibeho was used as an excuse by the EU temporarily to stop its aid to Rwanda.[11]

The present authors feel that since genocide must be the ultimate abuse of human rights, the observers' loss of interest is, at best, odd. Nonetheless, these changes of attitude encouraged by Western states and their organisations, have created the climate in which the 'problem' may be interpreted as a relatively straightforward case of feeding refugees until they can be repatriated. A dreadful irony becomes apparent here. Many authorities have made forceful cases for not treating refugees as victims; instead their resourcefulness and abilities must be recognised and built upon (for example, Harrell-Bond, 1986; Watkins, 1995). Perhaps no more formidable and unfortunate example of this exists than in the effectiveness of the extremist Hutu organisation of the camps and their capitalisation on the work of the INGOs.

Rwanda, more than any other humanitarian disaster, has changed the nature of the debate about the role of INGOs. It is no longer morally acceptable, if indeed it ever was, for expatriate NGOs to arrive at the scene explaining that their role is 'apolitical' and simply concerned with fulfilling a higher imperative to do with saving lives. Because such disasters are commonly politically and economically engendered, usually either proximately or finally caused by the very societies from which these NGOs spring, to behave in this way is simply to become part of whatever the immediate massive problem may be. Many INGOs are fully aware of the dilemma and we may see the titanic struggles of Oxfam to come to terms with it as one of several examples (see, in particular, Watkins, 1992, 1995). This awareness has yet to translate into practice and is, in any case, a commodity in limited supply.

JEEAR's report, in a passage dealing specifically with the case of Kibeho, includes a telling sentence which applies across the board: 'The NGOs understandably placed primary emphasis on the well-being of their humanitarian charges, perhaps without giving adequate consideration to the predicament and need for both security and justice, and, most importantly, the sense of urgency of the government', and it goes on to mention 'the anarchic system of NGO coordination' (Vol. 2, pp. 64–5). Anarchy was inevitable. Surprising numbers of NGOs have appeared in other humanitarian catastrophes, as many, the report suggests, as 80 and this had previously led to huge problems of coordination which tended to remain unresolved, Somalia being a case in point (IOV, 1994). Without counting organisations involved in programmes in Tanzania and Zaïre, two hundred NGOs responded to the Rwandan crisis, some of them quite small, many of them without African experience of any kind, all of them involved in the consequent chaotic duplication of effort and supplies. This should be borne in mind when assessing the outrage of some NGOs when they were expelled from Rwanda. People sent by NGOs to Rwanda were frequently

without experience and completely incompetent,[12] their competition
for local supplies and resources inflated prices and, we may safely
assume, damaged yet further an already crippled economy. A
succinct account of this invasion is to be found in the third volume
(pp. 152–3) of JEEAR's comprehensive report which adds that the
ICRC, together with certain, presumably more responsible, INGOs,
is drawing up a 'Code of Conduct for the International Red Cross
and Red Crescent Movement and NGOs in Disaster Relief' (p. 153).
We may hope that this will improve matters, but it seems to us that
it is unlikely to address the fundamental political problem.

The JEEAR report is very thorough, well balanced and naturally
cautious, but even it, in its careful fashion, points to the ways in
which none of this was inevitable (see, especially, Vol. 3). Although
the problem is now generally recognised (except among the most
obtuse of INGOs), it continues. Responsibility for the lack of
change seems to lie in a mixture of the failure of the UNHCR and
the INGOs to agree about priorities and the inability of UN
agencies to exercise any control over the activities of NGOs
(JEEAR, Vol. 3, p. 98). There is no reason to abrogate common
political sense when looking at disaster; in any other situation
where the outcome is so politically clear we should not hesitate to
say that those in whose hands some central answers lie, and who
fail to act, lack 'political will'. By that we mean that they prefer
the status quo to some other possible outcome. We are supported
in this view by the philosopher Anscombe who, 40 years ago,
made a powerful argument for looking at a person's actions for a
guide to their intention rather than simply accepting what they say
(Anscombe, 1957) and we may reasonably apply the principle to
organisations. Humanitarian intervention by the UN is compromised
by its dependence on the vagaries of the Security Council and while
there is an undeniable role for INGOs in any international response
to humanitarian disaster, it is one which, so long as they do not
intend to engage with the political nature of what they do, they
are incompetent to perform.

CHAPTER 8

Afghanistan

Afghanistan is just over 652,000 sq. km. in extent, 17 times the size of The Netherlands, two-and-a-half times the size of the UK. It contains three main geographic regions, the central highlands, the south-western plateau and the northern plains. These are formed, or bounded, by the Hindu Kush and its subsidiary ranges, outliers of the central Himalayas. There are four main river-drainage systems: the Amu Darya, part of which forms the border with the Central Asian Republics, debouches into the Aral Sea, Helmand ends in the lake Hamun-e-Saberi on the Afghan–Iranian border, Kabul which is a tributary system for the Indus, and Harirud which, for part of its course, forms the border with Iran before disappearing in the Karakumy Desert in Turkmenistan.

In the northern mountains rain is often heavy – up to 53 inches per annum, but in the arid west it can be as little as 3 inches. The south-west is a monsoon region and averages 15.8 inches each year. Summers, except in the monsoon region, are hot and cloudless; winters are very cold. Even in Jalalabad, where summer temperatures can reach 49 degrees, winter temperatures often fall to –15 degrees. In Kabul the lowest recorded temperature was –31 degrees. Southern and south-western Afghanistan has little vegetation outside the rainy season, and no trees; sandy deserts are the major form of terrain. In contrast the regions around and north of Jalalabad are rich in vegetation and in trees – the higher regions have extensive forests. There are substantial reserves of natural gas, which, in more settled days, were exploited and sold to the USSR, fairly large reserves of coal but only small amounts of oil. Afghanistan has large deposits of high-grade iron ore, some copper, lead, zinc and beryllium, and it also has lapis-lazuli and salt. Despite these substantial resources, its economy is mainly pastoral.

Its population is approximately 22 million and there are two principal languages: Pushtu, spoken by about half the population, and Dari, a Persian dialect spoken by about a third of the people. Turkic languages spoken in Turkmenistan, Uzbekistan and Tajikistan, all very closely related, are widely spoken around the borders with those states. There is a substantial number of other local languages. Pushtus (known to some westerners as Pathans) make up the largest group in the population and Tajiks probably account for a third. Although most of the policital parties and military alliances recruit along ethnic lines, there is little, if any, evidence of ethnic oppression in the areas in which each of them is influential. Religious antagonisms between traditional conservatives, modernising Islamicists and the puritanical *Taliban* are more commonplace.

Afghanistan emerged as an independent state in the course of the eighteenth century and succeeded, during the reigns of Nadir Shah (1736–47) and his successor, Ahmed Shah Durrani (1747–72), in advancing its frontiers deep into India, thus briefly making it one of the great Islamic empires. Successors to Ahmed Shah were unable to maintain these conquests, particularly in the face of British expansion. From the beginning of the eighteenth century and with increasing intensity throughout the nineteenth, both Russia and Britain had nurtured colonising designs in the region; Russia was anxious to ensure access to ports in the Persian Gulf and to protect itself from the hostility of the Ottoman Empire; Britain was determined to control the Indus Valley with the object of securing its Indian Empire. Russia furthered its expansionist aims by a mix of threat, diplomacy and bribery, Britain resorted to war.

The first Afghan War (1839–42) ended in defeat for Britain, but the second (1878–80) resulted in the British annexation of the Khyber Pass and the Afghani Pashtun territory to its south, beyond the 'Durand Line' (now part of Pakistan and sometimes called 'Pashtunistan'). During the British occupation, Afghanistan's

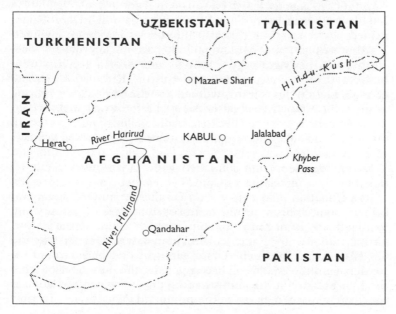

borders were also slightly expanded by the addition of a narrow gusset of land reaching through the Hindu Kush to the borders of China. This was to complete a *cordon sanitaire* between Britain's Indian Empire and Russia. So it is that Afghanistan is no exception among Third World states whose borders have been artificially defined by Western colonial adventures.

In 1919 a third war drove the British from the country and independence brought a modernising ruler to power in the person of Emir (subsequently Khan) Amanullah; it was his government that became the first in the world to recognise the revolutionary government of the Soviet Union. Stalin responded, in 1924, by declaring that 'The struggle of the Emir of Afghanistan for ... independence ... is objectively a *revolutionary* struggle' (Carrère d'Encausse and Schram, 1969). Amanullah Khan's rule was ended by a putsch organised by Tajiks who replaced him, in January 1929, with their own appointee, Bacha Saqqao, who was crowned as Habibollah II. His reign lasted for nine months when another coup, supported by Britain, installed Mohammed Nahir, one of Amanullah Khan's former generals, as Nadir Shah. By 1931 a system of autonomous, semi-federal, local leaders was in place and, in passing, we may note that this more or less traditional framework substantially conditions relatively recent internecine struggles. Nadir Shah was assassinated in 1933 and was succeeded by his son Zahir Shah, who reigned until 1973.

The system of local, autonomous, clan-based leadership survived without challenge until 1953 when central government, led by the Shah's brother-in-law, Prime Minister Muhammad Daud Khan, gained power and introduced a number of important changes. Roads were built, utilities nationalised, irrigation improved, hydro-electric schemes were begun, schools and medical facilities were built and the armed forces were modernised. There were even some changes in attitudes towards women and the compulsory wearing of the veil (*chador*) was abolished. Land reform was planned, but never actually introduced because traditionalist opposition led, in 1963, to Daud's abdication and the restoration of the absolute power of the monarchy.

Daud's developments coincided with, indeed were rendered possible by, the escalation of Cold War manoeuvrings in the region by the USSR and the US. With a familiar mixture of threat and bribery both empires did their utmost to achieve supremacy and for ten years, until the re-establishment of monarchical power, virtually all developments in the country were financed by the Cold Warriors. The Soviet Union was the principal source of aid to Afghanistan (US$ 2.5 billion compared with US$ 0.5 billion from the US) because in the long-standing dispute with Pakistan over the 'Pashtunistan' region, the US supported Pakistan, not the least because it had successfully recruited that country into its two major Asian military alliances, SEATO and CENTO; the latter is sometimes remembered as the Baghdad Pact (Rubin, 1996). Changes led to an increase in the role of the central state and a substantial change in its relations with the rest of society. In 1964, Zahir Shah established an elected, but solely consultative, parliament and introduced a constitution and a form of government known as the 'New Democracy' (ITeM, 1995). It survived for seven years, but lacked a broad, popular and participatory base and so was largely ineffectual and left monarchical power untouched. Political resistance to the monarchy had come principally from the People's Democratic Party of Afghanistan (PDPA – describing itself as 'Marxist-Leninist') which split into two major factions – one, the *Khalk*, led by Nur Muhammad Taraki and Hazifullah Amin, was an alliance of workers and peasants, the other, the *Parcham*, led by Babrak Karmal, tried to unite the urban middle classes, the military and the intellectuals (in 1977, the USSR pushed the two factions into reuniting). PDPA support and, come to that, Soviet covert assistance, allowed the army to stage a successful *coup d'état* in 1973 which abolished the monarchy and installed Daud Khan again, this time as President. It was, of course, government by permission of the army and like so many such regimes, was plagued by dissent – Daud was deposed in April 1978 and his successor was murdered. Early in 1979 the PDPA appointed Hazifullah Amin as Prime Minister who, once again, began the process of reform, largely by force rather than by persuasion. Land reform was high on his agenda, so, too, was the promotion of literacy and the ending of traditional forms of social control like the dowry system and wearing the *chador*. Later in the same year the US Ambassador to Kabul, Adolph Dubs, was murdered which led to the ending of US economic assistance to the country and to an increase in the CIA's support of armed activity hostile to what the US now denounced as a pro-Soviet state.

Other political forces were at work in this period. During the 'New Democracy' an Islamic politicising group had emerged in the University of Kabul; calling itself *Jamiat-i-Islami*, it was led by Burnahanuddin Rabbani and 'Abd al-Rabb al-Rasul Sayyaf from the staff – Gulbuddin Hekhmatyar was its most prominent student leader. This movement later gave rise to the three most important Islamic parties: the *Hezb-i-Islami* led by Hekhmatyar; the *Jamiat-i-Islami*, largely Tajik in membership and led by Rabbani; *Ittihad-i-Islami* led by Sayyaf is allied to *Jamiat* and several of its former commanders are now senior figures in the *Taliban* movement.

Hekhmatyar's party, radical and principally Pashtun in membership, maintained armed forces in most Sunni areas in Afghanistan, but controlled very little of the country. It was defeated by the *Taliban* in February 1995 and is no longer a serious military power. One of *Jamiat*'s most prominent commanders is Ahmed Shah Massud who was, at one time, patchily supported by Pakistan and in a more comprehensive way by the US. At the time of writing, he and his party still control north-east Afghanistan despite being under sustainmed attack by the *Taliban*. *Ittihad* has huge resources in armaments and money, but very little support on the ground; despite its connections with *Taliban*, it is, in theory allied to *Jamiat*.

Apart from these recent Islamicising parties there are several others. The *Mahaz-i Milli-yi Islami* or National Islamic Front of Afghanistan, *Jabha-yi Nijat-i Milli* or National Salvation Front, *Harakat-i Inqilab-i Islami* or Movement of the Islamic Revolution are all conservative and religious parties. *Harakat-i Islami* was closely linked to *Jamiat-ul-Ulema*, a clerical party in Pakistan which largely fostered the *Taliban* movement. There were also a number of Shi'a parties, many of them sponsored by Iran and some of them merged into what is now *Harakat-i-Islami* (Islamic Movement).

It was from within this confusing mix and from Islamic fundamentalist groups entering Afghanistan, largely from Pakistan and Iran, with the object of fighting 'Satan', that the CIA found and armed the opposition; its principal financial intermediary was Saudi Arabia (ITeM, 1995). Leonid Brezhnev responded by sending, in December 1979, an expeditionary force to topple the Afghan government and to control the country more directly. It attacked the PDPA headquarters and killed Amin; Babrak Karmal whose influence, during Amin's ascendancy, had been contained by his appointment as ambassador to Czechoslovakia was installed as President. His first act was to legitimise the Soviet presence under the terms of an older treaty between the two countries. Soviet intervention in Afghanistan combined with the US freezing of the Strategic Arms Limitation Treaty (SALT) to open what is sometimes referred to as the 'Second Cold War'. US military aid to opposition Islamic forces in Afghanistan during 1980 amounted to US$ 30 million, substantially more than it had given in aid; by 1987 this had risen to US$ 630 million a year. Funds from the US had been matched throughout by military aid from Saudi Arabia and both states supplied the *mujahedin* with very sophisticated weaponry which had, hitherto, been confined to NATO forces; these flows were maintained until 1989. 'During 1986–1989, total aid to the *mujahedin* from all sources exceeded US$ 1,000 million per year' (Rubin, 1996). We may, perhaps, contrast this largesse with the subsequent US demonisation of Islamic 'fundamentalism', particularly in Iran. Of course, Afghanistan must be pacified in the interests of a stable environment for an oil pipeline to be built from the Central Asian Republics to the Pakistan Coast and which is so central to the US's control of the region's oil reserves. Perhaps we should, in view of this, be a little less curmudgeonly in our praise for this remarkable aid commitment.

Despite the constant military interventions, Karmal tried, by less autocratic means than his predecessor, to continue the programme of reform, but his position was hopelessly compromised by the circumstances of his accession to power.[1] Changes in the USSR, begun with the advent, in 1985, of Gorbachev as Secretary-General of the Soviet Communist Party, led to its desire to withdraw from its expensive and futile engagement in Afghanistan. More-or-less at Soviet insistence Karmal resigned in 1986, offering 'ill-health' as the reason. In his place the PDPA appointed its Pushtu Secretary-General, Mohammed Najibullah. He presided over the completion of long-standing negotiations which resulted in an Afghan–Pakistan Accord (1988), guaranteed by the US and the USSR and, subsequently, over the agreement with the USSR which led to the withdrawal of Russian troops from Afghanistan.

In the course of Najibullah's presidency the Cold War ended and with it the financial interest of the US and the USSR; with the collapse of the latter the relationship with Afghanistan's three former Soviet neighbours, Turkmenistan, Uzbekistan and Tajikistan was also changed. At the same time, possibly also a consequence of the end of the Cold War, Saudi Arabia and Iran fell into dispute about the financing of the *mujahedin*, the fundamentalist irregulars, who were fighting against the regime in Kabul. Najibullah also presided over the change in the PDPA's name to the *Watan* (fatherland) Party, a change made in recognition of a growing nationalism but which seemed not to reduce its commitment to 'Marxist-Leninism' (ITeM, 1995).

The PDPA/*Watan* had been maintained in power by the USSR and the withdrawal of Soviet support left it unable to cope with the explosive mix of warring Islamic factions. Najibullah fled for protection to the UN offices in April 1992 where he remained until he was executed by the *Taliban* when they entered Kabul in September 1996. PDPA authorities, chief among whom was the provisional President Abdul Rahim Hatif, immediately negotiated a settlement with General Massud of the *Jamiat* who took command of the capital. This provoked the fundamentalist *Hezb-i-Islami*, led by Gulbuddin Hekhmatyar, into an attack on the *Jamiat* forces in Kabul ostensibly to restore the power of the government. It was an intermittent battle which ended with a peace agreement in 1993. Kabul had been devastated by the war and, in the confusion, Afghanistan's foreign reserves were mysteriously spirited away (ITeM, 1995).

Apart from Massud, who was allied to Sayyaf and *Harakat-i-Islami*, and Hekhmatyar with his Pushtan support, two other groups had also fought for control of Kabul: these were an amalgam of former

government militias calling themselves *Junbish*, under the command
of Abdul Rashid Dostum, and a smaller, Shi'a group backed by
Iran and called *Hizb-i-Wahdat*. Perpetual war, the obvious corruption
of so many politicians (Afghanistan had become the centre of the
world's opium trade and the CIA lists it as the world's second largest
producer) and increasing poverty led to the complete disenchantment
of ordinary Afghanis with politics. The sudden emergence in late
1994 of a new movement, the *Taliban*, seemed to offer a new start.
Earlier in the year, Dostum, in alliance with Hekhmatyar, attempted
yet another *coup* with the support of Pakistan whose hope was that
it might produce a stable government in Afghanistan; the *coup* failed
and this persuaded Pakistan finally to end its support for
Hekhmatyar.

Pakistan was anxious to make use of the disarray in Afghanistan
in order to secure its plan for opening trade links with the Central
Asian Republics along a highway and, possibly, by rail through
Afghanistan. Depending on the state of the war, the road route was
to be from Peshawar, through Kabul and along the Salang Highway
or from Quetta, through Qandahar to Herat and Turkmenistan.
In October 1994 an experimental convoy was dispatched by
Pakistan's Minister of the Interior, General Naseerullah Khan
Babar, along the second of these two routes and was met by an
armed party of Afghanis who demanded to be paid for allowing it
to proceed. Haggling continued for several days, but was abruptly
ended by an incursion of a heavily armed group consisting of a mix
of Afghan refugees and Pakistani Pashtuns calling themselves
Taliban – Students. The convoy was freed and the *Taliban* advanced
on, and took, Qandahar virtually without resistance. Whether or
not the beginning of the *Taliban* campaign was a deliberate act of
provocation by Pakistan, the inhabitants of Qandahar welcomed
the invaders as guarantors of some order and stability, even though
they seemed to resent the regulations imposed against women.

Taliban leadership was recruited from Pashtun graduates of
traditional private Sunni schools (*madrasas*) principally found in
Pakistani Baluchistan ('Pashtunistan') and it is worth noting, in
passing, that the same movement was involved in the removal of
Benazir Bhutto from power. The party seems to have been armed,
at least for the move to protect the convoy, by the Pakistani
intelligence agencies. Once it had taken Qandahar it widened its
ambitions and began to advance on Kabul; for this adventure it
was heavily supported by Pakistan. Popular support was widespread
with the consequence that the movement easily defeated the
assorted *mujahedin* irregulars in the southern Pashtun regions.

Support was also provided by the CIA among mutterings from
that organisation about *Taliban*'s ability to create a stable state in
Afghanistan. During the Cold War, the Shah of Iran, whose *coup*

against democratic government in 1953 had been so handsomely backed by the CIA, had been one of the US's most reliable supporters in the containment of the USSR. When his monarchical dictatorship was overthrown by Islamic extremists, led by the Ayatollah Ruhollah Khomeini, the US replaced its somewhat fundamentalist demonisation of the USSR with an equally obsessive opposition to Iran. With the collapse of the Soviet Union it had secured a major interest, through its TNC Unocal, in the oilfields of the Central Asian Republics. In the ordinary way a pipeline from that source should have been built through to the Iranian coast, but a deal with such a dangerous enemy could not be contemplated. Instead, the US determined to build its longer pipeline across Afghanistan to Pakistan's coast – hence its interest, to which we have already referred, in the *Taliban*'s ability to form a 'stable' government.

In mid-February 1995, Hekhmatyar ceded his main base to the *Taliban* in Kabul's neighbouring province, Lowgar, without a fight, while Massud occupied the remaining *Hezb-i-Islami* positions. Shi'a militias, maintained by Iran, had been operating in Kabul Province but were destroyed by attacks, on the one side, by the *Taliban* and, on the other, by Massud's forces. Massud succeeded in preventing the *Taliban* from reaching the capital city or from occupying its environs. Herat fell to the party in September without opposition and its attention was turned once more to Kabul where it opened a major battle for control on 10 October. *Taliban*'s subsequent victory, Massud's withdrawal and regrouping, his alliance with Dostum and subsequent uncertain fortunes are all current circumstances. Pakistan, realising that it was unable to control its creature and, should *Taliban* fail, that it will have severely compromised any relationship with another future administration, increasingly seemed to vacillate in its policy. By the beginning of the 1997 campaign and the increasing successes it brought to the *Taliban*, Pakistan once again stiffened its support.

Over the decades millions of refugees have been created (in the 1980s 3.5 million fled to Pakistan and 2 million to Iran), though many of them have returned either spontaneously or with the help of UNHCR. Between two and three million other people have become internally displaced, many of them settling around Kabul where the population has tripled (Rubin, 1996). Although many refugees have returned, few of them have been able to resume their former lives. Fighting is sporadic and breaks out in numbers of different places; as it continues new refugees and newly displaced people leave the areas of conflict and the situation has been further complictaed by the influx of refugees from troubled neighbouring states in Central Asia looking for safety in Afghanistan.

Another major humanitarian problem is caused by the extensive mining of substantial parts of the country; UN estimates suggest that somewhere in the region of ten million anti-personnel and two million anti-tank mines have been deployed. This estimate can only be of the crudest since untold numbers of butterfly bombs, particularly attractive to children, were dropped. War zones, of which there are many, are littered with unexploded ordnance (UXO), itself very dangerous but used also by inventive warriors to construct anti-personnel devices. Mines, as well as recycled UXO, are, of course, weapons of terror principally designed to attack non-combatants – a point carefully evaded by those political representatives of the arms trade, the British Conservative government, when they blocked an international move to ban these devices. They might, in their passion not to jeopardise British jobs, have paid some brief attention to the WHO report which states that over half the casualties of the war are mine victims, or to the even more troubling statistic offered by the Save the Children Fund that 78 per cent of the mine casualties are children.[2]

All normal state services in Afghanistan have collapsed and many urban centres, large parts of Kabul in particular, have been devastated. *Taliban* have taken over a notional civil government, but it is incapable of exercising normal governmental functions, not simply because it is principally engaged in fighting a war, but because it lacks the experienced human, as well as all the usual infra-structural, resources for doing so. For the foreseeable future, even if the present war were to end, much of the population will largely be dependent on emergency services provided by the international community. These are provided by the WFP, UNICEF, UNHCR, a variety of other, specialist, UN organisations, the ICRC and a sizeable assortment of other NGOs. The latter are particularly significant in the medical field in which the UN, at present, lacks an institutional structure for emergency interventions. But in December 1996, the ICRC issued a special report entitled 'Afghanistan: a forgotten and exhausted population' in which it remarked that 'the operation for victims of the Afghan conflict is the ICRC's third largest and it remains seriously underfunded'.[3]

Food production and distribution has also been ruined in many parts of the country by war and, to a certain extent, by *Taliban*'s meddling in social structures. According to the WFP[4] much of the shortfall in food supplies has been made up by the import, from Pakistan, of about 600,000 metric tonnes of wheat each year. As in many predominantly rural societies outside the industrialised world, Afghanistan's spring, even in normal circumstances, is a time of food shortages as new crops grow and, consequently, a time when food prices in the markets get higher. In the spring of 1997 prices were affected even more by Pakistan's inability to supply wheat because its own crops in the previous season had been poor as a result of drought.[5] Wheat in the Afghan markets tripled in price putting it out of the reach of huge numbers of poor people. This crisis is important in the context not because large-scale famine followed, too many international interests are at stake to allow that, but because it is an indicator of the general lack of food security throughout the country.

Medical facilities are scarce and are largely kept in being by UNICEF and a number of NGOs, including the ICRC. Schools and universities are being reopened in areas firmly under the control of the *Taliban*, but they cannot be said to be functioning normally and there are many places, including large parts of Kabul, where none are open at all. Many infrastructural services, like waste collection, are organised by UN agencies, often in food-for-work programmes and much food distribution itself is handled by WFP. It is a violent world in which, for the poor majority, ordinary civil human rights do not exist and compounding this neo-colonial mess is the much remarked upon *Taliban* policy for women.

Using, in justification, an account of Islam that can, at best, be described as odd, the *Taliban* are controlling the lives of women in a way which we may legitimately describe as misogynist. Unengagingly they respond to criticism of their rules with much the same rhetoric as the defenders of South Africa's apartheid – critics, they claim, fail to allow for their ancient religious culture. It is unnecessary for us to rehearse the familiar arguments against that position; these have adequately been addressed by Halliday (1996), Hourani (1991) and Said (1993). We need only remind ourselves that *any* culture, including our own, which denies human rights to half its people is unacceptable, a point made forcefully by the early Irish socialist, William Thompson (1825), over a century-and-a-half ago. Women in Afghanistan have been forbidden to work, to attend schools or universities, to appear in the streets unless covered form head to foot in *burqas*, to receive medical attention unless women doctors are available and have been beaten up for what armed thugs decide is an infringement of these rules.

Belatedly *Taliban* officials discovered that, in enormous numbers of families, women are the sole providers – for the males as well as the females in their families – and have partially relaxed their demands. WFP has been instrumental in organising a network of women's, largely widows', cooperative bakeries through which basic food is got to the needy. Similar cooperatives are engaged in making clothes, and several multilateral agencies, particularly UNICEF, have begun vocational and health training courses for women. CARE has its 'Relief for Widows Project' which 'is helping 1,000 widows and their children by providing them wheat as "payment" for their work making quilts. The women are provided

15.4 pounds of wheat per quilt, or 154 pounds of wheat per month for the 10 quilts which each woman can produce in that time.'[6] Other relaxations have also taken place, SCF-US has been permitted to employ women so long as they wear an Islamic veil (hejab) and are kept strictly apart from men; UNHCR has received 'encouraging indications' that some of their female staff will be allowed to return to work.[7] These limited concessions can be unreliable since local Taliban officials seem frequently to be out of touch, or in disagreement, with the policies of their central government.

Here, yet again, we meet that most notorious of dilemmas facing both multilateral agencies and NGOs – can immediate help be given to the needy if, by doing so, an unjust regime is supported which will, in the longer run, worsen their plight? There are no easy, certainly no general, answers; each case will be resolved in its own way. Nevertheless, recognising that the dilemma exists is an important precondition of not falling into the error of so many NGOs in the aftermath of the Rwandan genocide. In Afghanistan some organisations simply duck the issue; the ICRC, for example, in the context of its substantial and important campaign of relief, remarks that 'Taking cultural norms into account and with the agreement of all the parties, the ICRC has arranged for separate distributions of food and other basic necessities for women.'[8] Deciding to deal with women separately might well, as the organisation says itself, be pragmatic, but to maintain that it is a response to 'cultural norms' evades too many central questions.

The Red Cross is not, of course, alone in this, and all the other agencies feel it necessary to compromise if they are to be permitted to work at all. One UNDHA report remarks that 'SCF-US received permission from the Ministry of Public Health for women to work in the medical field under the condition that female staff strictly observe Islamic veil (Hejab) and work separated from male staff.'[9] Essential services for, or run by, women in the middle of a humanitarian catastrophe are thus made subject to the eccentricites of male religious ultras who, we must remind ourselves, are substantially the creatures of the US and Pakistani intelligence agencies. One of the most depressing examples of this misogyny may be found in another UNDHA report: 'A local NGO ... has secured funding ... for [four] ... centres for street children .... The centres provide boys (5–14) and girls (up to the age of 7) with general and health education, a daily meal and weekly medical check-ups.'[10] Clearly, at 7 girls become preilously close to being those dangerous and subhuman species, young women, and it is better that they should become diseased or starve rather than contaminate pubescent young men.

Taliban officials have offered the odd excuse that the war renders matters too dangerous for women to work but, quite apart from the standard macho view of women embodied in such a remark, even when things begin to return to some semblance of normality, their anti-women edicts continue. Thus a report from the WFP says that 'The schools in *Taliban* areas ... opened in March, but without girl students; Kabul University also opened, without women as students or instructors. Women have also not yet been allowed to return to work, except in the health sector.'[11] The report continues: 'United Nations Heads of Agencies ... briefed the Taliban on UN and agency policies and programs', not, apparently, with much success.

Whatever the outcome of this war, Unocal will have its pipeline and the US will keep as tight a rein as it is able on the political structures of the country. Much of the political future will also be conditioned by what happens in Iran, Pakistan and the Central Asian Republics. In the meantime, Afghanistan is a devastated country with an economy in ruins, its farmers increasingly dependent on opium as the only saleable crop and the prospect of a capricious and tyrannical government. Eight thousand people, most of them children, are killed or injured by landmines every year.[12] There are over two-and-a-half million refugees; most of them are in Iran and Pakistan but many others have fled to the CIS and India. How many people are displaced within Afghanistan is unclear because the number constantly fluctuates, but UNDHA says that 'between 1 October 1996 and 1 May 1997, more than a quarter of a million people were displaced within Afghanistan or became refugees in Pakistan'.[13] These people, of course, are in addition to the huge numbers already displaced. This massive human catastrophe, whose political origins lie largely in the ambitions of other states, is taking place in what is, potentially, a reasonably wealthy country since it has considerable natural resources. But rebuilding it is likely only to be possible with foreign assistance and, as things stand, this will mean accepting the meddling of the Bretton Woods institutions.

Bleak as this prospect may be, it will unquestionably be an improvement on the present state of affairs, but, no matter how improbable, there is an alternative. It would be entirely possible for a regional trading alliance to emerge from an association between Afghanistan and its immediate neighbours, many of whom are also potentially powerful and wealthy. Improbable because it would depend on the coming to power of mature, secular, democratic and forward looking governments which, in turn, must spring from appropriate political movements. Where these exist they are in hiding; we can only hope that their time will come.

CHAPTER 9

Azerbaijan

We have chosen to include Azerbaijan in our examples because apart from the wide, if not always very informative, news reporting at the time of the war between the Azerbaijan Azeri government and the Armenians of Nagorno-Karabakh from 1991 until an uneasy cease-fire in May 1994, it is rarely mentioned in the Western media. When it is, journalists commonly reach for that vapid 'tribal' analysis and one recent example spoke of Armenians as seizing territory by force 'from their ancient blood enemies, the Turkic Azerbaijanis'.[1] As an account of a war with clear political origins, in which 18,000 people died, 25,000 were wounded and roughly 1.2 million became refugees or were displaced (ETC UK et al., 1996), this is less than illuminating. That war has not really come to an end, its causes are still unresolved and no settlement has been reached, but what is happening there could, indeed should, be seen, not as some obscure tribal conflict, but in the context of a political and economic upheaval which is engulfing the entire Caucasus and its neighbours, both to the north and the south. Much of that upheaval is caused by miniature cold wars between Russia and the US over oil. We are examining only one country in the Caucasus and its neighbouring regions not just because regional upheavals break down into national disasters, but also because that is how humanitarian agencies continue to respond to them. Azerbaijan may stand as representative for a number of nearby and interconnected calamities.

Contemporary Azerbaijan is a relatively modern state. Over the last two-and-a-half millennia it was part, first, of the Arsacid (often known in the west as 'Parthian') and subsequently the Sassanid, Persian empires. Between the thirteenth and fifteenth centuries, came, variously, the Mongol and Turkish (Ottoman) occupations of the Caucasus; both of these were essentially part of the struggles for control of the Persian empire. Esmail I, a Shiite Muslim, whose distant ideological origins sprang from Muslim hostility to the Buddhism of the Mongols, had established an independent fiefdom in part of Azerbaijan and his principal political object in doing so was to establish a base from which to secure power over Persia. In 1501, he succeeded in supplanting the Turkish ruler in Azerbaijan; a decade later he had taken the greater part of what is now Iran and Azerbaijan became, once more, part of the Persian empire. It remained that way until the rise of the Russian empire in the nineteenth century which compelled the Ottomans, in the treaties of Gulistan (1813) and Turkmenchai (1828), to cede the northern half of the territory, contemporary Azerbaijan, to the Russians. The southern regions, now Azarbayjan-e Khavari and Azarbayjan-e Bakhtari are still provinces of Iran.

Until the Mongol and Turkish invasions and suzerainties, a variety of nomadic pastoralists, traders and settled farmers had made up the greater part of the Azerbaijani population but, during that period, their identity as a distinct ethnic group, the Azeris, was created. The construction of their ethnicity differed little, if at all, from all other examples (compare Fukui and Markakis, 1994, writing on the process in the Horn of Africa). What actually made an Azeri was a common political, commercial and social bond in the face of alien rulers as much as any supposed ancestry or even a language. Since most Azerbaijanis remained, without much complaint, in Persia after the Russian annexation of the north, the two elements of ethnicity most popularly seen as definitive, ancestry and language, seem not to have resulted in a pan-Azeri nationalism. Other ethnic groups are also native to Azerbaijan, particularly the Armenians and the Lezgins and we shall return to them, but the Azeris make up the greater part of the population (see Table 9.1). It is scarcely surprising that, following Russia's takeover, a colonial

bourgeoisie emerged, particularly in urban centres, 'being separated
from the fundamental mass of the people not only by their level of
life and culture, but also by language, as are the English in India'
(Trotsky, 1934). These were the forebears of that other significant
ethnic group in the country, the present Slavic population.

In 1918, following the Soviet revolution, British, American and
Turkish forces of intervention, in support of the southern
detachments of the White Russian army, headed by Anton Ivanovich
Denikin, who was busy waging war against the Bolsheviks in the
Ukraine, occupied the Caucasus, including Azerbaijan (Carr, 1979;
ITeM, 1995; Deutscher, 1954). Part of the attraction of Denikin's
cause for World War I's allies, aside from their hostility to
Bolshevism, lay in the substantial oil reserves known to exist in the
Caucasus, including the region around Baku. During their
occupation of Azerbaijan, they put into government a 'pan-Turkish
and pan-Islamic' party, the Musavatists (ITeM, 1995 – *Musavat*
means 'equality') which survived until the Red Army took the
region in 1920 and the Soviet Socialist Republic of Azerbaijan was
proclaimed. In March 1922 the Republic became, together with
Armenia and Georgia, part of the Transcaucasian Federation of
Soviet Socialist Republics, an arrangement which was brought to
an end in December 1936.

For a mix of economic and religious reasons, relations between
the Azeris and their Armenian neighbours were poor. Moscow
decided that the situation could be better contained if Nagorno-

Karabakh and Nakhichevan, both of them historically part of Armenia, were incorporated into Azerbaijan. In 1923 and 1924, the two were accorded the status of Autonomous Region (*Oblast*), dependent on Azerbaijan; Nakhichevan was largely cleared of its Armenian people who were driven into Armenia proper. In this Draconian solution, obviously unlikely, in the long term, to succeed in its purpose, we may see one of the principal elements in the current disaster. Despite this clumsy and inhumane attempt at segregation, Azerbaijan as a whole retained substantial numbers of Armenians, most of whom lived in the Nagorno-Karabakh enclave where they made up between 80 and 90 per cent of the population (ITeM, 1995). In succeeding decades, as Stalinist policies increasingly rendered peripheral republics economically precarious, the two groups, like so many others throughout the world, sublimated their problems into mutual hatred.

Unlike every other example that we have examined, Azerbaijan, by virtue of being a member republic of the USSR, was not an arena for the battles of the Cold War, but it is certainly one of its casualties. Once Gorbachev had introduced *glasnost,* that greater openness and accountability in government, the Armenians' long-suppressed, or sometimes repressed, desire to be united with their fellows in Armenia proper began vociferously to be expressed. Their demand was, unsurprisingly, not for repatriation, but for an extension of Armenia's borders to include the enclave, a demand resisted with equal vehemence by the national Azeri majority, particularly through the medium of their new and nationalist party, permitted in Gorbachev's regime, the Popular Front of Azerbaijan (PFA). In 1988, the Karabakh Regional Soviet passed a resolution that the enclave should be annexed to Armenia, a proposal which was vigorously supported by popular demonstrations among Armenians throughout Azerbaijan.

Glasnost had its limits, Moscow despatched Russian troops to suppress the demonstrations which they did, like most armies in such situations, with unnecessary violence; some commentators (Lawrence Sheets, for example, in *War Report,* June 1996) date the start of the Azeri–Armenian war from that episode. Nonetheless, in the autumn of the following year, Azerbaijan was declared to be a sovereign state within the Soviet Union and, in the fluctuating political situation, Azeris attacked Armenians in Sumgait and in Baku, killing a number of them and setting off large Armenian demonstrations. The government, still Communist, called in Soviet troops yet again and over one hundred more people died in the process of pacification. These episodes heightened the tension between the two groups and, even more importantly, as the Cold War drew to its messy end, encouraged yet further the emergence of the rival nationalisms. In December 1991, as the USSR was replaced by the Commonwealth of Independent States (CIS), Soviet-cum-CIS troops were investing Nagorno-Karabakh which was holding a plebiscite in which most people voted for independence. As the CIS came into existence, these regular forces were withdrawn and fighting between Azeri and Armenian militias erupted.

Azerbaijan was a colony of the Russian empire inherited by the Soviet Union, and we have already remarked on the division of the Azeri community between Persia and Russia in the course of that colonisation. Like most other colonies, the country's borders were created by the process, but before independence in 1991 Azerbaijan had never been united politically except as part of another empire. Uneasily placed between Persia and Russia (subsequently Iran and the USSR), Azeri demands for self-determination matured, in the late nineteenth and early twentieth centuries, into a nationalist campaign. Those struggles, concentrated within the borders created by the Russo–Persian treaties, were a necessary part of subverting first the Russian and then the Soviet imperial order, but success came to the Azeris not directly as a result of prolonged conflict in which national aims might have been more clearly worked out, but as a consequence of the defeat of the empire by an external force, the USA.

Armenian nationalism within Azerbaijan, and in the Nagorno-Karabakh enclave in particular, was subject to additional influences. It, too, takes much of its contemporary character from its opposition to the Russian and Soviet empires but its overall history of national struggle is far longer than that of the Azeris and has been tied, from time to time, to Armenia's periodic independence. Armenia's borders, like so many others, have changed with its fortunes, for example an eighteenth-century alliance between some of its leaders and the Czars ultimately led to the incorporation of the otherwise Armenian region of Nagorno-Karabakh into Azerbaijan. Within Azerbaijan confrontation between Armenians and Azeris is sharpened by religious differences; the former have been Christian since the fourth century, the latter are Muslims. Other Azeri nationalist disputes are with the urbanised Slavs who are by now, despite Trotsky's acerbic comment, natives of Azerbaijan, and with the Lezgins, a north-eastern Caucasian group living on both sides of the border with Dagestan. The Russian blockade of Azerbaijan, particularly along the Dagestan border during the Chechen war, led to a considerable heightening of tension between Lezgins, who at least in Baku were a well organised group, and Azeris. There is also some opposition to the Azeris from the Talish and the Kurds, but both groups are comparatively small.

The last reliable census before the war between Azerbaijan and Armenia was taken by the Soviet authorities in 1979, and from it may be derived the relative sizes of the various ethnic groups. These are given in Table 9.1 which is extracted from a larger table for the whole Caucasus constructed by Felix Corley in which he also gives his own estimates illustrating the devastating changes wrought by the Nagorno-Karabakh war. His estimates are given here because they include Lezgins and 'others'.

Table 9.1 Ethnic Composition of Azerbaijan (percentages of population)

	Soviet Census (1979)	Corley's estimate (1996)
Azeris	78.1	88.0
Slavs	8.4	4.0
Armenians	7.9	2.0
Lezgins	2.6	3.0
Others	3.0	3.0

Source: War Report, Jan/Feb 1997.

Conflict in Nagorno-Karabakh, which had been bubbling viciously since 1988, escalated in 1990 when the USSR first sent in the troops we have already described as investing the enclave during its plebiscite. In 1991 and 1992, following the collapse of the Soviet Union, the rise of the CIS and the withdrawal of its forces, the war became one fought solely between Azeris and Armenians. For a while military advantage alternated between the two (ETC UK et al., 1996): in 1992 Azeri artillery disrupted electricity and water supplies and damaged the hospital in Stepanakert (capital of Nagorno-Karabakh), while the Armenians controlled the Lachin corridor to Armenia proper and took the Azeri town of Susha. By the end of that year, 7700 people had died in the war and half a million people had become refugees in Azerbaijan; 'thousands of Azeri refugees [were] caught in the snow to the west' (ETC UK et al., 1996). In 1993 the Armenians took back territory that they had previously lost, including Agdam, an Azeri town just over their eastern border, from which an estimated 250,000 Azeris were compelled to flee, they also extended the Lachin corridor. From December 1993 until April 1994, the war was at its most intense. Azeri forces, by then provided with substantial technical assistance by Iran, Turkey and Russia, were fighting, with considerable success, on Nagorno-Karabakh's north-eastern front, while the Armenians (we refer below to the way they, too, were also armed by Russia), successful on another front, were preparing a major onslaught on the Azeri city of Gyandzhe in western Azerbaijan.

Fighting also spread to that other enclave, physically separated from Azerbaijan by Armenia, Nakhichevan. By May and the signing of the cease-fire, Nagorno-Karabakh's forces had seized as much as 20 per cent of Azerbaijan's territory, including the districts of Lachin, Kelbadjar, Zangelan and Kubatly, from all of which the Armenians expelled sizeable Kurdish populations.[2] Movement was not confined to one direction, and Azeri onslaughts led Azerbaijani Armenians to find refugee in Armenia; 200,000 came from Azerbaijan proper, 14,000 from Nagorno-Karabakh (14,000) and 3800 from the Shahumian district.[3]

Simultaneously with the nationalist conflict and, to a certain extent, consequent on it, rival Azeri parties, the Communists and the PFA, were also struggling for power. Azerbaijan has a dual presidential-parliamentary system of government and although, from time to time, Presidents of differing persuasions were installed, parliament remained largely in the control of the Communists until 1992. In June of that year, following a period of great political turmoil, the PFA occupied the parliament, took over the main government posts and agreed to an interim President. Elections were eventually held in June 1993, when Abulfaz Elchibei, the Popular Front's candidate, was installed as President and, in turn, appointed Heidar Aliev as Prime Minister. Elchibei was toppled in a *coup d'état* engineered by Colonel Surat Huseinov and Aliev became interim President; his rule has been notorious for its savagery towards minorities, particularly the Talish and the Kurds.

The birth of a nation out of the collapse of an empire and the end of a war, no matter how cold, would be an adequate explanation for such a melancholy history but, of course, there was more. Both the US and Russia, now the leading nation in the CIS, are competing for control of Caspian oil. In broad terms the Americans and their allies in the region have backed Azeri nationalism and Russia has supported the Communist or post-Communist opposition. Matters are further complicated by the tendency of some leading nationalists to regard the oil as their route to personal wealth. Thomas Goltz remarks: 'Not surprisingly, the putsch of ... Huseinov ... was timed to occur just before Elchibei ... was to sign the so-called Deal of the Century with the ... oil consortium composed of BP, Pennzoil, and other oil giants.'[4] Elchibei had already profited substantially from the negotiations leading up to the deal and would, no doubt, have continued to do so had it gone through.

Whichever power finally succeeds in controlling Azerbaijani oil, the country should become wealthy and able to reach for substantial social and economic development. International competition lies both in deals for the extraction and for the transport of oil; it is in the latter that the connections between Azerbaijan's troubles and those, not only of its neighbours, but even of distant Afghanistan are most clearly seen. Three principal routes for pipelines have been proposed. Russia hopes to extend an existing pipeline from Baku through Dagestan and Chechnya (this should be remembered in any consideration of the Chechen war) and, eventually to Novorossyisk on the Black Sea, a project which has some TNC cooperation. A consortium of twelve international oil companies, including the Russian LukOil, have refurbished the northern pipeline and expect to move oil from the Chirag field at the rate of 105,000 barrels a day from late summer 1997.[5] When full production of both on- and off-shore oil is achieved, US and European consortia most favour the shortest route from Baku through Azerbaijan and Georgia to the small port of Supsa, but this route is endangered by the existing unresolved divisions in both countries as well as the distinct possibility of a new battle in the Georgian province formerly known as the Adzhar Autonomous Republic.[6] Georgia, at the time of writing in June 1997, is also still embroiled in a rumbling semi-war with its breakaway province of Abkhazia and a grumbling dispute with the former autonomous *oblast* of South Ossetia. Two southern routes have also been considered by the Western companies, one from Baku through Armenia, across Nakhichevan and through Turkey to its Black Sea coast; the other through Iran to the Persian Gulf. Turkey's war against the Kurds has ruled out the first, and the second runs foul of US opposition to Iran. Since the increasing success of the *Taliban*, Western interest has also grown in a route across the Caspian to the Central Asian Republics, where it would join the production from the planned exploitation of Turkmenistan's and Uzbekistan's oilfields, through Afghanistan to Pakistan's Arabian Sea coast. We may see here a link, not entirely tenuous, between Azerbaijan's problems and those of Afghanistan (see Chapter 8).

One commentator working in Baku has suggested that all the states involved in the development of Caspian oil, including those who have, at least for the moment, been excluded from the business, are meddling in one way or another in the complex of regional conflicts. Different peaceful solutions are on offer, nationalist, Russian and Western, but other states see possible advantages in attacking those of their own ethnic minorities who may form a majority in a neighbouring state as a means of gaining some leverage in the region. All the peaceful solutions also differ – they could lead to some form of wide regional development, or they could produce Caucasian Mobutus or Abachas. Whatever the outcome may be, oil joins the other factors we have discussed as a background to an Azerbaijan possessed of a ruined economy and a huge population of refugees and displaced people.

Of the various agendas operating in the area, some of which combine with the battle for oil while others impinge only indirectly, there is one in which a number of elements combine. It is the sale, by Russia, of armaments to Armenia. For some time an informal alliance has existed within the CIS between the Ukraine, Georgia and Azerbaijan, a condition which has made Russia very uneasy since it adds to the chances that the problems besetting the Western pipeline will be resolved and Russia's route through Chechnya will become redundant except for such oil as its company, LukOil, can control. Considerable parts of Georgia, through which the pipeline would have to pass, are inhabited by Armenians and since Armenia has some territorial ambitions in them similar to those it entertains for Nagorno-Karabakh, arming the country adds to regional instability. Matters are rarely so conveniently compartmentalised; it is perfectly possible that Armenia was also a convenient intermediary in the provision of weapons to the Serbs or to other groups that Russia was anxious to support. Mixed into this particular brew are complications to do with Russia's internal power struggles and simple corruption; one authority, Azad Isa-Zade, has described it all as 'Armeniagate'.[7]

CARE remarks that 'Azerbaijan is one of the most economically depressed republics of the former Soviet Union. More than a million people were displaced as a result of the on-going conflict with Armenia ... . Of these, some 60,000 of the most vulnerable, including children under five, pregnant and nursing women, and the elderly, have no permanent shelter, are living in public buildings, railroad cars and make-shift tents, and are without sufficient food.'[8] Some among that 'more than a million' became refugees, others were displaced within Azerbaijan (549,000 according to the UNHCR),[9] yet others have fled to Azerbaijan from other conflicts. In its May 1997 report UNHCR remarks: 'Azerbaijan shelters some 233,000 refugees, including 185,000 ethnic Azeri refugees from Armenia and 48,000 Meshketians, who were forcibly deported during the Stalin era from Georgia to Central Asia, and who recently arrived in Azerbaijan.'[10]

War, together with the machinations of corrupt rulers, has reduced Azerbaijan's economy to ruins, though the CIA, in its website description of the country, attributes this economic distress, somewhat eccentrically, to a failure to implement 'economic reform'. It is a country which once had a sizeable industrial base, is still rich in natural resources and is reasonably fertile yet, for example, in 1996 its cereal production, in tatters following wartime disruption, was 35 per cent below its needs. It is no position, even if it were blessed with a popular and democratic government, to deal with its proportionately enormous population of displaced people and refugees. Because of its resources there is no lack of donors, United Nations, US and European Union agencies, together with several individual countries operating bilateral aid policies, are all working away there and have brought with them the customary train of INGOs.

Goltz refers to a malady, common among countries afflicted by major disaster, called 'NGO-itis'. It is, he says an 'affliction [which] usually manifests itself ... through ... symptoms that can be summed up as an ... over-reliance on outside funding to promote internal political and social change'. He goes on to point out that this 'malady' is commonly treated by the INGOs with 'an over-zealous approach to social change in societies they know very little about'.[11] In Azerbaijan's case that excess of zeal is added to by an attitude succinctly expressed by USAID:

> Azerbaijan's oil and natural gas resources make it attractive to US investors. Although US assistance is primarily aimed at relieving suffering of vulnerable segments of the population, the potential for market development and trade expansion provide other avenues for United States private support of Azerbaijan's peaceful transition to sustainable economic and democratic governance.[12]

Such beady-eyed philanthropy was no doubt fully justified by the huge deal made by Aliev, in June 1997, with a consortium of AMOCO and BP. USAID's aims are, of course, reproduced in those of the EU and, despite double dealing in the matter of arms sales to Armenia, by Russia. All of them are giving tacit, if not overt, support to Aliev's authoritarian and repressive regime. It is difficult, in such circumstances, to disentangle UN agency and INGO policies and attitudes from the foreign policies of the organisations and states from which they come, even in those cases where their work is unexceptionable.

Feeding and housing the refugees and the displaced will, for the foreseeable future, depend on substantial subventions from outside. Recovery demands not only substantial foreign involvement in the development of the oil and natural gas industries but also finding a credible and sustainable resolution of the conflict over Nagorno-Karabakh. The two are linked, as we have already remarked, by the territorial and economic aims of other states in the region. But they are linked in other, more obvious, ways since if the customary pattern of oil exploitation is followed in which predatory TNCs buy the local government, as in Nigeria, in exchange for the cheapest possible extraction, then Azerbaijan's marginalised population will grow exponentially – 'ethnic' conflict is a common consequence of alienation. It is also perfectly possible that, as the TNCs carve up Azerbaijan's oil between them, they will shore up otherwise shaky repressive governments in order to get the oil out. Ultimately, real and democratically controlled recovery in which the greatest differences are settled can probably only be realised in some kind of Trans-Caucasian federation of independent states. The South-Asian subcontinent and Africa both offer several examples of multilingual, multicultural and multireligious countries, even though some of them are racked by tensions. Differences in the Caucasus are no greater, 'ethnic' wars are suspect, and the common economic grounds for cooperation are substantial.

We have little room for optimism since the Bretton Woods machinery is in full operation, the World Bank has provided loans and the IMF its combined ESAF–EFF financing.[13] The IMF has attached its usual conditions, everything in sight is to be privatised and monetary policies must conform to its market oriented practices. Privatisation is not, of course, wholly to be attacked – Azerbaijan suffers from the legacy of the Soviet command economy and the effects of Stalinist hostility to any form of private enterprise – but opening up all sections of the economy to the world market in an unregulated way will merely substitute, as we have argued throughout this book, in a new colonialism, divisive and exploitative like all others.

Part 3

Riches grow in Hell (*Paradise Lost*, 1: 691)

CHAPTER 10

Deus ex Machina or Devil in the Detail

Our argument, in Part 2, has depended on using examples of humanitarian disasters which have very obviously been politically engendered. We have not considered, for example, flooding in Bangladesh, earthquakes in Mexico, storms in the Caribbean or volcanoes in the Philippines, all of which might be thought to be less obviously political, even though, in all of them, the poor have suffered most. Putting aside, for a moment, the valid and plainly cognate argument offered by Wijkman and Timberlake (1984) that many possibly catastrophic 'natural' events are the product of human activity, we need only observe that disaster and natural hazard are phenomena that differ in kind. Natural hazards, in this context, are events which may imperil life and limb, but they are only implicated in disasters if certain other humanly created conditions exist. Disasters following all, or any, of these hazards typically happen to the poor and the deprived, not, on the whole, to the wealthy. They are phenomena consequent on the relationships of class and power; in short they are political happenings. This view is underlined by the growing public consciousness that some of the most horrifying contemporary disasters which have, as part of their horror, an element of natural hazard, for example Ethiopia and Somalia, were politically and economically engendered – even though that same consciousness may fall far short of encompassing the nature of those politics and economics.

Evidence that this public perception cannot be ignored is not hard to find and a single example may stand for many. ECOSOC, in its briefing dated 19 July 1996, reports Yasushi Akashi as attributing the rise in humanitarian disasters to failures in development and observes that:

> Complex crises, rather than being aberrations, have deep roots in the ways in which societies are structured. Humanitarian assistance is provided in a political context which all too frequently constitutes the only effective response of the international community when political will and resources are lacking to tackle the root causes of crises.

It is, possibly, a little too much to expect of this kind of briefing that content might be given to some of its larger concepts, but they unquestionably point to significant shifts in the debate. Some of them, of course, spring from the massive growth in projects of humanitarian assistance, to which we referred in Chapter 2. Perhaps the largest of them is the shift from seeing humanitarian interventions as discrete interruptions in the process of development which must be ended as soon as practicable, to recognising that ways must be found to ensure that their *modi operandi* go, so far as possible, hand-in-hand with those of development. This may be both an acknowledgement of the scale of contemporary humanitarian crises and of their intimate links with development processes for the absolutely poor.

Akashi's observation, that 'complex crises, rather than being aberrations, have deep roots in the ways in which societies are structured', may be correct, but takes us little further since the world is sharply divided over the question of remedies. Before we consider those issues we have to return to the question of the 'complexity' of crises. The use of the adjective springs from an earlier account of large-scale catastrophes fashioned when the model for analysing them, in which disaster sprang simply from some natural event, was beginning to be found inadequate. Humanitarian catastrophe was better understood if it was seen as arising from a complex, a web, of causes, disparate in nature but mutually reinforcing. This was undeniably an advance on past analyses, but it still allowed both theorists and practitioners to isolate the event, or events, and to propose solutions related only to national or, in some cases, regional circumstances. As we pointed out in Part 1, that blight is evident in *At Risk*. Our argument, based on the cases that we have offered, is that while the *effects* of disasters are complex, cumulative and commonly self-perpetuating, the ultimate causes, to use language prompted by Blaikie et al.'s relentlessly Thomistic logic, are simple. Colonialism and its successors, the aftermath of the Cold War and the triumph of ruthless, monetarist free-marketeering, despite a history as labyrinthine as that of the rise of capital, may legitimately be seen as a unified construct which may be complex to analyse, but is simple to recognise; collectively they amount to a single and ultimate cause of all the disasters we have discussed. Proximate causes, in virtually every instance, are, as it were, tentacles of the ultimate cause. Corrupt governments, the loss of control over resources, internecine strife, inadequate social institutions and so on, may all be traced to the hegemony of the industrialised world.

One of the objectives of the authors of *At Risk* is to provide analytical tools for the use both of those in power who might be unaware of the consequences of their actions and for the relatively powerless who have to cope with those consequences. What, of course, they cannot do, not the least because of their self-limiting ambitions, is to deal with the issue of those who have power but who feel that no matter how regrettable it is that there should be casualties in the process of perfecting markets, even in enormous numbers, they are inevitable. In a sense Blaikie et al. are forced to abandon the attempt without a struggle because, when they describe the audience they hope to reach (Blaikie et al., 1994, pp. 6–9), they think first of individuals and not of the institutions responsible. We are offered here a version of the entryist argument which maintains that converting individuals within institutions is a means of changing policies, it has always ignored the power of institutional dynamics; an error repeated, in a different form, by so many INGOs which, often for reasons related to their charitable status, fail to come to terms with their own political roles in humanitarian disasters.

We remarked in the first chapter of this book that, for the poor, everyday life is dangerous; they must struggle with poverty, disease and the effects of national economies which, at best, are weighted against them and, at worst, are spiralling out of control. Very many, if not most, of those whom the World Bank categorises as 'absolutely poor' are living in *chronic* humanitarian crises. Adequate interventions would be relatively simple to describe: they would include the restoration of stolen resources, support for remaking livelihoods, assistance in constructing services and institutions, including government, controlled by the people, making room for their trading networks and so on. Inadequate, indeed inappropriate, interventions are those typified by the extraordinary events we have described in Kenya where 'humanitarian' actions further and seriously undermine the conditions of those they were supposed to assist. In the present climate, one in which the most honest of all the international agencies, USAID, feels no need to make a secret of its function as an arm of US interests simply because it cannot conceive that the world does not see that those interests are the best for us all, adequate responses are improbable. But the present authors argue that distinguishing between a chronic disaster, like that of the dispossessed in northern Kenya, and an immediate crisis, like the genocide in Rwanda, is crucial if egregious political and, consequently, humanitarian choices are to be avoided. This, of course, begs the question of whether it is right to see any immediate crisis other than as a moment in a chronic disaster. We do so because in this book we are dealing with the categories imposed by development theorists and adopted by multilateral agencies.

To move the issue away from the self-defeating counsel of prudence proclaimed in *At Risk* (Blaikie et al., 1994), we have to consider, in the broadest terms, the nature of the neo-liberal revolution informing the projects of contemporary capital. Ownership of the means of production and virtually all trading has, in the course of this century, increasingly shifted into the hands of conglomerates of shareholders who attempt to multiply their capital by trading in that ownership. Known as *rentier* capitalism, its dangers, particularly when unregulated, have been extensively analysed by legions of writers (among them, for example, are Marx, 1981, 1973; Keynes, 1973; Mandel, 1968; Hutton, 1996). In such a system primary investment is not in infrastructure, plant, research and development and an educated, responsible, respected and cooperative workforce, but in ownership which gives high rates of return on investment. So far as its practitioners have an interest outside their returns on investment, then it is in the expansion of the market control by the corporations whose shares they have bought. Keynes described this as 'the separation between ownership and management' which leads to an inherently volatile and unstable market (Keynes, 1973, pp. 150–1).

Companies may increase the rate of dividend they pay to shareholders, at least in the short term, by lowering wage costs, by cutting back on investment in production technology, research and development. Competition is, in the first instance, about the increased value of company shares in the international bourses and, as Hutton points out so well and so devastatingly, this has become so much the norm that national economic performance, throughout the world, is commonly measured by share-price indices; national productivity is scarcely mentioned. Britain is one of the nations which has taken this course to its extreme and Hutton adds his voice to all those others who see its capital markets, rather than its industrial development, as the springboard of its earlier imperialist adventures. Christopher Hill (1975) makes the same point as he defines the 'Protestant ethic', not, as we have come to see it, as one of work, but as the sanctity of private property. In such an ethic finance, rather than production, is of the first importance. Hutton goes on to make the case that unregulated *rentier* competition leads inexorably to an unsustainable short-termism: since greater and greater returns are demanded for capital thus 'invested', the tendency to switch to more and more profitable shares grows. The consequent uncertainty in capital underpinning then makes long-term industrial development even more difficult, particularly, as Hutton argues, because successful industrial growth depends precisely on satisfied workforces, on investment in technology and in research and development.

Will Hutton's *The State We're In* is predominantly about Britain's economic squalor and, even though he quotes, in his introduction, the case of the drug corporation, Glaxo, taking over another, Wellcome, 'explicitly to maintain the growth of dividends to its shareholders' (p. xv), he does not set out to deal with the extent to which economic short-termism has spread to TNCs. He does, however, effectively extend his critique to the mechanisms of the market. Substantially basing himself on Keynes, he makes an astutely argued case for maintaining that market mechanisms are always and inevitably short-termist, exclusive because competitive (there are always winners and losers) and, because they can only treat people as '"customers" ... who consume products ... the capacity to be a citizen depends on spending power, without which citizenship disappears' (p. 218), at best, they execute social functions 'poorly'.

Hutton is, as one reviewer has pointed out,[1] an optimist and he sees ways out of free-market induced problems as coming in happier relationships between state, corporations, unions and workers along the lines developing in the more civilised European states. These are relationships in which the state helps to create a social climate favourable to corporate industry in return for agreement by the corporations to conform to acceptable social practices. He offers The Netherlands and Germany and their relative economic security as two of his examples of how this can be achieved. In his support we might note the increasing tendency among corporations, even in Britain, to feel that the EU's 'social chapter' (in itself scarcely a threat to anyone's profit margins) would improve matters for employer and worker alike, particularly following the Labour government's decision, shortly after its accession to power, to endorse it.

Space, in Hutton's book, is devoted to the origins of 'free-market' dogma, but, because he is writing primarily about Britain, there is less about the extent to which it has captured international territory. In addition to some European states in which industry is prepared to see social harmony as in its interests, Hutton quotes Japan but not, interestingly, the US, home to the greatest number of TNCs. The point, of course, is that TNCs do not, as a rule, produce anything; their function is the ownership and expansion of numbers of subsidiary companies; they are, in a sense, the private, corporate and giant version of the individual shareholder, though their role as parent companies is usually greater than that. Many of them are the principal investors in industrial and other forms of research and development, but one large part of their purpose is to manipulate the stock markets in pursuit of rapid returns and dividends. Even so, it is perfectly possible, indeed not uncommon, for TNCs to ensure that their organised and vocal workforces are more or less adequately compensated while simultaneously exploiting the market and its mechanisms quite ruthlessly.

This dichotomy may appear in, for example, a TNC acting as a perfectly reasonable employer, or at least no worse than its rivals, in the US while, at the same time, being somewhat less than impeccable in Bhopal. Even more deadly than callous indifference to many Third World workers is the motivating force behind

TNCs. The need constantly to expand, even in the currently fashionable form of smaller and more manageable component units, no matter how unsustainable this may prove to be in the long run, leads to the transformation of everyone and their institutions into customers, that cant word so beloved of the privatised utilities of Britain. Where those 'customers' have alternative modes of production and alternative economies, TNCs can only see them as competitors to be defeated and it is from this position that they approach the rural Third World. Bretton Woods and its organisations were, as we remarked in Chapter 2, created to solve economic difficulties standing in the way of a free market, hence there is a real sense in which the GATT agreement, leading to the creation of the WTO, is the TNCs' charter. Together with the World Bank and the IMF it is offering, in the face of all the evidence pointing to its failure, the *market* as the solution to the world's economic ills. Nothing, not even practices defending small producers or measures to defend a threatened environment, may stand in the way of this new Moloch (George and Sabelli, 1994).

Hutton maintains that contemporary capitalism is not homogeneous and suggests that there are four distinct versions of it divided, one from the other, by geography and social custom .They are Japanese capitalism, American capitalism, European Social Market capitalism and British capitalism. He makes a convincing case in claiming that the most efficient forms are those which are socially inclusive and which do not try unjustly to exploit their workforces. Despite the tendency of capital to homogenise, Hutton suggests that the existence of at least four differing systems provides, in the interstices, room for social manoeuvre and, as a precondition of that, room for the construction of the machinery of the necessary social control of corporate activity. Necessary, not simply to the well-being of employees, but, because the stability and certainty provided by regulation and a cooperative workforce are essential to the efficient working of the market, necessary also to the well-being of the corporations.

His book is devoted to the problems of Britain, so it is scarcely surprising that he has no more than a passing paragraph in which he mentions the Third World. In it he makes the unexceptionable points, that for universal well-being poor countries need greater fiscal power and a radical change in the structural adjustment programmes of the World Bank and IMF. What he does not do, because it is not his subject, is to consider the ways in which the Bretton Woods institutions, because they are the homogenous and homogenising instruments of all four capitalisms, do not reflect the differences that he discerns. Above all the WTO is designed specifically to ease the way for the free operation of the market – it is the contemporary neo-liberal institution *par excellence* and, like its siblings, it is deeply informed by the ideology of the neo-liberal new right. Concerned only in ensuring that what it determines as barriers to trade are removed, it treats all trading nations as if they were equal. In Chapter 2, we referred to Watkins' remark that the OECD estimates that every farmer in the US is subsidised to the tune of US$ 29,000 is sufficient indication that few, if any, farmers in the Third World are in a position to make use of this presumed 'equality'. Both the World Bank and the IMF, responding to the demands of their major shareholders, the US, Japan and Germany, continue to ensure that impoverished Third World states maintain their debt repayments. Even if old debt is eventually cancelled, new finance will carry with it the conditions now common to all three major institutions: reductions in the role of the state, harnessing economic effort to the international trading system and increasing competition – the articles of short-termist, profit-taking, *rentier* faith. For the Third World the consequences of this are ruinous since indebted states, trapped in Bretton Woods' embrace, are compelled to allow such assets as they possess to pass into the TNC and commodity market ambit. Whatever they have of value must increasingly be given over to the profit-takers – a major example of the process is offered by Stoneman and Thompson (1995) in their description of the effects on Zimbabwe's agriculture of a World Bank/IMF structural adjustment programme adopted in 1990.

In each of the seven catastrophes that we have examined, the hands of the terrible triplets of Bretton Woods may be discerned. We do not suggest that these institutions are solely and directly responsible for the tragedies; indeed we have taken pains in each case to look at imperial pasts, at the nexus of political, social and economic forces, even at the cupidity of indigenous élites and so on, all of which are implicated in the miseries to which we refer. But all three institutions are the principal financial and regulating tools of the industrial world's attempt at world market domination, in the scheme of which alternative economic arrangements must be anathematised. In every disaster that we have examined we find that concomitant with programmes of relief is the joint programme of the IMF and the World Bank to advance their own form of economic reconstruction. For the world's poorest countries, those most prone to the crises we are dealing with, the IMF offers financing at very low rates of interest – one half of 1 per cent – through its enhanced structural adjustment facility (ESAF). As its name implies, the real price of the financing lies in surrendering control of the national economy to the Fund and its associates and in accepting their market driven priorities (Masson and Mussa, undated).

Obviously enough we are seeing in all this a familiar conflict of values which, with some justification, may also be seen as a conflict between urban and rural societies. In Somalia, Kenya and Sudan contemporary land-looting brings to mind the land enclosures in England from the sixteenth to the nineteenth centuries. Where it was felt necessary to justify the wholesale dispossession of peasants in England, agrarian 'improvement' or the demands of modern farming were offered. It is well described by E.P. Thompson (1980) who remarks that 'Enclosure ... was the culmination of a long secular process by which men's customary relations to the agrarian means of production were undermined' (p. 239). The outcome, of course, was the proletarianisation, that is, the absorption into an urban working class, of the consequent landless and displaced peasantry in circumstances which bear comparison with those facing refugees and the displaced in the catastrophes we have described in Part 2 of this book. Christopher Hill (1988), in his compelling and detailed case for the revolutionary nature of the politics of *The Pilgrim's Progress*, writes of the way that John Bunyan, in the episode of the encounter between Pilgrim and Giant Despair, represented the 'repression and social contempt' heaped on those whose ancient customary rights to land have been removed by enclosure. We may call to mind, by way of comparison and illustration, the racialist contempt involved in Khartoum's looting of Nuban land.

In every disaster that we have discussed, not simply those in which land-looting has played a substantial part, that 'secular process' is discernible and its results are much the same. These disasters are not simply the unintended consequence of market processes, they become, no matter how much they may be regretted, one of the instruments of major social change. Hill has a superb account of that change in his history of seventeenth-century radicals in the English revolution (Hill, 1975). He describes the extent to which most people, particularly in the early part of the century, 'lived in a world of magic, in which God and the devil intervened daily ... . Most villages had their "cunning man", their white witch: they were cheaper than doctors or lawyers.' This he contrasts with our utterly altered world in which acts of God have been replaced by all the contemporary social comforts and institutions, from social insurance to brick houses, from the control of disease to winter food for cattle 'so that spring is no longer starvation time', but, he adds, 'The traditional insecurity of medieval life had been intensified by the new insecurity of the capitalist market', first experienced, particularly by the new urban poor, in slumps in the 1620s (1975, pp. 87–8).

When left to itself, that 'capitalist market', from its beginnings to the present day, is always a dangerous structure. Its insatiable hunger for swifter and greater returns on its 'investment' is simply not conducive to long-term development in any form and is notorious for its inclination to reduce labour costs, whatever the consequences for its workforce. We scarcely need to remind ourselves of the horrors it produced in pursuit of its returns in its European and American past, they have been immortalised in literature,[2] but there is one record which bears particularly on our argument. James Larkin, the fiftieth anniversary of whose death is celebrated in the year this chapter is written, was a champion of the Irish working class in the first decades of this century. Although conditions in Dublin, when he came to Ireland to organise trades unions, were worse even than those in most English cities, Larkin had been radicalised by his experiences as a social worker in Liverpool. Part of his very well-known attack on extreme poverty in that city bears repetition; he had gone to a particular slum in Christian Street where families were crowded into noisesome, lightless cellars:

> It was dark, bitterly dark. We passed into the first orifice and then the next, and then we heard a moan, and we looked through and we saw nothing, it was so dark, and I went out and got a candle and came back, and lit the candle, and then we found it. In the corner laid [sic] the body of a woman, and on its dead breast is the figure of a child, about two months old, sucking, trying to get the life blood out of the breast of the dead woman. And then there were two little girls, one seven years old, and one of nine, and that was in the year 1902, and the City of Liverpool, in a Christian City, in a street called Christian – Christian Street, and Christian people ... . (quoted in Larkin, 1989)

Market forces had rendered that woman and her children unnecessary and we cannot now right the injustices done to them, but there are two reasons for remembering them. The first bears only generally on our purpose and may be seen in the recent recrudescence of the diseases of poverty in Britain and that, since water was privatised (1988–9), nearly 94,000 households, including many with children, have had their supplies disconnected because they could not meet their bills (MFS, 1996). The second reason is obvious, the ideology lying at the root of the miseries attacked by Larkin differs little, if at all, from contemporary neo-liberal ideology; in extreme, but frequent, cases it led directly to the starvation to death of the poor – sometimes, as in Ireland, to mass famine. Hunger, disease and hideously circumscribed lives have been the norm for most of the European working class for centuries; our argument is that colonialist adventure, with its neo-liberal ideological baggage, reproduced that process in the Third World. It was an industrialised urban ideology and process, confronting a predominantly rural Third World and neo-colonialist successors keep it alive today. Contemporary sisters of the woman in Christian Street may be seen in most of the catastrophes we have discussed.

Here it is worth making a short digression. Numbers of INGOs have, in recent years, dropped famine iconography from their appeals because, they say, these images are degrading, intrude on misery and are unrepresentative of Third World societies where much that is hopeful and creative is going on. They are, without question, absolutely right, but have, not unusually, missed the point. Liverpool, when Larkin was active, was also inhabited by a prosperous middle and trading class, even a sort of upper-working class that could, no matter how uncertainly, boast of some small prosperity. It, too, was a city, a society, in which much that was hopeful and creative could be found. Larkin's poor were the dispossessed, either from land or from industrial employment, living in enormous numbers on the wretched margins of urban economies and, it should be recalled, often seen as a necessary consequence of mercantile 'progress'. Many of those INGOs made uncomfortable by that iconography (some call it the 'pornography of suffering') may be right in questioning its use, but have, by wanting to substitute happier images, fallen into the trap that Blaikie and his fellow authors laid for themselves. In short, with few exceptions, they have not recognised that humanitarian disasters, particularly those that occur in fragile ecologies, are commonly an inevitable consequence of the same market forces that so skew the local economies in which their stock-in-trade, the hopeful endeavours, are fighting for survival. To take an extreme example, enclosing land for the large-scale production in Sudan of irrigated crops for the international market, a process actively encouraged by the IMF, does not sit well with the INGOs' desire to help peasant agricultural communities. It is, however, a significant element in the destitution and starvation of huge numbers of the dispossessed – the displaced people and the refugees. The missed point lies in the failure to recognise that those afflicted by humanitarian disaster are, by that calamity, commonly cut off from what is hopeful and creative, cut off, that is, from the means of production, often indefinitely.

Even if the wilder excesses of structural adjustment programmes were to be curbed, and the class prejudices that lead, among other things, to worries about 'dependency syndromes' were to be moderated, we should still be left with the problems created by the unfettered prosecution of free trade. It is improbable, for example, that such changes would make much difference to the US's ambitions in Central Asia. Nor would they affect its support for the *Taliban* in Afghanistan, consequent partly on its obsession with Iran and partly on its determination that the TNC, Unocal, should be enabled to build its oil pipeline from Turkmenistan to the Pakistani coast.[3] Equally doubtful would be any supposition that these changes would seriously affect French adventures in Central Africa or Khartoum's appropriation of land and scarce water resources. All these phenomena, and so many more like them, are ultimately to do with the control of resources and their integration into the globalised market. Because of its inherent instability, its fetish of liquidity (Keynes, 1973; Hutton, 1996) and its tendency always to create losers, 'The actual, private object of the most skilled investment to-day is "to beat the gun" ... to outwit the crowd, and to pass the bad, or depreciating, half-crown to the other fellow' (Keynes, 1973, p. 155), the market continues to create a new geography of poverty. Recipients of, to change the currency, the wooden nickels now include not only the '14 million children under the age of five [who] die in the developing world, not in a drought and famine year, but in an "ordinary" year' (Timberlake and Thomas, 1990), but also, for example, the two-and-a-third million children of poor families at risk of malnutrition, rickets and TB in British cities (MFS, 1996).

Class and racialist attitudes which underlie, as we have pointed out, a good deal of the analysis of both humanitarian assistance and development, demonstrably inform responses in the industrialised world. Obvious examples were seen in the repellent defences, by Thatcher's epigones, the Howards, Widdecombes and Portillos, in the decaying months of the now departed Tory government, of plainly unprincipled law and regulation, but they may be seen even more starkly in the effects of their policies. Milk for Schools (1996, p. 11) suggests that in Britain 40 per cent of Asian, 30 per cent of Afro-Caribbean and 20 per cent of Caucasian children of pre-school age and from low-income families 'have a nutrition related iron deficiency in the majority of inner cities'. It is enough to remark that the same language is used of the poor in industrialised inner cities as development theorists use of the poor in the Third World; they may not be helped too much or they will become dependent, they are unwilling to work when 'over-generous' state assistance is available to them and so on – the mantras of a creed as blind and as monstrous as the unregulated market forces which bred it.

To adopt the prescriptions of neo-liberalism is to make a political choice; there is no inexorable natural law demanding such a course which, like gravity, cannot, in the ordinary way, be denied. Arguments embodying the concept of the 'perfectibility of the market' trotted out by, among others, the IMF (see, for example, Masson and Mussa, undated) have repeatedly been refuted. Evidence against it runs from the destruction of British industry to the overwhelming and worldwide exploitation of poor workers.

We have pointed to the opposition between what we have suggested is the urban nature of neo-liberal economic values and the continuing rural nature of the still enormous Third World peasantry. We neither suggest that urbanisation of itself is bad, nor do we propose some alternative rural idyll; our argument is that neo-liberalism is a particular kind of urban creed and is, where adopted, an irresistibly urbanising force. Its clearances and enclosures are creating a huge and dispossessed urban under-class, not only in and around existing cities, but also in those extraordinary new towns, the semi-permanent refugee camps – both constituting a massive, unprepared and commonly catastrophic urbanisation. To use Hutton's words, that under-class is, to a substantial degree, robbed of citizenship because it lacks purchasing power. Not only is its creation a direct consequence of the political choice of neo-liberalism, but it is a series of humanitarian catastrophes waiting to happen.

Urban values and urbanisation are, by themselves, neutral concepts, but, of course, they cannot be seen in that way since our primary account of them is drawn from our historical experience of urban organisation. Occasional flirtations with utopianism apart, any common understanding, or criticism, of the cultural construct of the city must begin with what we have in front of us, or what we live in ourselves. This is why we must see that the almost universal lack of planning and resources for growing cities flows directly from the predominance of market values and short-term financial interest; these forms of urbanisation are political and economic choices. We have already made the same point about the increasing despoliation of Third World agriculture and the progressive destruction of its rural, peasant societies. With the dubious exception of Kenya, all the catastrophes that we have examined have emerged from wars, the most extreme of all political events. Each of them may be interpreted as wars about the control of resources and in each we may see the unbridled prosecution of the objectives of *laissez-faire* free trade, often, as we have pointed out with the active support of the institutions of the industrialised countries. Opposition to the process exists, much of it springing from the poorer countries, but it is still weak and divided and the institutions built around neo-liberal political and economic agendas show little sign of being constrained. Some limited comfort may, we suppose, be drawn from Hutton's view that the instability and inefficiency of the free market will eventually compel reform along more or less social democratic lines, but, the present authors feel, it would be rash to expect too much.

CHAPTER 11

Conclusions

Philanthropy seems to have crept into English (out of classical Greek) in the seventeenth century when writers, like Francis Bacon in his *Essays* (1625 edition), used it to mean a general love of humanity. It gradually became a grand word for charity and one which, somehow, lent gentility to what was, fundamentally, a degrading relationship – that between the haves and the have-nots. Patronising, not to say patriarchal, ways of thinking about the poor entered into European and US consciousness, as we have observed, along with the sanctification of property. Hill (1975) points to the later writings of both Luther and Calvin in which the elect seem only to be of the propertied classes and the rejected, the damned, are always the poor. Mechanisms, schemes, for alleviating poverty have also been dominated by that consciousness and although 'do-goodery' is often derided, it remains, to a surprising degree, a motivating force in those with power of any kind who engage with the powerless. Such attitudes may be unavoidable in a world which has a vested interest in not seeing that greater equality is a surer means of creating long-term security for everyone. Many INGOs, and particularly individual workers within them, have struggled mightily, some with considerable success, against this cultural legacy, but they are commonly struggling not only with their own ideological baggage, but with the momentum of their institutional history combined with that of the states from which they spring. Increasingly, as in the case of Sudan, they are also obliged to work within the practical and ideological constraints imposed by the UN and other international agencies.

Most industrialised states allow INGOs charitable status which usually brings with it substantial tax advantages, both for donors and for the organisations, but they usually do so on the condition that these 'charities' keep out of politics. The present authors have commented elsewhere (Middleton et al., 1993) on this fatal flaw, particularly as it affects the activities of INGOs in advocacy in their parent states. Further restraints are imposed as donor governments increasingly recognise that aid for development projects is often more effectively administered by INGOs than through inter-governmental agreements. Many INGOs make valiant efforts to preserve their independent policies and, up to a point, they often succeed, but it is obviously difficult for them to stray too far from the policies of their respective governments. Several industrialised states have relatively benign overseas development authorities, though their more senior fellows in government, treasuries and the ministries involved in trade, are commonly less so, but benignity is no substitute for coherence in policy, or for relinquishing control. Controlling mechanisms are familiar; INGOs frequently bid for government aid contracts, they have to satisfy the state that they are the appropriate organisation, that they posses whatever skills seem necessary for a given programme or project and that they will observe government aid guidelines, conform to international standards and build in adequate systems of accountability. Government aid departments, naturally enough, prefer to deal with tried and tested agents and a sensible, even cosy, relationship between the state and certain INGOs develops.

Belief that development can only be effective when people and their communities participate fully in the proposal, design and management of the programmes and projects affecting them, is becoming widespread. It is still unusual to find that belief put into practice, and, we think, unheard of for donor governments and their INGO agents to recognise, let alone to accept, how much power they would have to surrender for such participation to be real. In the case of humanitarian disaster, general practice suggests that no one imagines participation to be possible. Somalia provided the most infamous examples of interventions in which all the controlling instincts of governments and multilateral agencies came into play (see Chapter 3 and IOV, 1994). In Sudan a number of INGOs are struggling, not only to relieve suffering, but to help people to rebuild their own livelihoods, but, as we pointed out in Chapter 5, they are only able to operate within the limits set out by OLS which works closely with the oppressive state responsible for the situation in the first place.

Rwanda, in the two years following the genocide, was one of the most dispiriting cases in point. There most INGOs joined the industrialised nations in largely ignoring the new RPF government and concentrated instead on what they defined as the most urgent need. That they effectively made possible the survival of a murderous regime in exile, which has since played a large part in the tragedies in Burundi and what is now the Democratic Republic of the Congo, and that they are thus complicit in the subsequent large-scale slaughter and refugeeism, that some even became 'accessories after the fact', has yet to be widely acknowledged, though some INGOs, to their credit, have begun to express concern. Unilateral action, fired by some antiquated and confused notion of flying to the rescue, is thought by otherwise intelligent people to be more effective in disasters than any form of participation. What this indicates is an extraordinary lack of political sophistication which the present authors are inclined to think has a multiplicity of roots.

Within industrialised societies, twentieth-century *Weltschmerz* has increasingly led to a widespread suspicion of, not to say a contempt for, politics and there are political agendas, particularly of the neo-liberal right, which encourage this – not the least Thatcher's notorious attack on the concept of society. Clinging to the view that politics is, among other things, the principal language of social organisation, the grammar, so to say, of living together, the articulation of social morality, is often thought to be, at best, eccentric and, more commonly, to be totally out of touch with reality. Corruption in government, both in Europe and the US, the 'democratic deficit' in, for example, Britain or the EU, have left people with a universal suspicion of parties in power. The Cold War has also had its effect in spawning a dangerous political myopia. It is within this culture that the INGOs have, as it were, grown up. If we add to this the extent to which, because they are charities, they are expected to steer clear of politics, then we may be moving towards a reason, if not an excuse, for their persistent failure to make sensible political judgements about their activities and their tendency to look outside politics for motivation.

We are thus faced with a paradox. The UN, the World Bank, the IMF and the WTO are in no doubt that their activities in development are political events, and that it is also necessary for them to link their political objectives to their interventions in humanitarian disasters, and USAID (as we saw, for example, in the case of Kenya) recognises that humanitarian intervention is an economic and political issue affecting US interests. Yet many INGOs, including some who work with one or more of these and similar institutions, seem to regard what they do as somehow apolitical, as having no political agenda of its own, or even, except by accident, of having no political effects. Their philanthropic ancestry, their close connections with 'donor' governments, their disbarment from overtly political activity within their parent countries, their existence within that culture of political world-weariness all conspire towards this self-defensive, but ultimately irresponsible, reaction.

Political quietism combined with past attitudes and present institutional rules frequently compromises INGO effectiveness both in humanitarian disasters and in development. Even within relatively politically sophisticated INGOs like, for example, Oxfam, the need to pacify the Charity Commission's censors inevitably adds to this problem. It does so not simply because criticism must be muted, but because the 'pragmatism' engendered by such accommodation obscures huge political difficulties. The complexity of the relationships between the institutions of the developed world, including the UN and the Bretton Woods Three, with development and humanitarian assistance which we have been setting out, cannot easily be tackled by INGOs. Willingly or unwillingly, and no matter what alternative ideologies lie trapped within them, the INGOs are as surely compromised by the neo-liberalism of the multilateral organisations as any individual committed to entryist views. A first step in changing matters would be for all INGOs to reject the limitations put on them by charitable status – even if that means losing consequent financial benefits – while, at the same time, recognising that a politically sophisticated self-examination of their interventions, together with an openness to serious evaluation by their 'clients' must be the base on which their work is built.

Much ink has been spilt over the relationship, or lack of it, between development and humanitarian assistance. For the purposes of organisation or budgeting it may be useful, even necessary, to distinguish sharply between them, but in each of the catastrophes that we have examined in this book, including the complicated case of Rwanda, it is impossible to separate the disaster from issues of development with any meaningful political or economic sense. The extent to which multilateral agencies have tied recovery from disaster to the prosecution of market objectives – a process most evident in the case of Kenya – could lead the unwary to suppose that they almost feel that the absence of total integration into the world market led to the disaster in the first place. We prefer to think that most crises emerge from chronic difficulties and have made plain our view of their connection with the workings of contemporary capital and, by derivation, with development.

It is here that we must look more closely at the agendas adopted by donors and the agencies acting for them in the relief of disaster. Throughout all our examples we make the point that, no matter in how discontinuous a manner, the objectives of the market are an integral part of the rescue and rehabilitation package. This would follow from the apparent conviction among the donor states and organisations that real development, whatever that may mean, can only flow from economic and market globalisation. We may note, in passing, that this belief proposes a world revolution far more thoroughgoing and uncertain in its effects than anything dreamt of by socialists. Be that as it may, changing international relations, dependent on market neo-liberalism, like, for example, the political and economic reappraisals prompted by the formation of the European Union, have led to substantial reductions in aid budgets and, as we remarked in Part 1, increasing costs in humanitarian assistance. Because of this change in direction many development theorists have felt obliged to construct a new analytical model, sometimes referred to as the 'disaster cycle' (Frerks et al., 1995). It is used both to establish the relationship, rather than the disjunction, between assistance and development, and to try to understand the processes that produce it. Sense, say its protagonists, can only be made of rehabilitative activity if the link with development is understood (see, for a well-argued example, Brigaldino, 1995).

A model of the cycle, based on the experience of numerous disasters, has been constructed. Crises are seen typically as lasting for up to five years or so and are divided into three overlapping phases: relief, rehabilitation and reconstruction, each continuing, respectively, for six months to a year, twelve to about twenty months and one to four years and each of them costing substantially more than undisturbed development. Throughout these phases it is assumed that development expenditure remains constant (see Figure 11.1). Frerks et al. remark that, in this model, the points in the curves at which the phases overlap are the points at which the subsequent phase takes over – the final graceful decline in reconstruction leads back to normal development. It is very elegant, but, as Frerks et al. make clear, it has little to do with reality; so little that it is doubtful whether the model can serve any purpose at all. In its place they offer a model which is closer to what actually happens and which describes more accurately the levels of cumulative expenditure (see Figure 11.2).

Adopting the second of these two models leads to a recognition of a basic flaw in much humanitarian thinking, not the least in that of some of those more enthusiastic INGOs rushing to scenes of disaster determined to 'help' at all costs. In both models the inevitable organisational delay in getting humanitarian assistance

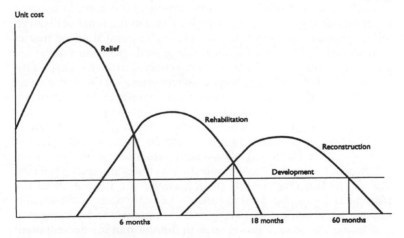

Figure 11.1 The disaster recovery cycle

Source: Frerks et al., 1995.

to people caught by disaster is recognised and, in both, so is the probability of arriving after the first very high rates of mortality have begun to decline. Because careful assessment of the needs engendered by humanitarian crises is at least thought to be impossible, and may even be so, there will always be an excess over need in the volume of relief supplies. The first model both leads to, and is based on, the assumption that the excess of supply over demand will be narrow and will decline with the rate of mortality until normality is restored. The second model shows that this is quite false, that supplies grossly exceed need throughout the crisis and have a deleteriously distorting effect on any recovery.

Both models suffer from the oversimplification discussed at length in Part 1 of this work – disasters rarely, if ever, affect everyone even-handedly, though the second model points obliquely in that direction. In Part 2 we gave a number of examples in which humanitarian relief offered temporary welfare provision for the dispossessed, though there are instances where that provision seems almost to be permanent. What the models are incapable of distinguishing is the difference between the dispossessed and those for whom development is largely conceived. In general those dispossessed by catastrophe remain dispossessed after the crisis is over. Some linger on in the hope of recovering a semblance of their former lives, or in the hope of living off the survivors, others drift to the towns or to temporary settlements, all of them largely excluded from development processes. Because the agenda of most

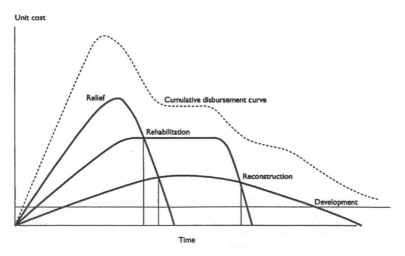

Figure 11.2 Real disaster recovery cycle

Source: Frerks et al., 1995.

donors and their agencies has to do with market integration as the route to recovery, at least in rural areas dispossession continues after the crisis is theoretically over; both Sudan and Kenya offer dismaying examples of governing élites looting land and justifying it in the name of progress. Our second model has the advantage over the first in allowing for this distinction; the first model simply ignores it.

Into the Daedalian relationship between disaster and development we must insert yet another factor: participation. We have already pointed to the way in which any fragile support for the principle of participation vanishes in the face of what Western agencies, sometimes in collusion with dubious governments, decide is a disaster. Repeated failure, arriving too late and with inappropriate responses, leaving with ill-defined objectives not yet reached, capitulation to state terrorism, are all common features of humanitarian intervention. Despite all this, it is rare for the intervening powers to consult, or to work closely with, those whom they have determined are 'victims' and who are about to be transformed into 'beneficiaries'. UNHCR's QIPs are a possible exception, but they can only emerge after the greater conflagration, of whatever kind, has died down. It ought to be a matter of common sense that helping people in trouble to harness their own well-demonstrated skills of survival in face of appalling odds must be the most effective way of coping with catastrophe. To do so, of course, would mean accepting their political choices and we may turn to the recent history of Somalia for an example of how these are disregarded (Prendergast, 1997).

Current disputes about the meaning of participation in development frequently turn on the question of degree; the present authors are inclined to feel that the minimalists in the debate, those who equate participation with little more than free labour from the 'beneficiaries' in projects, have, consciously or otherwise, understood just how political the real concept is. When groups, communities, of the poor decide for themselves, with whatever assistance they require in making those decisions, what forms of development they feel are needed; when they invite the agencies and INGOs to provide the expertise and resources that they feel to be appropriate; when they are the 'owners' of their projects, then they take the first major steps in politicisation. This is not the place to discuss the difficulties – discrimination against women, cultural conservatism, power and hierarchy, land and resource ownership and so on – that discussion belongs in another book. Here it is enough to remark that until decisions about development projects are given over to the people for whom they are intended, whatever the INGOs do to promote their participation, in some sense they will always be manifestations of power.

In the case of humanitarian crises created, at the very least in part, by the institutions and policies of the developed world, serious and rapid responses are morally imperative. It must also be obvious, even to the most blinkered, that any move, in a notoriously shrinking world, towards an equitable stability is a matter of self-interest. But high-handed intervention of the kind described in most of our seven cases is not only self-defeating, it is also liable to perpetuate the problem. Humanitarian interventions can be legitimate only when those dismissed as 'victims' become the agents of their own regeneration. Current crises, large and small, are numerous; East Timor, Bhutan, Iraq, Algeria, Palestine, Sierra Leone, Angola and Albania are just a few which spring instantly to mind. Possible future crises are just as common; Nigeria, Venezuela, Colombia, Bangladesh and Pakistan are just a few cases in point. What, then, is to be done?

There is, of course, a body of authors in the development field which sees nothing wrong with the status quo and which persists in seeing present catastrophes as mere hiccoughs in an otherwise excellent system and for whom our question is simply irrelevant. Such theorists we may class among the unregenerate; particularly when reports like the failure of a river in Kenya, on which farmers have always depended, consequent on excessive drainage for up-river irrigation schemes for fresh vegetables for Northern supermarkets,[1] are everyday phenomena. Faced with the question most development theorists first turn to other issues simply because they find it too large in compass, or because there are other, unquestionably important, matters to be addressed first. Some authors, and we may include Blaikie et al. (1994) among their number, feel that sufficient attention to the smaller detail will eventually force changes in the macro-economic and social conditions leading to the problems. If myriad smaller, even micro, projects, rescues, rehabilitations are successful, then conditions may be created which would compel the institutions of the market to adapt. In a sense, which may not be pushed too far, their argument is supported by Hutton's view (1996) that some rein will be put on the present unbridled free-marketism simply because it is inefficient, and that inefficiency is added to by too great a population living in acute poverty. The present authors are not so sanguine.

We are inclined to agree with Hutton that the present mix of catastrophe, unequal development, absolute poverty, debt, protectionism and subsidy within industrialised nations, closed commodity markets and nakedly extractionist policies towards Third World assets may be seen, even by its protagonists, as ultimately self-destructive. What seems to us less certain is that the will, or the ability, to remedy the disease lies within the complex of institutions which have caused it. Financial short-termism may have been carried to ludicrous extremes in Britain and the US, but its tentacles are global in reach. Despite the models of reasonable practice offered by some European states, far too many financial institutions, including the TNCs themselves, have immense interests in precisely this short-term return on capital. Devastation, to which this leads, takes place in the long term and is ignored until, as in Bhopal, it is too late – then these institutions, which always arrange effective escape hatches for themselves, tip-toe away to plusher and, as yet, productive regions. It cannot be said too often that the purpose of a TNC is to make profits which, in general, it does through the medium of its ownership of profitable enterprises. Its sole interest in social and economic reform lies in its effect on the market; it will moderate its practices only when it feels itself to have no alternative. In the case of the Bretton Woods institutions we may, at least until the moment of writing, take their record rather than their rhetoric, as a serious indication of their support for neo-liberal attitudes – it has repeatedly been pointed out that they are net extractors of profit from the Third World.

Nonetheless, despite our melancholy view of the matter, even within the industrialised world there are some causes for guarded optimism. In the case of the industrialised world, so long as economically successful social democracy, that sure foundation for a political conscience, flourishes in Northern Europe (The Netherlands, Germany and Scandinavia, for example) and Canada, then some pressure for reform will continue. Combined with a measure of self-criticism from within the TNCs and their financial institutions, this might even lead to some change, but it will be change designed to ensure the survival of the global market. The worst excesses of neo-liberalism which, directly or indirectly, lead to increased impoverishment and to humanitarian catastrophe may, eventually, be overcome, but only in the interests of a more efficient market which will still polarise the world into rich and poor, will still be subject to cyclical depressions, will still lay claim to the world's resources, and will still be subject to all the ills endemic to global capitalism. Our optimism in this arena stretches, with difficulty, only so far as to envisage the possibility of a less directly destructive global market – we are the first to admit that this is cold comfort.

A much more powerful ground for optimism or, rather, for hope, must be acknowledged even if it is difficult to analyse. Third World intellectuals, writers and artists constantly remind us that they and their fellow country-people are not simply passive creatures moved solely by the vagaries of the industrialised world. Many of them are fighting for democracy against corrupt regimes which have been either installed or supported by the industrialised world and there is at least some evidence that they may succeed. We may legitimately hope that, where these struggles are successful, the resulting governments do not automatically become prey to the Bretton Woods triplets. Further, rapid urbanisation will continue, either in the form of expanding existing towns and cities, or in the form of more-or-less permanent refugee camps – it is impossible to tell what political growths might emerge as a result, but there is no reason to suppose that, in their own terms and in those of their histories, they will fail to produce movements as socially progressive as those which appeared in similar conditions throughout the earlier history of the industrialised world and, later, in the course of decolonisation. Detailed analysis, out of place in this book, even if the present authors were capable of it, would be necessary seriously to assess these grounds for hope. We simply observe that they exist and should not lightly be discounted.

Africa may be the continent in which the greatest number of catastrophes and of disintegrating states may be found, it may also have the highest proportion of people living in absolute poverty, but it is also the continent most capable of resisting the destructive power of the global organisations. Those organisations have made massive inroads into African economies, both as the extractors of materials and as the barkers for, and salespeople of, the products of the industrialised world; but they, like the states in which, throughout the continent, they operate, are hamstrung, at least in part, by economies rendered unstable by external debt and the costs of servicing it. This very weakness could be the instrument of change, the means by which alternative economic solutions might be engendered within Africa.

Despite endless promises, little has been done by the industrialised world's banking system to resolve the issue of debt, which bears most heavily on African states. Even when proposals for debt cancellation are advanced, their prosecution is at best dilatory and, of course, they are modest – they rarely, if ever, amount to more than small percentages of the total. Such proposals are also hedged about with conditions binding the state concerned even more closely to the global market. Most importantly, debt cancellation seems never to be considered in regional, but only in national terms – banks, including the multilaterals, deal piecemeal. All of this has been admirably described and analysed in the work of, for one of the best examples, Susan George (1976, 1988, 1992, 1994). It was she (1995) who pointed out the two main advantages of piecemeal dealing for the Bretton Woods triplets: it is easier to keep individual states in thrall than it is to control groups of them deciding to work economically together, and it makes the bribery of ruling élites simpler. George also points out that debt cancellation, by itself, may do little to assist the poor, serving only to line, yet further, the pockets of corrupt rulers. Nonetheless, one of the most obvious consequences of the incubus of overwhelming external debt is economic stasis in the countries afflicted by it.

We have referred already to the rapid rise in urbanisation and have suggested that it is not unreasonable to expect this to be followed by, for example, an increase in African trade-unionism. We have mentioned the growth of oppositional movements to the present corrupt élites. Both these elements contain at least the possibility for new relationships between urban and agrarian workers which may yet compel more rational and just economic arrangements. Success in such endeavour will depend on breaking away from the economic isolation at present imposed on separate nation states and in creating at least regional, if not continent-wide, economic unions. This case has long been made, certainly by the Pan-Africanist independence leaders (obvious examples are Lumumba, Nkrumah, Ben Bella and Moumié) and by numerous writers since (see for examples, Green and Seidman, 1968; Davidson, 1994; Barratt Brown, 1995). Indeed many attempts have been made by groups of African states to combine into regional customs or trading unions and they have met with varying success. UDEAC, ECOWAS, CEPGL, PTA and, most significant of all, SADC are all examples and there are several others, even though some have either perished or have been reduced to shells (Barratt Brown, 1995).

Such unions are not necessarily solutions in themselves; they may, after all, simply be constructed for some small increase in advantage when operating within the confines of the existing market order, but this course is unlikely either to meet with much success or to satisfy the growing demands of the poor and marginalised. Yet even moderately successful combination in intra-African trading would give greater power to the member states in resisting the depredations of the multilateral banks, of the commodity markets and of the TNCs. Extractive TNC operations are widespread in Africa, so no union is likely to emerge which is miraculously free of their influence and SADC is no exception, but we may look to it as the strongest example of an African trading and customs union.

South Africa's membership of the SADC has clearly confirmed it as one of the most important unions. During the years of white domination, business, including the TNCs, treated South Africa as an extension of the industrialised world's club, successfully excluding most of the population and using them as a reserve pool of low-paid labour, allowing some a marginal existence as smallholders. With the collapse of apartheid this has become decreasingly workable, even though many industries still offer appalling conditions to their underpaid black workers and though present levels of unemployment and deprivation among the poor are patently unacceptable. That there has not been an enormous explosion of anger at continuing want may be a result of residual euphoria following the end of the old regime, and of the regard that so many grass-roots organisations and individuals have for the ANC – they can still feel it to be their party and their government. Nevertheless, that something must be done to relieve the circumstances of that considerable proportion of South Africa's people living in penury is clearly recognised by the incumbent government.

It is perfectly possible that, against all good sense but bowing to *force majeure*, South Africa will succumb to the onslaughts of the Bretton Woods trio and decide that integration into the neo-liberal global market is the way forward. Yet in joining SADC, it has widened its scope for manoeuvre and has also tapped more directly into a number of differing, but also similarly polarised economies. Despite the poverty of so many of its citizens, South Africa is a relatively powerful economy, and it is possible that, together with its new partners, it could form a regional trading and manufacturing bloc powerful enough to resist further unbridled extractionism by the TNCs and to dictate its own terms to the Bretton Woods bureaucracies. All the states of the SADC have large impoverished populations and most of them have wealthy élites; the latter have visibly done remarkably well out of existing trade and financial relations and this is a fact probably not lost on the poor. Since existing relationships between most African states and the world's financial institutions have largely been discredited, it may not be too much to expect that SADC governments may feel that alternative ways of meeting their obligations to the poor should be tried.

For such a transformation to take place within SADC, pressure must come from the grass-roots. Women are becoming increasingly politicised in their struggle against discrimination, particularly through the medium of cooperatives and numberless informal groups (Barratt Brown, 1995; Waterhouse, 1996). Cooperatives and other forms of working partnership are forming the basis for new agrarian movements. In urban centres, both political organisation and trades union activity are capable of giving the dispossessed a voice. For all these reasons we are at least permitted to hope that SADC may come to realise that its interests are best served by resisting the industrialised world's marketing juggernaut and that increased intra-African trade is one way of building the resource and financial security essential to ending the cycle of catastrophe. Any success in shifting the balance achieved by SADC would be a powerful signal to the other, often virtually dormant, African trading unions.

There are, of course, myriad social groups, many of them springing from among the world's poorest, trying to secure for themselves and their children a world not utterly inhuman. It would be foolish to imagine that they are completely without power. It is even the case, as we have observed, that there are governments with at least some sympathy for an equitable world view. There are, too, those within the institutions of governance in the global banking and market system who are calling for reform, precisely because they are not completely blind to the dangers of extreme inequity; unfortunately these reformers have, so far, contented themselves with pieties. Yet the world economy, although it remains largely in the power of the 'grab-the-money-and-run' marketeers, is changing rapidly. It is difficult, for example, to predict the effect on it of an increasingly powerful China. But in spite of these caveats, the present authors are uncomfortably aware that much economic optimism on behalf of the poor and marginalised, those who are most commonly afflicted by grotesque catastrophes, is little more than whistling in the dark. We have used seven humanitarian disasters to illustrate our view that the principal culprit is the complex form of domination exercised by the rich world over the poor; seven others could easily have been substituted. What emerges from daily newspaper reports of our examples, and of many others, is that the chief reaction of the developed world to catastrophe is, while offering assistance on terms designed to strengthen its market dominance, to construct insurmountable barriers to keep the poor at a distance. We may legitimately paraphrase the Synoptics: 'It is easier for a camel to go through the eye of a needle than for a poor economic refugee to enter into the kingdoms of the European Union or the United States.'

Indeed, one of the more distasteful of the preoccupations of public figures in the industrialised world, who are frequently abetted by complicit mass media, is their determination to distinguish between 'economic' and 'political' refugees. Political refugees, those forced by some form of persecution to leave their countries, are thought to be sufferable, if only barely and when they can satisfy the most preposterous of conditions. Economic refugees, on the other hand, forced to leave their countries by a poverty more or less created by the resource predators of the developed world and their local satraps are anathematised as immoral scroungers preying on our generosity. It matters little to the propagandists that only the tiniest proportion of economic refugees actually leave their own regions; what is important is that those few who do should not be allowed to become our social responsibility – whatever profit may have been made from their countries in the first place. We should not be surprised by this, it is the self-righteous cant of those who have bought the neo-liberal package. Nevertheless, the position has to be resisted, it is window-dressing which diverts attention from the central issue, the failure politically to control the Bretton Woods circus and the TNCs. That failure can only result in the rapid escalation of humanitarian disasters in which the poor, in unimaginable numbers, will die, become displaced in their own countries or fly to others as refugees. There are solutions, there is a common sense which may prevail over the idiocies of capital, we are entitled both to hope and to work for their triumph, but realistic expectation must remain grim.

Notes

Chapter 1

1. The *Guardian*, the *Irish Times*, 1 February 1996.
2. Here we deliberately beg the question of how 'natural' many events thus described may be. Is it, for example, right to call major flooding caused by precipitate deforestation natural?
3. A body of English colonial law in Ireland governing, *inter alia*, religion, language and land-holding.
4. Richard Thomas, 'Britain "squeezing Third World debtors"', *Guardian*, 23 September 1996.

Chapter 2

1. See, for example, Dan Atkinson, 'Letting Gatt out of Mrs T's bag', *Guardian*, 19 February 1996.
2. See, for example, 'Tory Story in a Hall of Mirrors', Will Hutton in the *Guardian*, 19 February 1996, in which he takes the word to refer, primarily, to the possible mobility of TNCs.
3. 'Seeds of Discontent' in the supplement *Developing World*, in the *Irish Times*, Dublin, 22 November 1995.
4. 'World Bank Joins Billion-Dollar Argentina Rescue', Martin Walker in the *Guardian*, 14 March 1995.
5. Kevin Watkins in the 'Society' supplement, the *Guardian*, 5 February 1997.
6. Ibid.
7. The *Guardian*, 22 January 1997.

Chapter 3

1. The authors owe this expression to African Rights – October 1993 – and have used it throughout the book to mean the forcible alienation of peasant customary land rights.
2. African Rights, directed by Rakiya Omaar and Alex de Waal, is a research and reporting organisation 'dedicated to working on issues of conflict, famine and civil reconstruction in Africa in an integrated manner'. Its offices are in London.
3. The *Guardian*, 25 February 1994.
4. Quoted in African Rights, May 1993.
5. The *Guardian*, 13 August 1996.

6. When the UN was most active in the emergency its agencies working in Somalia were: UNDHA, UNHCR, UNICEF, WFP, WHO, FAO and UNDP.
7. One report may stand for many, see the *Irish Times*, 1 May 1996.

Chapter 4

1. For much of the rest of this chapter the authors are indebted to ETC UK et al., October 1995.
2. Press Release No. 96/21, dated 26 April 1996.
3. Michel Camdessus is General Manager of the IMF.
4. 'Moi raises the devil to keep Kenya in line', Chris McGreal in the *Observer*, 6 October 1996.

Chapter 5

1. This US report maintains that there are three million internally displaced people in Sudan, a figure based on those of the US Committee for Refugees.
2. Shyam Bhatia, the *Observer*, 17 September 1995.
3. Ian Black, the *Guardian*, 16 May 1996.
4. David Hirst, the *Guardian*, 26 May 1997.
5. For the material on Nuba the authors are indebted to African Rights, July 1995.
6. Alice Martin, the *Guardian*, 23 January 1997.
7. See note 5.
8. For this small catalogue of interventions the authors are grateful to *Human Rights Watch World Report 1995*.
9. David Hirst, the *Guardian*, in the second of three articles on Sudan, published 26–28 May 1997.
10. David Hirst, the *Guardian*, 26 May 1997.
11. InterPress Third World News Agency (IPS), 23 April 1997.
12. David Hirst, the *Guardian*, 28 May 1997.

Chapter 6

1. Jean-Francois Durieux, UNHCR Division of International Protection, undated article UNHCR website.
2. For a detailed account of South Africa's military strength one year after the embargo see ACAS, 1978, Chapter 6, written by Sean Gervasi.
3. Professor Cynthia Enloe has written Chapter 5 in the ACAS collection; it describes the relationship of European and US mercenaries to their own governments.
4. A valuable analysis of the forms and effects of famine and war on the civil populations of sub-Saharan Africa may be found in Macrae and Zwi (1994).
5. Andrew Meldrum, 11 June 1996.

Chapter 7

1. James McCabe, the World Bank's representative responsible for development projects in Rwanda in the mid-1980s, writing in the *Irish Times*, 7 May 1994.
2. Thus Fiona Foster in the December 1995 issue of a journal eccentrically, for a journal of the political right, titled *Living Marxism*.
3. For example, JEEAR refers to R. Lemarchand, *Rwanda: The Rationality of Genocide* (1995) and G. Prunier, *The Rwandese Crisis 1959–1994* (London: Hurst, 1995).
4. JEEAR quote 'Rwanda: Background to Genocide' by F. Reyntjens in *Bulletin des séances* (Académie Royale des Sciences d'Outre-Mer, Brussels, 4/95) in support of this.
5. *Africa Confidential*, 15 April 1994, quoted in African Rights, September 1994.
6. François Mitterrand, 'Présence Française et abandon' in *Tribune Libre 12*. Quoted in African Rights, September 1994, p. 667.
7. Chris McGreal, the *Guardian*, 15 November 1996.
8. Paul Webster, the *Guardian*, 8 January 1997.
9. A private communication to one of the authors.
10. Reported by Mark Huband in the *Observer*, 31 July 1994.
11. Lindsey Hilsum, 'Europe Rubs Salt in Wounds of Rwanda', in the *Observer*, 30 April 1995.
12. See, for example, Alex de Waal, the *Observer*, 20 October 1996.

Chapter 8

1. Jonathan Steele, the *Guardian*, 6 June 1996.
2. Quoted in the UNDHA Afghanistan Weekly Update, 12 November 1996.
3. ICRC, *Afghanistan: A Forgotten and Exhausted Population*, 1 December 1996.
4. Emergency Report No. 15, 11 April 1997.
5. Afghanistan Weekly Update, 8 April 1997, UNDHA.
6. CARE, *Afghanistan Country Profile*, 17 March 1997.
7. UNDHA, Afghanistan Weekly Update, 18 December 1996.
8. ICRC, *Afghanistan: A Forgotten and Exhausted Population*, 1 December 1996.
9. UNDHA, Afghanistan Weekly Update, 18 December 1996.
10. UNDHA, Afghanistan Weekly Update, 8 April 1997.
11. WFP Weekly Emergency Report, 11 April 1997.
12. UNDHA, Afghanistan Emergency Report, May 1997.
13. Ibid.

Chapter 9

1. James Meek, the *Guardian*, 9 June 1997.
2. Arif Yunusov in *War Report*, January/February 1997.
3. UNHCR situation report, 1 May 1997.
4. Thomas Goltz, *War Report*, September 1996.

5. Hasan Guliev, *War Report*, April 1997.
6. Azerbaijan Situation Report No. 1, 1–28 Feb 1997, UNDHA.
7. Hasan Guliev, *War Report*, April 1997.
8. An excellent summary of the story is provided by Azad Isa-Zade in *War Report*, May 1997.
9. Azerbaijan Country Profile, 18 March 1997, CARE.
10. Azerbaijan Situation Report, May 1997, UNHCR.
11. Thomas Goltz, *War Report*, September 1996,
12. February 1997 Assistance to the NIS, Request to Congress.
13. IMF Press Release, 20 December 1996.

Chapter 10

1. David Marquand in the *Observer*, quoted on the jacket of the 1996 edition.
2. Quite aside from *Pilgrim's Progress*, we may recall *Hard Times*, by Charles Dickens, *The Ragged Trousered Philanthropist* by Robert Tressell and the powerful non-fictional account of the US Southern poor in W.J. Cash's *The Mind of the South* as only three examples of an enormous literature of anger.
3. David Hirst in the *Guardian*, 4 February 1997.

Chapter 11

1. The *Guardian*, 11 March 1997.

References

ACAS (Association of Concerned African Scholars), 1978 *US Military Involvement in Southern Africa*, Boston: South End Press.

Ackroyd, Peter, 1995, *Blake*, London: Christopher Sinclair-Stevenson and Minerva.

African Rights, May 1993, *Somalia: Operation Restore Hope: A Preliminary Assessment*, London: African Rights.

—— September 1993, *The Nightmare Continues: Abuses Against Somali Refugees in Kenya*.

—— October 1993, 'Land Tenure, the Creation of Famine, and Prospects for Peace in Somalia', *Discussion Paper No.1*.

—— May 1994, *Rwanda: Who is Killing? Who is Dying? What is to be Done?*

—— September 1994 (1st edn) *Rwanda: Death, Despair and Defiance*.

—— July 1995, *Facing Genocide: the Nuba of Sudan*.

—— December 1995, 'Imposing Empowerment? Aid and Civil Institutions in Southern Sudan', *Discussion Paper No. 7*.

Amin, Samir, 1973, *Neo-Colonialism in West Africa*, New York and London: Monthly Review Press.

Anscombe, G.E.M., 1957, *Intention*, Oxford: Basil Blackwell.

Baran, Paul A. and Sweezy, Paul M., 1966, *Monopoly Capital*, New York and Harmondsworth: Monthly Review Press and Penguin Books (1968).

Barratt Brown, Michael, 1995, *Africa's Choices*, Harmondsworth: Penguin Books.

Bello, Walden, 1990, *Dragons in Distress: Asia's Miracle Economies in Crisis*, San Francisco: Institute for Food and Development Policy.

Bernstein, Henry; Crow, Ben; Mackintosh, Maureen; Martin, Charlotte, 1990, *The Food Question: Profits versus People?* London: Earthscan Publications.

Blaikie, Piers; Cannon, Terry; Davis, Ian; Wisner, Ben, 1994, *At Risk*. London and New York: Routledge.

Brigaldino, Glenn, 1995, *Using Rehabilitation to Bridge the Institutional Gap between Relief and Development*, Maastricht: European Centre for Development Policy Management (ECDPM).

Browne, Harry with Sims, Beth; Barry, Tom, 1994, *For Richer, For Poorer: Shaping US–Mexican Integration*, Albuquerque, New Mexico and London: Resource Center Press and Latin America Bureau.

Carr, E.H., 1979, *The Russian Revolution From Lenin to Stalin, 1917–1929*. London: Macmillan.

Carrère d'Encausse, Hélène and Schram, Stuart R., 1969, *Marxism and Asia*, Harmondsworth: Allen Lane the Penguin Press.

Chisholm, Nick, 1996, *Irish Aid Involvement in Sustainable Agriculture, Rural Development and Food Security*. Dublin: The Irish Aid Advisory Council.

Collins Concise Dictionary, 1989, London and Glasgow: Collins.

Commission on Global Governance, 1995, *Our Global Neighbourhood*, Oxford and New York: Oxford University Press.

Dankelman, Irene and Davidson, Joan, 1988, *Women and Environment in the Third World*, London: Earthscan Publications.

Davidson, Basil, 1964, *The African Past*, London: Longmans, Green and Co.

—— 1971 (3rd edn), *Which Way Africa? The Search for a New Society*, Harmondsworth: Penguin Books.

—— 1994 (3rd edn), *Modern Africa: a Social and Political History*, London and New York: Longman.

Deutscher, Isaac, 1954, *The Prophet Armed*, Oxford and New York: Oxford University Press.

Eagleton, Terry, 1991, *Ideology: an Introduction*, London and New York: Verso.

—— 1995, 'Ascendancy and Hegemony' in: *Heathcliff and the Great Hunger*, London and New York: Verso.

ETC International, November 1994, *UNHCR Mozambique, Evaluation Report*, Unpublished.

ETC UK; Fellows International; ACTS; Kenya Pastoralists Forum, October 1995, *Evaluation of the WFP and UNICEF Emergency Relief Operations Kenya (1992–1994)*. Unpublished.

ETC UK; Kirkby, John; Convery, Ian, July 1996, *Evaluation of the ICRC and Netherlands Red Cross Emergency Programme in the South Caucasus 1995*, Unpublished.

Fatimson, T. and Keshav Rao, G., December 1996, *ILEIA Newsletter*.

Frerks, G.E.; Kliest, T.J.; Kirkby, S.J.; Emmel, N.D.; O'Keefe, P.; Convery, I., 1995, 'A Disaster Continuum?', Letter in *Disasters*, Volume 19, Number 4. Oxford: Blackwell Publishers.

Fukui, Katsuyoshi and Markakis, John, 1994, *Ethnicity and Conflict in the Horn of Africa*, London: James Currey; Athens, Ohio: Ohio University Press.

Gaffney, Patrick D., C.S.C., 1994 (Fall), 'Rwanda a Crisis of Humanitarian Security' in: *Report*, Washington: The Joan B. Kroc Institute for International Peace Studies.

GATT, 1994, *The Results of the Uruguay Round of Multilateral Trade Negotiations: the Legal Texts*, Geneva: The GATT Secretariat.

George, Susan, 1976, *How the Other Half Dies*, Harmondsworth: Penguin Books.

—— 1988, *A Fate Worse than Debt*, Harmondsworth: Penguin Books.

—— 1992, *The Debt Boomerang*, London: Pluto Press.

—— 1995, 'Rethinking Debt', paper presented at the North South Roundtable on Moving Africa into the 21st Century, held in Johannesburg, 15–18 October.

George, Susan and Sabelli, Fabrizio, 1994, *Faith and Credit: the World Bank's Secular Empire*, Harmondsworth: Penguin Books.

Green, Richard H. and Seidman, Ann, 1968, *Unity or Poverty? The Economics of Pan-Africanism*, Harmondsworth: Penguin Books.

Grunberger, Richard, 1971, *A Social History of the Third Reich*, London: Weidenfeld and Nicolson.

Halliday, Fred, 1996, *Islam and the Myth of Confrontation*, London: I.B. Tauris.

Harrell-Bond, B.E., 1986, *Imposing Aid: Emergency Assistance to Refugees*, Oxford: Oxford University Press.

Harris, Nigel, 1983, *Of Bread and Guns: the World Economy in Crisis*, Harmondsworth: Penguin Books.

Hill, Christopher, 1975, *The World Turned Upside Down*, Harmondsworth: Penguin Books.

—— 1988, *A Turbulent, Seditious, and Factious People*, Oxford: Oxford University Press.

Hobsbawm, Eric, 1987, *The Age of Empire, 1875–1914*, London: Weidenfeld and Nicolson.

—— 1994, *Age of Extremes: the Short Twentieth Century 1914–1991*, London: Michael Joseph.

Hodgkin, Thomas, 1956, *Nationalism in Colonial Africa*, London: Frederick Muller.

—— 1961, *African Political Parties*, Harmondsworth: Penguin Books.

Hourani, Albert, 1991, *A History of the Arab Peoples*, London: Faber and Faber.

HRW, Annual, *Human Rights Watch World Report*, New York, Washington, Los Angeles, London, Brussels: Human Rights Watch.

—— 1995a, *Playing the 'Communal Card': Communal Violence and Human Rights*.

HRW/A, June 1993, *Beyond the Rhetoric: Continuing Human Rights Abuses in Rwanda*, New York, Washington, London, Brussels: Human Rights Watch, Africa.

—— July 1994, *Kenya, Multipartyism Betrayed in Kenya*.

—— November 1994a, *Sudan 'In the Name of God'*.

—— November 1994b, *Sudan, the Lost Boys, Child Soldiers and Unaccompanied Boys in Southern Sudan*.

—— April 1995, *Somalia Faces the Future: Human Rights in a Fragmented Society*.

—— July 1995, *Kenya, Old Habits Die Hard: Rights Abuses Follow Renewed Foreign Aid Commitments*.

HRWAP, January 1994, *Arming Rwanda: the Arms Trade and Human Rights Abuses in the Rwandan War*, New York and Washington: Human Rights Watch Arms Project.

—— May 1995, *Rwanda/Zaire: Rearming with Impunity; International Support for the Perpetrators of the Rwandan Genocide*.

Hutton, Will, 1996, *The State We're In*, 2nd edn, London: Vintage.

ILO (International Labour Office), 1972, *Employment, Incomes and Equality: a Strategy for Increasing Productive Employment in Kenya*, Geneva: ILO.

IOV (Inspectie Ontwikkelingssamenwerking te Velde), 1991, *A World of Difference: A New Framework for Development Cooperation in the 1990s*, Den Haag: Ministerie van Buitenlandse Zaken.

—— 1994, *Humanitarian Aid to Somalia*.

—— 1997, *Review of Development Aid 1984–1994*.

ITeM (Instituto del Tercer Mundo), 1995, *The World: a Third World Guide 1995/96*, Montevideo: ITeM.

Issa-Salwe, Abdisalam M., 1994, *The Collapse of the Somali State*, London: The Author and Haan Associates.

Jennings, Frank, August–September 1995, 'Equality by the Year 2000' in: *Amnesty International*, Irish Section, No. 90, Dublin: Amnesty International.

Joint Evaluation of Emergency Assistance to Rwanda, March 1996, *The International Response to Conflict and Genocide: Lessons from the Rwanda Experience*, Copenhagen: The Steering Committee.

—— Vol. 1 *Historical Perspective: Some Explanatory Factors.*

—— Vol. 2 *Early Warning and Conflict Management.*

—— Vol. 3 *Humanitarian Aid and Effects.*

—— Vol. 4 *Rebuilding Post-War Rwanda.*

—— *Synthesis Report.*

Kariuki, J.M., 1963, *Mau Mau Detainee*, Oxford: Oxford University Press.

Kaunda, Kenneth D., 1966, Letter to Colin M. Morris, in: *A Humanist in Africa*, London: Heinemann.

Keynes, John Maynard, 1973, *The General Theory of Employment, Interest and Money* (2nd edn, the Complete Works vol. VII), London: Macmillan.

Kiberd, Declan, 1995, *Inventing Ireland*, London: Jonathan Cape.

Kirkby, John; Kliest, Ted; Frerks, Georg; Flikkema, Wiert; O'Keefe, Phil, November 1995, *UNHCR the Cross Border Operation in Somalia: the Value of Quick Impact Projects for Refugee Settlement*, Unpublished.

Lappé, Frances Moore and Collins, Joseph, 1986, *World Hunger: 12 Myths*, New York: Grove Press; London (1988): Earthscan Publications.

Larkin, Emmet, 1989, *James Larkin, Irish Labour Leader* (2nd edn), London: Pluto Press.

MacRae, Joanna and Zwi, Anthony (eds), 1994, *War and Hunger*. London and Atlantic Highlands, NJ: Zed Books and Save the Children Fund-UK.

Machiavelli, Niccolò, 1961, *The Prince*, translated by George Bull. Harmondsworth: Penguin Books.

Mandel, Ernest, 1968, *Marxist Economic Theory*, London: Merlin Press.

Marx, Karl, 1867, (edition used 1975-81), *Capital*, Harmondsworth: Penguin Books.

—— 1968, *Theories of Surplus Value*, Moscow: Progress Publishers.

—— 1973, *Grundrisse: Foundations of the Critique of Political Economy*, Harmondsworth: Penguin Books.

Marx, Karl and Engels, Frederick, 1965, *The German Ideology* (1st complete edition), London: Lawrence and Wishart.

Masson, Paul R. and Mussa, Michael, Undated, *The Role of the IMF Financing and Its Interactions with Adjustment and Surveillance*, IMF Pamphlet No. 50. Worldwide Web: IMF.

Mbilinyi, Marjorie, 1990, '"Structural Adjustment", Agribusiness and Rural Women in Tanzania' in: Bernstein, Henry; Crow, Ben; Mackintosh Maureen; Martin, Charlotte, *The Food Question: Profits versus People?* London: Earthscan Publications.

Middleton, Neil; O'Keefe, Phil; Moyo, Sam, 1993, *The Tears of the Crocodile: From Rio to Reality in the Developing World*, London and Boulder, Colorado: Pluto Press.

MFS (Milk for Schools), 1996, *The Hunger Within: a Report into Children/Poverty/Nutrition*, Stafford: Milk for Schools.

Moyo, Sam; O'Keefe, Phil; Sill, Michael, 1993, *The Southern African Environment: Profiles of the SADC Countries*, London: Earthscan.

Ngũgĩ, wa Thiong'o, 1967 (revised 1987), *A Grain of Wheat*. London: Heinemann.

Nkrumah, Kwame, 1963, *Africa Must Unite*, London: Heinemann.

O'Dowd, Liam, 1990, 'New Introduction' to: Memmi, Albert, *The Colonizer and the Colonized*, London: Earthscan Publications.

Ó Gráda, Cormac, 1993 *Ireland Before and After the Famine*, Manchester and New York: Manchester University Press.

—— 1995, 'The Great Famine and Today's Famines' in: Póirtéir, Cathal, *The Great Irish Famine*, Dublin and Cork: Radio Telefis Éireann and Mercier Press.

Oliver, Roland and Fage, J.D., 1970, *A Short History of Africa*, 3rd edn, Harmondsworth: Penguin Books.

Oxfam, 1995, *The Oxfam Poverty Report*, Oxford: Oxfam.

The Oxford English Dictionary, 1971, Oxford: Oxford University Press.

Peters, Chris, 1996, *Sudan: a Nation in the Balance*, Oxford: Oxfam Publications.

Póirtéir, Cathal (ed.), 1995, *The Great Irish Famine*, Cork: Mercier Press.

Prendergast, John, 1997, *Crisis Response: Humanitarian Band-Aids in Sudan and Somalia*, London and Chicago: Pluto Press.

Rubin, Barett R., *Afghanistan: the Forgotten Crisis*, UK: Writenet, February 1996.

Said, Edward, 1993, *Culture and Imperialism*, London: Vintage.

Sen, Amartya, 1981, *Famines and Poverty*, Oxford: Oxford University Press.

—— September 1994, 'Population: Delusion and Reality' in *The New York Review*, New York.

Sen, Gita and Grown, Caren (for Development Alternatives for a New Era – DAWN), 1988, *Development Crises and Alternative Visions: Third World Women's Perspectives*, London: Earthscan Publications.

Sogge, David, with Biekart, Kees and Saxby, John (eds), 1996, *Compassion and Calculation: the Business of Private Foreign Aid*, London and Chicago: Pluto Press.

Sontheimer, Sally (ed.), 1991, *Women and the Environment: A Reader*, London: Earthscan Publications.

Stolz, Walter, 1996, *Donor Experiences in Support of Human Rights: Some Lessons*, Den Haag: Ministerie van Buitenlandse Zaken.

Stone, I.F., 1960, 'The Writing on the Synagogue Walls' in *I.F. Stone's Weekly*, Washington: 18 January 1960.

Stoneman, Colin and Thompson, Carol, September 1995, 'The GATT Uruguay Round: Implications for Agriculture in Zimbabwe', paper presented at the Development Studies Association Annual Conference, University College, Dublin.

Swift, Jeremy, 1996, 'Understanding Food Security Crises', paper presented at the Seminar on Drought Related Disasters in Kenya, Machakos.

Tandon, Yash, 1996: see Sogge, David with Biekart, Kees and Saxby, John.

Thompson, E.P., 1980, *The Making of the English Working Class*, 3rd edn, Harmondsworth: Penguin Books.

Thompson, William, 1825, *Appeal of One-Half the Human Race*, London: Virago (1983).

Timberlake, Lloyd and Thomas, Laura, 1990, *When the Bough Breaks ...*, London: Earthscan Publications.

Trotsky, Leon, 1934, *The History of the Russian Revolution* (single volume edition), London: Victor Gollancz.

UNDHA, *Retrospective DHA 1995*, Geneva: United Nations Department of Humanitarian Affairs.

UNDP, Annual, *Human Development Report*, New York and Oxford: Oxford University Press.

UNHCR, 1990, *Policy on Refugee Women*, New York: UNHCR.

—— 1991, *Guidelines on the Protection of Refugee Women*, New York: UNHCR.

—— 1993, *The State of the World's Refugees: The Challenge of Protection*, Harmondsworth: Penguin Books.

—— 1994, *Final Project Monitoring Report* (Mozambique), UNHCR, unpublished.

—— March 1996, *Briefing Note on Reintegration Activities Targeting Women and Community Participation*, UNHCR: privately published.

—— July 1996, *Rebuilding a War-Torn Society: A Review of the UNHCR Reintegration Programme for Mozambican Returnees.*

UNICEF, Annual, *The State of the World's Children*, New York and Oxford: Oxford University Press.

USAID, 1995, *Agency Performance Report, 1995*, Washington: United States Agency for International Development.

United States Department of State, 30 January 1997, *Human Rights Report*, Washington: US Government.

Vidal, John, 1997, *McLibel*, London: Macmillan.

Walker, Peter, 1989, *Famine Early Warning Systems*, London: Earthscan Publications.

Waterhouse, Rachel, 1996, *Mozambique Rising from the Ashes*, Oxford: Oxfam Publications.

Watkins, Kevin, 1992, *Fixing the Rules*, London: CIIR.

—— 1995, *The Oxfam Poverty Report*, Oxford and Dublin: Oxfam Publications.

Watts, Michael, 1990, 'Peasants Under Contract' in: Bernstein, Henry et al., *The Food Question: Profits versus People?* London: Earthscan Publications.

Whelan, Kevin, 1996, *The Tree of Liberty: Radicalism, Catholicism and the Construction of Irish Identity, 1760–1830*, Cork: Cork University Press.

Wijkman, A. and Timberlake, L., 1984, *Natural Disasters: Acts of God or Acts of Man?* London: Earthscan.

WCRWC (Women's Commission for Refugee Women and Children) Delegation Visit to Mozambique, August 1995, *Refugee Women in Mozambique*, New York: WCRWC.

World Bank, Annual, *World Development Report*, New York and Oxford: Oxford University Press.

Index

179